Mobil
Travel Guide®

SOUTHERN GREAT LAKES

ACKNOWLEDGEMENTS

We gratefully acknowledge the help of our representatives for their efficient and perceptive inspections of the lodging and dining establishments listed, the establishments' proprietors for their cooperation in showing their facilities and providing information about them, and the many users of previous editions who have taken the time to share their experiences. Mobil Travel Guide is also grateful to all the talented writers who contributed entries to this book.

Front cover photos:
Sim Smith's Bridge, Indiana: U.S. Landmarks and Travel/Getty Images
Lake Michigan: U.S. Landmarks and Travel/Getty Images
Chicago River At Night: U.S. Landmarks and Travel 2/Getty Images
Cleveland at Dusk: © Barry Howe/Corbis

ISBN: 0-8416-0319-7 or 978-0-8416-0319-6
Manufactured in the Canada.

10 9 8 7 6 5 4 3 2 1

CONTENTS

MAPS

SOUTHERN GREAT LAKES

CELEBRATING 50 YEARS

Because time is precious and the travel industry is ever-changing, having accurate, reliable travel information at your has fingertips is essential. Mobil Travel Guide provided invaluable insight to travelers for 50 years, and we are committed to continuing this service into the future.

The Mobil Corporation (known as Exxon Mobil Corporation since a 1999 merger) began producing the Mobil Travel Guide books in 1958 following the introduction of the U.S.-interstate highway system in 1956. The first edition covered only five Southwestern states. Since then, our books have become the premier travel guides in North America, covering all 50 states and Canada.

Since its founding, Mobil Travel Guide has served as an advocate for travelers seeking knowledge about hotels, restaurants and places to visit. Based on an objective process, we make recommendations to our customers that we believe will enhance the quality and value of their travel experiences. Our trusted Mobil One- to Five-Star rating system is the oldest and most respected lodging and restaurant inspection and rating program in North America. Most hoteliers, restaurateurs and industry observers favorably regard the rigor of our inspection program and understand the prestige and benefits that come with receiving a Mobil Star rating.

The Mobil Travel Guide process of rating each establishment includes:
★ Unannouced facility inspections
★ Incognito service evaluations for
★ A review of unsolicited comments from the general public
★ Senior management oversight

For each property, more than 450 attributes, including cleanliness, physical facilities and employee attitude and courtesy, are measured and evaluated to produce a mathematically derived score, which is then blended with the other elements to form an overall score. These scores form the basis that we use to assign our Mobil One- to Five-Star ratings.

This process focuses on guest expectations, guest experience and consistency of service, not just physical facilities and amenities. It's fundamentally a rating system that rewards those properties that continually strive for and achieve excellence each year. The very best properties are consistently raising the bar for those that wish to compete with them.

Only facilities that meet Mobil Travel Guide's standards earn the privilege of being listed in the guide. Deteriorating, poorly managed establishments are deleted. A Mobil Travel Guide listing constitutes a positive quality recommendation. Every listing is an accolade, a recognition of achievement.

★★★★★The Mobil Five-Star Award indicates that a property is one of the very best in the country and consistently provides gracious and courteous service, superlative quality in its facility and a unique ambience. The lodgings and restaurants at the Mobil Five-Star level consistently continues their commitment to excellence, doing so with grace and perseverance.

★★★★The Mobil Four-Star Award honors properties for outstanding achievement in overall facility and for providing very strong service levels in all areas. These award winners provide a distinctive experience for the ever-demanding and sophisticated consumer.

★★★The Mobil Three-Star Award recognizes an excellent property that provides full services and amenities. This category ranges from exceptional hotels with limited services to elegant restaurants with a less-formal atmosphere.

★★The Mobil Two-Star property is a clean and comfortable establishment that has expanded amenities or a distinctive environment. These properties are an excellent place to stay or dine.

★The Mobil One-Star property is limited in its amenities and services but provides a value experience while meeting travelers' expectations. Expect the properties to be clean, comfortable and convenient.

We do not charge establishments for inclusion in our guides. We have no relationship with any of the businesses and attractions we list and act only as a consumer advocate. We do the investigative legwork so that you won't have to.

Restaurants and hotels—particularly small chains and stand-alone establishments—change management or even go out of business with surprising quickness. Although we make every effort to update continuously information, we recommend that you call ahead to make sure the place you've selected is still open.

We hope that your travels are enjoyable and relaxing and that our books help you get the most out of every trip you take. If any aspect of your accommodation, dining, spa or sightseeing experience motivates you to comment, please contact us. Mobil Travel Guide, 200 W. Madison St., Suite 3950, Chicago, IL 60611, or send an e-mail to info@mobiltravelguide.com.
Happy travels.

HOW TO USE THIS BOOK

The Mobil Travel Guide Regional Travel Planners are designed for convenience. Each state has its own chapter, beginning with a general introduction that provides a geographical and historical orientation to the state and gives basic statewide tourist information. The remainder of each chapter is devoted to travel destinations within the state—mainly cities and towns, but also national parks and tourist areas—which, like the states, are arranged in alphabetical order.

MAPS

We have provided state maps as well as maps of selected larger cities to help you find your way.

DESTINATION INFORMATION

We list addresses, phone number and web sites for travel information resources—usually the local chamber of commerce or office of tourism—and a brief introduction to the area. Information about airports, ground transportation and suburbs is included for large cities.

DRIVING TOURS AND WALKING TOURS

The driving tours that we include for many states are usually day trips that make for interesting side excursions. They offer you a way to get off the beaten path. These trips frequently cover areas of natural beauty or historical significance.

WHAT TO SEE AND DO

Mobil Travel Guide offers information about thousands of museums, art galleries, amusement parks, historic sites, national and state parks, ski areas and many other attractions.

Following an attraction's description, you'll find the months, days and, in some cases, hours of operation, address, telephone number and web site (if there is one).

SPECIAL EVENTS

Special events are either annual events that last only a short time, such as festivals and fairs or longer, seasonal events such as horse racing, theater and summer concerts. Our Special Events listings also include infrequently occurring occasions that mark certain dates or events, such as a centennial or other commemorative celebration.

LISTINGS

Hotels, restaurants and spas are usually listed under the city or town in which they're located. Make sure to check the nearby cities and towns for additional options, especially if you're traveling to a major metropolitan area that includes many suburbs. If a property is located in a town that doesn't have its own heading, the listing appears under the town nearest it. In large cities, hotels located within 5 miles of major commercial airports may be listed under a separate Airport Area heading that follows the city section.

THE STAR RATINGS
MOBIL RATED HOTELS

Travelers have different needs when it comes to accommodations. To help you pinpoint properties that meet your particular needs, Mobil Travel Guide classifies each lodging by type according to the following characteristics.

★★★★★The Mobil Five-Star hotel provides consistently superlative service in an exceptionally distinctive luxury environment, with expanded services. Attention to detail is evident throughout the hotel, resort or inn, from bed linens to staff uniforms.

★★★★The Mobil Four-Star hotel provides a luxury experience with expanded amenities in a distinctive environment. Services may include automatic turndown service, 24-hour room service and valet parking.

★★★The Mobil Three-Star hotel is well appointed, with a full-service restaurant and expanded amenities, such as a fitness center, golf course, tennis courts, 24-hour room service and optional turndown service.

★★The Mobil Two-Star hotel is considered a clean, comfortable and reliable establishment that has expanded amenities, such as a full-service restaurant on the premises.

★The Mobil One-Star lodging is a limited-service hotel, motel or inn that is considered a clean, comfortable and reliable establishment For every property, we also provide pricing information. The pricing categories break down as follows:

★ **$** = Up to $150
★ **$$** − $151-$250
★ **$$$** = $251-$350
★ **$$$$** = $351 and up

All prices quoted are accurate at the time of publication, however prices cannot be guaranteed. In some locations, special events, holidays or seasons can affect prices. Some resorts have complicated rate structures that vary with the time of year, so confirm rates when making your plans.

SPECIALITY LODGINGS

A Speciality Lodging is a unique inn, bed and breakfast or guest ranch with limited service, but appealing, attractive facilities that make the property worth a visit.

MOBIL RATED RESTAURANTS

All Mobil Star-rated dining establishments listed in this book have a full kitchen and most offer table service.

★★★★★The Mobil Five-Star restaurant offers one of few flawless dining experiences in the country. These establishments consistently provide their guests with exceptional food, superlative service, elegant décor and exquisite presentations of each detail surrounding a meal.

★★★★The Mobil Four-Star restaurant provides professional service, distinctive presentations and wonderful food.

★★★The Mobil Three-Star restaurant has good food, warm and skillful service and enjoyable décor.

★★The Mobil Two-Star restaurant serves fresh food in a clean setting with efficient service. Value is considered in this category, as is family friendliness.

★The Mobil One-Star restaurant provides a distinctive experience through culinary specialty, local flair or individual atmosphere. Each restaurant listing gives the cuisine type, street address, phone and website, meals served, days of operation (if not open daily year-round) and pricing category. Information about appropriate attire is provided, although it's always a good idea to call ahead and ask if you're unsure; the meaning of "casual" or "business casual" varies widely in different parts of the country. We also indicate whether the restaurant has a bar, whether a children's menu is offered and whether outdoor seating is available. If reservations are recommended, we note that fact in the listing. When valet parking is available, it is noted in the description. Because menu prices can fluctuate, we list a pricing category rather than specific prices. The pricing categories are defined as follows, per diner, and assume that you order an appetizer or dessert, an entrée and one drink:

★ **$** = $15 and under
★ **$$** = $16-$35
★ **$$$** = $36-$85
★ **$$$$** = $86 and up

All prices quoted are accurate at the time of publication, but prices cannot be guaranteed.

MOBIL RATED SPAS

Mobil Travel Guide is pleased to announce its newest category, hotel and resort spas. Until now, hotel and resort spas have not been formally rated or inspected by any organization. Every spa selected for inclusion in this book underwent a rigorous inspection process similar to the one Mobil Travel Guide has been applying to lodgings and restaurants for five decades. After researching more than 300 spas and performing exhaustive incognito inspections of more than 200 properties, we narrowed our list to the best spas in the United States and Canada.

Mobil Travel Guide's spa ratings are based on objective evaluations of more than 450 attributes. Approximately half of these criteria assess basic expectations, such as staff courtesy, the technical proficiency and skill of the employees and whether the facility is maintained properly and hygienically. Several standards address issues that impact a guest's physical comfort and convenience, as well as the staff's ability to impart a sense of personalized service and anticipate clients' needs. Additional criteria measure the spa's ability to create a completely calming ambience. The Mobil Star ratings focus on much more than the facilities available at a spa and the treatments it offers. Each Mobil Star rating is a cumulative score achieved from multiple inspections that reflects the spa management's attention to detail and commitment to consumers' needs.

★★★★★The Mobil Five-Star spa provides consistently superlative service in an exceptionally distinctive luxury environment with extensive amenities. The staff at a Mobil Five-Star spa provides extraordinary service beyond the traditional spa experience, allowing guests to achieve the highest level of relaxation and pampering. A Mobil Five-Star spa offers an extensive array of treatments, often incorporating international themes and products. Attention to detail is evident throughout the spa, from arrival to departure.

★★★★The Mobil Four-Star spa provides a luxurious experience with expanded amenities in an elegant and serene environment. Throughout the spa facility, guests experience personalized service. Amenities might include, but are not limited to, single-sex relaxation rooms where guests wait for their treatments, plunge pools and whirlpools in both men's and women's locker rooms, and an array of treatments, including a selection of massages, body therapies, facials and a variety of salon services.

★★★The Mobil Three-Star spa is physically well appointed and has a full complement of staff.

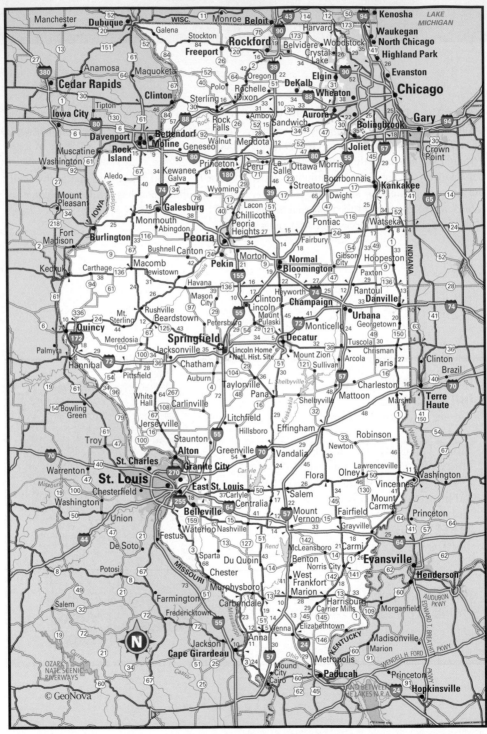

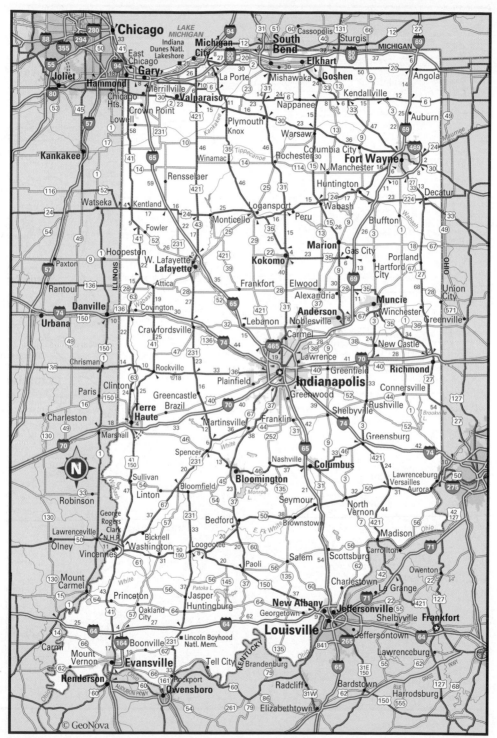

© GeoNova

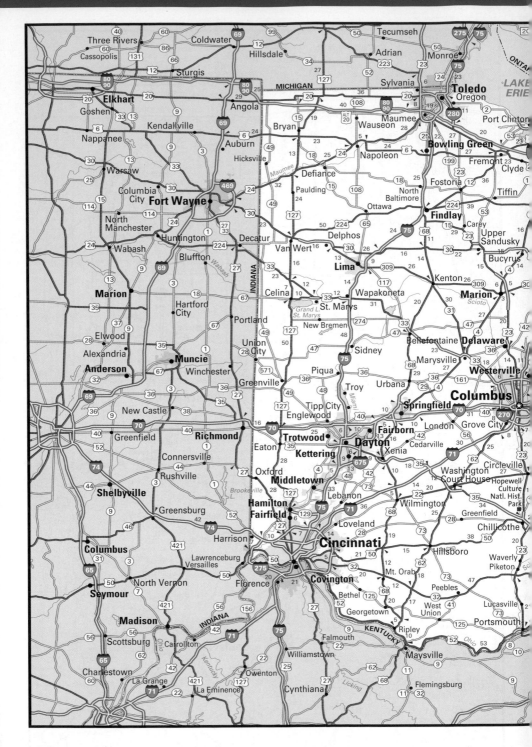

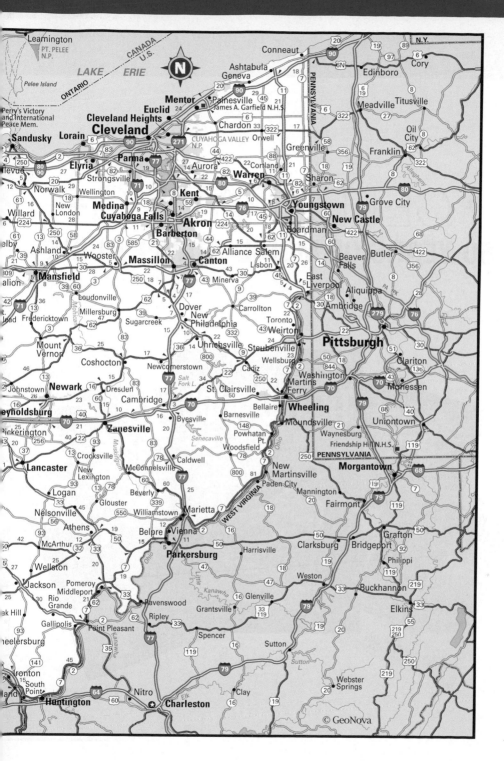

★ CELEBRATING ★
50 YEARS OF MOBIL TRAVEL GUIDE

| 1962 | 1964 | 1968 | 1971 |

| 1973 | 1976 | 1978 | 1979 |

← 1986 ——— 1988 ——— 1989 ——— 1992 →

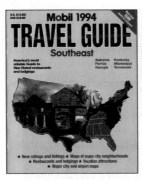

← 1994 ——— 1997 ——— 1998 ——— 2003 →

ILLINOIS

WHERE DO YOU START IN ILLINOIS? WITH AN URBAN ADVENTURE BENEATH TOWERING skyscrapers in Chicago? Or ambling the charming streets of the state's touristy towns? No matter which road you follow, you'll find an ideal getaway.

If you do start in Chicago, you'll be busy. With its famed architecture, legendary blues and jazz scenes and world-renowned museums like the Art Institute and the John G. Shedd Aquarium, Chicago is celebrated for its thriving cultural scene almost as much as its culinary classics: hot dogs and deep-dish pizzas.

When you're in Chicago, you'll want to experience the city like native Chicagoans do. That means catching a Cubs game at Wrigley Field, strolling Millennium Park, taking an architectural boat cruise on the Chicago River or twirling with the kids on Navy Pier's Ferris wheel.

If the only sights you're interested in seeing are designer labels, make Michigan Avenue your first stop. The mile-long stretch isn't named the "Magnificent Mile" for nothing. Highlighted by the seven-level Water Tower Place and big-name stores like Gucci, Chanel and Hugo Boss, the avenue is among the world's most cosmopolitan shopping districts. If you really feel like splurging, check out the high-end boutiques on Oak Street, just a step away from Michigan Avenue.

Even die-hard urbanites need a break from the city. If you're starved for nature, take a breather at Utica's Starved Rock State Park, featuring sandstone canyons, gushing waterfalls and miles of hiking trails. Or stop at the 8,000-acre Pere Marquette State Park—Illinois' largest—known for its 20-mile scenic bike trail and towering limestone cliffs.

Love golf? Have fun at southern Illinois' Rend Lake. The 18,000-acre manmade reservoir in Wayne Fitzgerrell State Recreation Area is popular with fishermen and boaters, but the Rend Lake Golf Course is an even bigger draw. The 27-hole championship course is considered one of the best in the Midwest.

For a more historic look at Illinois, take the family to Springfield and tip your hat to the 16th president at the Abraham Lincoln Presidential Library and Museum. Or drive toward the Illinois-Iowa border for Galena, an old lead-mining town known for its historic 19th century architecture, gorgeous vistas and boating trips down the Mississippi and Galena rivers;
Information:
www.enjoyillinois.com

1

ILLINOIS

★
★
★
★
★

 SPOTLIGHT

★ The world's first skyscraper was built in Chicago in 1885.

★ The abbreviation "ORD" for Chicago's O'Hare airport comes from the old name "Orchard Field."

★ The Hostess Twinkie was first produced in Chicago in 1930.

★ The first McDonald's franchise opened in Des Plaines in 1955. Oak Brook is now the international headquarters for the fast food giant.

ALGONQUIN

Before it was founded in 1834, this area was home to the Pottowatomi Indians. With the introduction of the railroad in 1855, Algonquin grew and became a popular summer destination for Chicagoans. www.algonquin.org

SPECIALTY LODGING

Victorian Rose Garden Bed and Breakfast
314 Washington St., Algonquin,
847-854-9667, 888-854-9667;
www.sleepandeat.com
Blacksmith James Philip built this house as a wedding present to his son, James Harvey Philip, and his bride Emma back in 1886 on what is now a lovely, tree-lined street in suburban Algonquin.
4 rooms. Children over 8 years only. Complimentary full breakfast. High-speed Internet access. **$**

RESTAURANT

★★**Port Edward**
20 W. Algonquin Rd., Algonquin,
847-658-5441;
www.portedward.com
Seafood menu. Lunch, dinner. Sunday brunch. Bar. Children's menu. **$$**

THE GREAT RIVER ROAD

Illinois has more than 500 miles of distinctive state, county and U.S. highways comprising its Great River Road, which runs along the Mississippi River from East Dubuque to Cairo. One of the most scenic drives in Illinois, the Great River Road is meandering to say the least; it winds back and forth over the river, changes direction frequently and wanders in and out of towns long-since forgotten.

The portion of the route that runs through Illinois (the Great River Road also runs through nine other states) is particularly well marked. Keep your eyes peeled for the green-and-white signs with a steamboat design in the middle, and that will be the indicator that you're on the right road.

From Rockford, take Highway 20 to Route 84, the starting point for this tour. Nearby Galena is one of Illinois' most treasured historic towns. Spend some time exploring the many mansions and buildings listed on the National Historic Register, poke through tiny antique stores, take a guided walking tour or go wine tasting at the Galena Cellars Winery.

Farther south along the Mississippi is the town of Grafton, home to Pére Marquette, Illinois' largest state park. Grafton is also where some of the prettiest stretches of the Great River Road are located. If you are traveling during the winter, stop in nearby Alton to see the 200 to 400 bald eagles that winter in this area every year. South of Carbondale, the cool woods of Shawnee National Forest provide a welcome respite from the heat of an Illinois summer. Acres of hiking trails are available for stretching your legs.

★
★
★
★
★

ALTON

Located on the bluffs above the confluence of the Illinois, Mississippi and Missouri rivers, Alton is rich in history. In 1837, Elijah Lovejoy, the abolitionist editor, died here protecting his press from a proslavery mob. Young Abraham Lincoln dueled on a sandbar in the river, and later debated Stephen Douglas in Alton in 1858. Alton was also the home of Robert Wadlow, the tallest man in history. The "Gentle Giant" is celebrated with a life-size nine-foot statue on College Avenue.

Information: Greater Alton/Twin Rivers Convention and Visitors Bureau, 200 Piasa St., 618-465-6676, 800-258-6645; www.altoncvb.org

WHAT TO SEE AND DO

Alton Museum of History and Art
2809 College Ave., Alton,
618-462-2763;
www.altonmuseum.com
Founded in 1971, the Museum is in Loomis Hall, the oldest building in Illinois. There are displays on local history and culture, including an exhibit on Alton's Robert Wadlow. Wednesday-Saturday 10 a.m.- 4 p.m., Sunday 1 p.m.- 4 p.m.

Brussels Ferry
Hwy. 100, near Grafton,
618-786-3636
This ferryboat navigates the Illinois River at its junction with the Mississippi River.

HOTEL

★★Holiday Inn
3800 Homer Adams Pkwy., Grafton
618-462-1220, 800-655-4669;
www.holiday-inn.com
137 rooms. Pets accepted; fee. High-speed Internet access. Restaurant, two bars. Fitness room. Indoor pool, whirlpool. Airport transportation available. Business center. $

3

PERE MARQUETTE STATE PARK

This is Illinois' largest state park, with 8,000 acres at the confluence of the Illinois and Mississippi Rivers. It is named after Pre Jacques Marquette, who passed the site with Louis Jolliet in 1673. They were the first white men to enter the present state of Illinois.

Fishing, boating (ramp, motors). Hiking and bridle paths (horses may be rented), hunting, picnic areas, playground, concession, lodge, restaurant, campgrounds (fees). Interpretive center. Schedule of free guided trips is posted in the visitor center. For information, contact the Park Superintendent, P.O. Box 158, Grafton, 62037. 618-786-3323, 618-786-2331 (lodge).

ANTIOCH

Founded prior to the Civil War, this village became a popular summer destination for Chicagoans in the 1890s. One famous summer resident was Al Capone. Most of the town was destroyed by fire by 1904 but it was rebuilt and has grown steadily since.

Information: Chamber of Commerce, 882 Main St., 847-395-2233; www.antiochchamber.org

CHAIN O'LAKES STATE PARK

8916 Wilmot Rd., Spring Grove. 6 miles W. on Hwy. 173.
815-585-5512;
www.dnr.state.il.us.
This park near the Illinois Wisconsin border is one of the most popular recreation areas in Chicagoland near the Illinois Wisconsin border. The parks' 2,793 acres adjoin a 3,230-acre conservation area and border three lakes and a river, which makes it ideal for boating, canoeing, rafting, fishing and wildlife watching (including white-tailed deer, mink, foxes, beavers, coyotes and eagles). However, this is truly a year-round playground; there are plenty of opportunities to camp, bike, ski, sled, ride horses, toboggan, snowmobile and take advantage of extensive running trails. (Daily)

WHAT TO SEE AND DO
Chain O' Lakes Area
This year-round recreational facility offers boating, fishing, ice fishing, cross-country skiing and snowmobiling.

HOTEL
★Best Western Regency Inn
350 Hwy. 173, Antioch,
847-395-3606, 800-780-7234;
www.bestwestern.com
68 rooms. Pets accepted, some restrictions; fee. Complimentary continental breakfast. Bar. Indoor pool, whirlpool. $

4

ILLINOIS

ARCOLA

Known as the "Broom Corn Capital of the World," Arcola is located in Illinois' Amish Country and is the state's largest Old Order Amish settlement.
Information: Chamber of Commerce, 135 N. Oak, 217-268-4530, 800-336-5456; www.arcola-il.org

WHAT TO SEE AND DO
Illinois Amish Interpretive Center
111 S. Locust St., Arcola,
217-268-3599, 888-452-6474;
www.amishcenter.com
This museum is dedicated to central Illinois' Amish community. Exhibits include antique buggies, quilts and handicrafts. Local tours available. April-November: Monday-Saturday; December-March: Wednesday-Saturday $

Rockome Gardens
125 N. County Rd. 425E., Arcola,
217-268-4106
For about 80 years, these gardens have housed native rocks inlaid in concrete to form fences, arches and ornamental designs. There are ponds, a petting zoo and train and buggy rides. There is a re-creation of an Illinois frontier village on 15 acres that includes a blacksmith shop, old country store and candle shops. Admission includes all attractions except buggy ride. Memorial Day-late August: daily; late August-October: Monday-Friday; mid-April-Memorial Day: days vary.

SPECIAL EVENT
Raggedy Ann Festival
135 N. Oak St., Arcola,
217-268-4530
This festival celebrates the creator of the Raggedy Ann and Andy characters, Johnny Gruelle, and includes carnival and petting zoo. Early June.

HOTEL

★ Comfort Inn
610 E. Springfield Rd., Arcola
217-268-4000, 800-228-5150;
www.comfortinn.com
41 rooms. Pets accepted, some restrictions; fee. Complimentary continental breakfast. Outdoor pool. $

RESTAURANTS

★Dutch Kitchen
127 E. Main St., Arcola,
217-268-3518
American menu. Breakfast, lunch, dinner. Closed two weeks in January, children's menu. $$

★Rockome Family Style
125 N. County Rd., Arcola,
217-268-4106.
Amish, American menu. Lunch, dinner. Closed November-mid-April. Children's menu. $

ARLINGTON HEIGHTS

Twenty-five miles northwest of Chicago, Arlington Heights possesses numerous public parks, tree-lined neighborhoods and a thriving downtown with an eclectic mix of shops and restaurants. The village may be best known for Arlington Park, where the Arlington Million thoroughbred race is held annually in August.
Information: Chamber of Commerce, 311 S. Arlington Heights Rd.,847-253-1703; www.arlingtonhtschamber.com

WHAT TO SEE AND DO

Arlington Park
2200 W. Euclid, Arlington Park,
847-385-7500;
www.arlingtonpark.com
From mid-May to mid-September, you can spend a day at the races here and bet on your favorite horse. Tours of the park and its 1 1/8-mile track are offered (Saturday-Sunday); register at the Clubhouse Information Booth. Crafts for children in Arlington Craft Stable most Sundays and holidays.

Kemper Lakes Golf Club
24000 N. Old McHenry Rd., Kideer,
847-320-3450;
www.kemperlakesgolf.com
A regular host of PGA events in the Chicago area is Kemper Lakes, which was the site of the 1989 PGA Championship, as well as several Champions Tour and LPGA events. Located in Long Grove, northwest of the city, the course plays 7,217 yards long, a challenging length for almost any golfer. The greens fee may be steep, but with the course's twilight rates you can save a bundle. The course's state-of-the-art global positioning system helps players judge yardage to a given hole from every golf cart.

Long Grove Confectionary Company
333 Lexington Dr., Buffalo Grove,
847-459-3100, 888-459-3100;
www.longgrove.com
Take a tour of this family-owned confectionary which produces more than 300 sweet treats. Learn how the chocolates are made, sample the products and then purchase discounted goodies from the outlet store. Store, Monday-Saturday 9:30 a.m.-5:30 p.m., Sunday 11 a.m.-4 p.m. Tours, Monday-Thursday 9 a.m., 11 a.m., noon, 1 p.m., other times by appointment; reservations are required.

RESTAURANTS

★★★Le Titi de Paris
1015 W. Dundee Rd., Arlington Heights,
847-506-0222;
www.letitideparis.com
The wine list at this French restaurant has more than 800 selections. Chefs Pierre Pollin and Michael Maddox serve innovative cuisine with nearly impeccable service. Save room for one of the creatively presented desserts.
French menu. Dinner. Closed Monday. Bar. Business casual attire. Reservations recommended. Outdoor seating. $$$

5

ILLINOIS

★
★
★
★
★

★★Palm Court
1912 N. Arlington Heights Rd., Arlington
Heights, 847-870-7770;
www.palmcourt.net

American menu. Lunch, Monday-Friday;
dinner. Closed July 4. Bar. Children's menu.
Casual attire. Reservations recommended.
$$

AURORA

Potawatomie chief Waubonsie and his tribe inhabited this area on the Fox River when
pioneers arrived from the East in the 1830s. Waterpower and fertile lands attracted more
settlers. Today, the city prospers because of its location along a high-tech corridor.
Information: Aurora Area Convention and Tourism Council, 44 W. Downer Pl.,
630-897-5581, 800-477-4369; www.ci.aurora.il.us

WHAT TO SEE AND DO

Aurora Art & History Center
20 E. Downer Place, Aurora,
630-897-9029;
www.aurorahistoricalsociety.org
In the restored Ginsberg building, the museum
contains displays of 19th-century life, a col-
lection of mastodon bones, a history center
and research library and public art displays.
Wednesday-Sunday noon-4 p.m.

Blackberry Farm's Pioneer Village
100 S. Barnes Rd., Aurora,
630-892-1550;
www.foxvalleyparkdistrict.org
This rural spot has an 1840s to 1920s liv-
ing history museum and working farm.
Exhibits include a children's animal farm,
discovery barn and train. There are also
craft demonstrations, wagon and pony rides
and a farm play area. Early April-Labor
Day: Monday-Friday 9:30 a.m.-3:30 p.m.;
Labor Day-early October: Friday-Sunday

Chicago Premium Outlets
1650 Premium Outlets Blvd., Aurora,
630-585-2200;
www.premiumoutlets.com/chicago
This outlet mall has approximately 120
stores, including staples like Gap and Nike
as well as upscale brands like Versace and
Giorgio Armani. Monday-Saturday 10 a.m.-
9 p.m., Sunday 10 a.m.-6 p.m.

Paramount Arts Centre
23 E. Galena Blvd., Aurora,
630-896-6666;
www.paramountarts.com

This theater was built in 1931 to compete
with the opulent movie palaces of the area.
It has been restored to its original appear-
ance and stages a variety of productions
throughout the year. Guided backstage
tours. Monday-Friday

Schingoethe Center for Native American Cultures
347 S. Gladstone Ave., Aurora,
630-844-5402;
www.aurora.edu/museum
On the campus of Aurora University, this pri-
vate collection contains thousands of Native
American artifacts, including jewelry, tex-
tiles, pottery and baskets. Tuesday-Friday
10 a.m.-4 p.m., Sunday 1-4 p.m. during the
academic year; closed August

SciTech-Science Hands-On Museum
18 W. Benton, Aurora,
630-859-3434;
www.scitech.mus.il.us
Housed in a historic post office building, this
interactive center provides more than 150
hands-on learning exhibits using motion,
light, sound and science principles. Memo-
rial Day-Labor Day: Monday-Saturday
10 a.m.-5 p.m., Sunday noon-5 p.m.; Labor
Day-Memorial Day: Monday-Tuesday
10 a.m.-2 p.m.,Wednesday, Friday-Sunday,
until 5 p.m., Thursday until 8, Sunday noon-
5 p.m.

HOTELS
★Comfort Inn
111 N. Broadway., Aurora,
630-896-2800

82 rooms. Complimentary continental breakfast. Fitness room. Indoor pool. Business center. **$$**

★Super 8
901 S. Tenney St., Kewanee,
309-853-8800;
www.super8.com
41 rooms. Check-in 1 p.m., check-out 11 a.m. **$**

RESTAURANT
★★Walter Payton's Roundhouse
205 N. Broadway Ave., Aurora,
630-264-2739;
www.walterpaytonsroundhouse.com
American menu. Lunch, dinner. Bar. Children's menu. Casual attire. Reservations recommended. Valet parking. Outdoor seating. **$$**

BARRINGTON
Located 35 miles northwest of Chicago, the village of Barrington was home to the Pottawatomi and Mascouten Indians, and later settlers from New York, Vermont and Massachusetts. It was called Miller Grove and was later changed to Barrington Center.
Information: Chamber of Commerce, 325 N. Hough St., 847-381-2525; www.barringtonchamber.com

RESTAURANT
★★Barrington Country Bistro
700 W. Northwest Hwy., Barrington,
847-842-1300;
www.barringtonbistro.com
French menu. Lunch, dinner. Bar. Casual attire. Outdoor seating. **$$**

7

BELLEVILLE
Named Belleville by its early French settlers, this city is now populated by people of German descent. Belleville is the headquarters of Scott Air Force Base.
Information: Belleville Tourism, Inc., 216 East A St., 618-233-6769, 800-677-9255; www.belleville.net

HOTELS
★Hampton Inn
150 Ludwig Dr., Fairview Heights,
618-397-9705, 800-426-7866;
www.hamptoninn.com
62 rooms. Complimentary continental breakfast. High-speed Internet access, wireless Internet access. Indoor pool, whirlpool. Airport transportation available. **$**

★★Ramada Inn
6900 N. Illinois, Fairview Heights,
618-632-4747, 800-272-6232;
www.ramadafairviewheights.com
High-speed Internet access, wireless Internet access. Restaurant, bar. Fitness room. Indoor pool, outdoor pool, whirlpools. **$**

RESTAURANT
★★Fischer's
2100 W. Main St., Belleville
618-233-1131;
www.fischersrestaurant.com
American menu. Breakfast, lunch, dinner. Bar. Children's menu. Casual attire. **$$**

BENTON

This town has seen some famous faces in its time. George Harrison visited his sister here in September of 1963 and performed at the local VFW hall in close-by Eldorado, Illinois. His sister's house is now the Hard Day's Night Bed and Breakfast. Actor John Malkovich and NBA coach Doug Collins are both hometown boys.

Information: Benton/West City Area Chamber of Commerce, 211. Main St., 618-438-2121; www.bentonillinois.com

WHAT TO SEE AND DO
Rend Lake
12220 Rend City Rd., Benton,
618-724-2493
Created from the Big Muddy and Casey Fork rivers, the Y-shaped Rend Lake covers 19,000 acres adjacent to 21,000 acres of public land with six recreation areas. The area has two beaches, riding trails, a restaurant and a golf course. April-October.

HOTELS
★★Rend Lake Resort
11712 E. Windy Lane, Whittington.
618-629-2211, 800-633-3341;
www.rendlakeresort.net

105 rooms. Pets accepted, some restrictions. Restaurant, bar. Beach. Outdoor pool, children's pool. Tennis. **$**

★Super 8 Motel—Benton West City Area
711 W. Main St., Benton,
618-438-8205
57 rooms. Pets accepted; fee. Restaurant. Fitness room. **$**

RESTAURANT
★★Bittersweet on the Bluff
7010 Donna's Dr., East Dubuque, 815-747-2360
www.bittersweetonthebluff.com
This family-owned and -operated business overlooks the Mississippi River. American menu. Dinner. Closed Sunday. **$$**

8

ILLINOIS

★ ★ ★ ★ ★

BLOOMINGTON

The Illinois Republican Party was formed here in 1856 at the Anti-Nebraska convention, where Abraham Lincoln made the famous "lost speech" spelling out the principles that helped win him the presidency. Bloomington was also the home of Adlai E. Stevenson, vice president under Grover Cleveland. His grandson, Illinois Governor Adlai E. Stevenson II, twice Democratic candidate for president and U.S. Ambassador to the United Nations, is buried here. The founding of Illinois Wesleyan University and the selection of North Bloomington (now the twin city of Normal) as the site for Illinois State University helped determine the town's economic future.

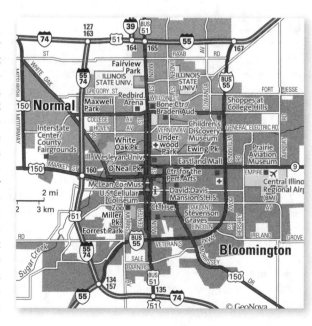

WHAT TO SEE AND DO

Illinois State University
220 N. Main St., Normal,
309-438-7000;
www.ilstu.edu
The first state university in Illinois founded in 1857 now has 22,000 students. Also on campus is the **Adlai E. Stevenson Memorial Room** (309-438-5669) which contains personal memorabilia, photographs. (Monday-Friday)

Miller Park Zoo
1020 S. Morris, Bloomington,
309-434-2250;
www.millerparkzoo.org
This zoo has big cats, river otters in natural settings, sea lions, a tropical rain forest and a children's zoo. Other activities include swimming, fishing, boating, picnicking, tennis and miniature golf. Band concerts are held in season. Daily 9:30 a.m.-4:30 p.m.

SPECIAL EVENTS

Illinois Shakespeare Festival
Ewing Manor, Normal,
Emerson and Towanda Streets,
309-438-8110;
www.thefestival.org
Shakespearean performances preceded by Elizabethan-era music and entertainment in June-early August.

HOTELS

★Best Western University Inn
6 Traders Circle, Normal,
309-454-4070, 800-780-7234;
www.bestwestern.com
101 rooms. Pets accepted; fee. Complimentary continental breakfast. Fitness room. Indoor pool. Airport transportation available. $

★Eastland Suites Lodge
1801 Eastland Dr., Bloomington,
309-662-0000, 800-537-8483;
www.eastlandsuitesbloomington.com

112 rooms, all suites. Pets accepted. Complimentary continental breakfast. High-speed Internet access. Fitness room. Indoor pool. Airport transportation available. $

★Hampton Inn
604 1/2 IAA Dr., Bloomington,
309-662-2800
108 rooms. Complimentary continental breakfast. High-speed Internet access. Outdoor pool. Airport transportation available. $

★★Holiday Inn
8 Traders Circle, Normal,
309-452-8300, 800-465-4329;
www.holiday-inn.com
160 rooms. Pets accepted; fee. Complimentary full breakfast. High-speed Internet access. Restaurant, bar. Children's activity center. Fitness room. Indoor pool, whirlpool. Airport transportation available. Business center. $

★★★The Chateau Hotel and Conference Center
1601 Jumer Dr., Bloomington,
309-662-2020, 866-690-4006;
www.chateauhotel.biz
This hotel is located near Illinois State University and has an indoor pool, sauna and whirlpool. Dining is made easy with an on-site restaurant and lounge.
180 rooms. Pets accepted, some restrictions; fee. Restaurant, bar. Children's activity center. Fitness room. Indoor pool, whirlpool. Airport transportation available. $

RESTAURANT

★★Central Station Cafe
220 E. Front St., Bloomington,
309-828-2323;
www.centralstation.cc
American menu. Lunch, dinner. Closed Sunday-Monday. Bar. $$

9

ILLINOIS

BURBANK

The city, located less than two miles from Midway airport, was incorporated in 1970 and shares a border with the southwest edge of the city of Chicago.
www.burbankil.gov

RESTAURANT

★★Old Barn
8100 S. Parkside Ave., Burbank
708-422-5400;

www.theoldbarn.biz
American menu. Lunch, dinner. Bar. Children's menu. Casual attire. Reservations recommended. Outdoor seating. $$

CARBONDALE

Carbondale is surrounded by lakes and rivers, including Crab Orchard and Little Grassy lakes and the Big Muddy River. Railroad yards, Southern Illinois University and surrounding coal fields give this community a unique personality.
Information: Convention and Tourism Bureau, 1201 E. Main St., 618-529-4451, 800-526-1500; www.cctb.org

WHAT TO SEE AND DO

Bald Knob
3630 Bald Knob Rd., Alto Pass,
618-893-2344
View three states from this high point in the Illinois Ozarks.

Giant City State Park
235 Giant City Rd., Makanda,
618-457-4836.
There are picturesque rock formations and a prehistoric "stone fort" on 4,055 acres at the park. Fishing, hunting, hiking and riding trails are available as well as picnicking, concession, lodge and dining room. Camping is permitted. Daily.

Golconda Marina and Smithland Pool
R.R. 2, Golconda,
618-683-5875
This marina is the gateway to Smithland Pool, a 23,000-acre recreational area off the Ohio River.

HOTELS

★Best Inn
1345 E. Main St., Carbondale
618-529-4801, 800-237-8466;
www.bestinn.com
82 rooms. Complimentary continental breakfast. Outdoor pool. $

★Super 8
1180 E. Main St., Carbondale
618-457-8822, 800-800-8000;
www.super8.com
63 rooms. Pets accepted. Complimentary continental breakfast. $

★★★Mansion of Golconda
515 Columbus St., Golconda;
618-683-4400
Built in 1894, this gabled 21-room Victorian mansion is a full-service inn included on the National Historic Register. 4 rooms. $

SPECIALTY LODGINGS

River Rose Inn
1 Main St., Elizabethtown,
618-287-8811
Located in a Greek Gothic mansion on the banks of the Ohio River in the Shawnee National Forest. 5 rooms. Check-in 2 p.m., check-out 11 a.m. $

RESTAURANTS

★★Mansion of Golconda
515 Columbus, Golconda; 618-683-4400
American menu. Lunch, dinner. Closed Monday. $$

★Tres Hombres
119 N. Washington St., Carbondale.
618-457-3308.
Mexican menu. Lunch, dinner. Bar. $

CENTRALIA

Centralia, named for the Illinois Central Railroad, and its neighbors, Central City and Wamac, form a continuous urban area that is the trading center and labor pool for four counties in south central Illinois.

Information: Chamber of Commerce, 130 S. Locust St., 618-532-6789; www.centralia.com

WHAT TO SEE AND DO

Fairview Park
Broadway and Buena Vista, Centralia; 618-532-6789

This is the site of Engine 2500, one of the largest steam locomotives ever built, weighing in at 225 tons. The engine was donated to the city by the Illinois Central Railroad. Swimming, picnicking and playgrounds are available on park grounds. Daily.

Lake Centralia
Green Street Rd., Centralia

Enjoy swimming, fishing, boating and picnicking.

RESTAURANT

★★Centralia House
111 N. Oak St, 618-532-9754

Cajun, American menu. Dinner. Closed Sunday. Bar. **$$**

CHAMPAIGN/ URBANA

Champaign and Urbana, separately incorporated, are united as the home of the University of Illinois. Champaign started as West Urbana when the Illinois Central Railroad ran its line two miles west of Urbana, the county seat. Defying annexation by Urbana in 1855, the new community was incorporated in 1860 as Champaign and prospered as a trade center. Today, the two communities are geographically one; Champaign continues as a commercial and industrial center, with the larger part of the university

falling within the boundaries of Urbana. Lincoln Square, the second downtown covered mall in the United States, is a forerunner in the revitalization of downtown districts.

Information: Convention and Visitors Bureau, 1817 S. Neil St., Champaign, 61820-7234, 217-352-1045, 800-369-6151; www.visitchampaigncounty.org

WHAT TO SEE AND DO

Lake of the Woods County Preserve
109 S. Lake of the Woods Rd., Mahomet, 217-586-3360

This preserve offers swimming, boating rentals, fishing and golf. The Early American Museum and botanical gardens is located here. Memorial Day-Labor Day:

★
★
★
★
★

daily; after Labor Day-early October: weekends. Park. Daily.

Orpheum Children's Science Museum
346 N. Neil St., Champaign/Urbana
217-352-5895
Located in the historic Orpheum Theatre, this museum has hands-on exhibits for kids. Wednesday-Sunday 1 p.m.- 6 p.m., Tuesday 9 a.m.-6 p.m.

University of Illinois
919 W. Illinois St., Champaign/Urbana
217-333-4666;
www.uiuc.edu
Founded in 1867, U of I now has a student population of 37,000 students. Included among the 200 major buildings on campus are the main library, which is the third-largest academic library in the United States. Also on campus is the **Krannert Art Museum,** which has a collection of 8,000 works including European and American paintings and decorative arts, as well as Asian art and African art.

HOTELS
★Best Western Paradise Inn
709 N. Dunlap St., Savoy,
217-356-1824, 800-780-7234;
www.bestwestern.com
62 rooms. Pets accepted, some restrictions; fee. Complimentary continental breakfast. Outdoor pool, children's pool. Airport transportation available. $

★Comfort Inn
305 W. Marketview Dr., Urbana,
217-352-4055, 800-228-5150;
www.comfortinn.com

67 rooms. Complimentary continental breakfast. Indoor pool, whirlpool. $

★Eastland Suites
1907 N. Cunningham Ave., Urbana,
217-367-8331, 800-253-8331;
www.eastlandsuitesurbana.com
127 rooms. Pets accepted; fee. Complimentary full breakfast. Bar. Fitness room. Indoor pool. Airport transportation available. $

★La Quinta Inn
1900 Center Dr., Champaign,
217-356-4000, 800-509-5507;
www.laquinta.com
122 rooms. Pets accepted, some restrictions. Complimentary continental breakfast. Outdoor pool. $

★★Historic Lincoln Hotel
209 S. Broadway, Urbana,
217-384-8800
130 rooms. Pets accepted, some restrictions; fee. Restaurant, bar. Indoor pool, whirlpool. Airport transportation available. $

RESTAURANTS
★Ned Kelly's
1601 N. Cunningham Ave., Urbana,
217-344-8201;
www.nedkellyssteakhouse.com
Steak menu. Lunch, dinner. Bar. Children's menu. $$

★★Timpone's
710 S. Goodwin Ave., Urbana,
217-344-7619.
Italian, American menu. Lunch, dinner. Closed Sunday; and one week in Aug. Bar. $$

CHARLESTON
One of the great Lincoln-Douglas debates was held here on September 18, 1858. As an itinerate lawyer riding the circuit, Abraham Lincoln practiced law in the area. His father, Thomas Lincoln, and stepmother once lived in a cabin eight miles south of Charleston.
Information: Charleston Area Chamber of Commerce, 501 Jackson St., 217-345-7041; www.charlestonchamber.com

WHAT TO SEE AND DO

Coles County Courthouse
651 Jackson Ave., Charleston,
217-348-0501
This courthouse sits on Charleston Square, where Lincoln practiced law in an earlier courthouse and where the Charleston Riot took place. The Riot involved 300 men in armed conflict during the Civil War.

Fox Ridge State Park
18175 State Park Rd., Charleston,
217-345-6416
This is a rugged area of 1,500 acres including Ridge Lake and maintained by the Illinois Natural History Survey.

Lincoln Log Cabin State Historic Site
400 S. Lincoln Hwy. Rd., Lerna,
217-345-1845
This 86-acre site contains the Thomas Lincoln Log Cabin, reconstructed on the original foundation that Abraham Lincoln's father built in 1840. A reconstructed farm surrounds the cabin. In nearby Shiloh Cemetery are the graves of Thomas Lincoln and Sarah Bush Lincoln, the president's father and stepmother. Interpretive program offered May-October. Picnicking. Wednesday-Sunday.

HOTEL

★★Best Western Worthington Inn
920 W. Lincoln Ave., Charleston,
217-348-8161, 800-528-8161;
www.bestwestern.com
67 rooms. Pets accepted, some restrictions. Complimentary continental breakfast. Restaurant. Outdoor pool. Airport transportation available. **$**

RESTAURANTS

★★Allies American Grille
200 Lee St. E., Charleston,
304-345-6500, 800-228-9290;
www.charlestonmarriott.com
American menu. Breakfast, lunch, dinner, late-night. Brunch bar. Children's menu. Casual attire. Reservations recommended. **$$**

★★Athletic Club Grill
300 Court St., Charleston,
304-347-8700, 800-362-2779;
www.embassysuites.com
American menu. Lunch, dinner. Bar. Children's menu. Casual attire. **$$**

★★Fifth Quarter Restaurant
201 Clendenin St., Charleston,
304-345-3933
Steak menu. Lunch, dinner. Bar. Children's menu. Casual attire. Reservations recommended. Outdoor seating. **$$$**

CHICAGO

Rudyard Kipling wrote of Chicago, "I have struck a city, a real city and they call it Chicago." The city is thriving, with a vibrant downtown, growing population, booming industry and world-class dining and entertainment. Wicked winter weather aside, the Windy City is one of the country's top tourist destinations.

Chicago's past is distinctive, built on adversity and contradiction. The city's worst tragedy, the Great Chicago Fire of 1871, was the basis for its physical and cultural renaissance. In the heart of one of the poorest neighborhoods, two young women of means, Jane Addams and Ellen Gates Starr, created Hull House, a social service institution that has been copied throughout the world. A city of neat frame cottages and bulky stone mansions, it produced the Chicago school of architecture whose innovative style was carried on by Frank Lloyd Wright and Ludwig Mies van der Rohe. Even its most famous crooks provide a study in contrasts: Al Capone was the Prohibition gangster, while Samuel Insull was the financial finagler whose stock manipulations left thousands of small investors penniless in the late 1920s.

In 1803, the fledging U.S. government took possession of the area and sent a small military contingent from Detroit to select the site for a fort. Fort Dearborn was built at a strategic spot on the mouth of the Chicago River; on the opposite bank, a settlement slowly grew. There was little activity until Chicago was selected as the terminal site of the proposed Illinois and Michigan Canal. This started a land boom that carries on today.

Chicagoans are proud of their world-famous symphony orchestra, their Lyric Opera and their numerous and diverse dance companies. Chicago's theater community is vibrant, with more than 100 theaters. The collections at the Art Institute of Chicago, Museum of Contemporary Art and galleries in the River North area are among the best in the country. The 1996 relocation of Lake Shore Drive made it possible to create the Museum Campus. This 57-acre extension of Burnham Park provides an easier and more scenic route to the Adler Planetarium, Field Museum of Natural History and Shedd Aquarium, and surrounds them with one continuous park featuring terraced gardens and broad walkways. No visit to Chicago is complete without touring Millennium Park. This new downtown park area includes the Harris Theater for Music and Dance, the 50-foot-high water-spewing towers of the Crown Fountain, the Frank Gehry–designed band shell and bridge or the Cloud Gate sculpture, which locals lovingly call "the bean."

Information: Chicago Office of Tourism, Chicago Cultural Center, 78 E. Washington St., 312-744-2400, 800-226-6632; www.enjoyillinois.com

ILLINOIS

★
★
★
★
★

SPOT★ LIGHT

★THE FIRST SKYSCRAPER WAS BUILT IN CHICAGO IN 1885.

★CRACKER JACK DEBUTED AT THE CHICAGO WORLD'S FAIR IN 1893.

★CHICAGO SOARS—IT'S THE HEADQUARTERS FOR BOTH BOEING AND UNITED AIRLINES.

WHAT TO SEE AND DO

Adler Planetarium and Astronomy Museum

1300 S. Lake Shore Dr., Chicago
312-322-0300;
www.adlerplanetarium.org

One of the oldest observatories in the country, the Adler Planetarium offers a high-tech look at the night sky. Exhibits commemorate the Space Race of the 1960s, as well as new techniques to learn more about the Milky Way. If you want a bargain, go on Monday or Tuesday between September and December, when admission is free. Monday-Friday 9:30 a.m.-4:30 p.m., Saturday-Sunday 9 a.m.-4:30 p.m.; Memorial Day-Labor Day: daily until 6 p.m.

American Girl Place

111 E. Chicago Ave., Chicago
312-943-9400, 877-247-5223;
www.americangirlplace.com

When strolling around downtown Chicago, you're bound to see legions of girls toting red shopping bags from American Girl Place. Dolls are the major draw here, but the store also sells clothing and accessories for the dolls (and their owners), as well as doll furniture and toys. American Girl Place also features a cafe (reservations recommended); various special events and a Broadway-style show. Sunday 9 a.m.-7 p.m., Monday-Thursday 10 a.m.-7 p.m., Friday 10 a.m.-9 p.m., Saturday 9 a.m.-9 p.m.

Apollo Theatre
2540 N. Lincoln Ave., Chicago,
773-935-6100; www.apollochicago.com
An intimate theater in Chicago's Lincoln Park neighborhood, the Apollo has been home to both famous and infamous productions over the years. Built in 1978, the theater saw many productions by the Steppenwolf Theater Company, as well as native Chicagoan Jim Belushi starring in David Mamet's *Sexual Perversity in Chicago*.

Art Institute of Chicago
111 S. Michigan Ave., Chicago,
31-443-3600; www.artic.edu
Adjacent to Millennium Park on South Michigan Avenue, this 1879 Beaux Arts building, originally part of the Columbian Exposition, houses more than 300,000 works of art within its 10 curatorial departments. The museum has what is considered the finest and most comprehensive modern and contemporary art collection in the world, one of the largest arms collections in America and one of the two finest collections of Japanese woodblock prints. Highlights include Georges Seurat's *A Sunday on La Grande Jatte 1884*, Grant Wood's *American Gothic*, Edward Hopper's *Nighthawks* and 33 Monet paintings. A new Renzo Piano-designed modern wing is under construction and set to open in the summer of 2009. Free admission on Tuesday. Monday-Wednesday, Friday 10:30 a.m.-4:30 p.m., Thursday 10:30 a.m.-8 p.m., Saturday-Sunday 10 a.m.-5 p.m.

Auditorium Building
430 S. Michigan Ave., Chicago
This landmark structure built in 1889 was designed by Chicago School architects Louis Sullivan and Dankmar Adler. The interior is noted for its intricate system of iron framing, ornamentation and near-perfect acoustics. Now houses Roosevelt University.

Auditorium Theatre
50 E. Congress Pkwy., Chicago
312-922-2110,
www.auditoriumtheatre.org
The Auditorium Theatre building, designed by architects Louis Sullivan and Dankmar Adler, underwent a face-lift in 2003, getting a new state-of-the-art stage and orchestra pit. The stage was returned to its original height, as designed in the 1880s. The Joffrey Ballet opened the new stage, and the historic building begins yet another era.

Briar Street Theatre
3133 N. Halsted St., Chicago,
773-348-4000
The Briar Street Theatre has been the Chicago home of the national sensation, *Blue Man Group*, which incorporates everyday objects like metal drums and pipes into a musical experience rife with color and comedy. It's easily accessible by CTA rapid transit, and tickets are less pricey than at many other theaters in the city.

Brookfield Zoo
8400 W. 31st St., Brookfield,
708-485-0263, 800-201-0784,
www.brookfieldzoo.org
Located just 14 miles west of downtown Chicago, the Brookfield Zoo is a world-class, 216-acre facility that houses more than 2,800 animals. Long known for its progressive approach to wildlife, the zoo was the first in the country to install animals in near-natural habitats instead of in cages. Children get special attention here: a two-acre, 300-animal Family Play Zoo enables kids and their families to interact with the animals. The zoo also features botanical gardens, a dolphin show, several restaurants, a store, roving naturalists and ongoing special programming. Memorial Day-Labor Day: daily 9:30 a.m.-6 p.m.; April-Memorial Day and Labor Day-October: Monday-Friday

ART DECO CHICAGO

Chicago is an Art Deco lover's dream. To see just some of the city's Art Deco buildings, begin at the Chicago Board of Trade (141 W. Jackson Blvd.), home to the world's oldest and largest futures exchange, formed in 1848. Ceres, the Roman goddess of grain and harvest, receives a nod with a 31-foot-tall statue that sits atop the original 1930 building as well as in a mural in the atrium, which was added in the 1980s. The three-story lobby, a dazzling Art Deco masterpiece, gleams with contrasting black and buff-colored marble trimmed with silver.

Walk a couple of blocks north to the American National Bank Building (1 N. LaSalle St.). This 49-story limestone building with typical Art Deco setbacks and dominant vertical lines occupies an entire block of Chicago's financial district. A stunning lobby features dark marble contrasted by gleaming metalwork and exquisite carved wood sconces. Outside, at the fifth-floor level, relief panels chronicle the 17th-century explorations of René Robert Cavelier and Sieur de La Salle.

Turn east to the former Chicago Daily News Building (400 W. Madison St.). The careers of Horace Greeley, Joseph Pulitzer and other famous journalists, as well as events from Chicago's rich newspaper history, are chronicled with stylized bas-relief figures carved by Alvin Meyer. The limestone building with dramatic setbacks and an open riverfront plaza was originally designed to house the newspaper's offices and plant. Inside are ornate metal elevator doors, grillwork and terrazzo floors in a geometric pattern.

Finally, travel north to the Carbide and Carbon Building (230 N. Michigan Ave.). This skyscraper is dramatically dark, but is offset with striking dark green masonry and gold terra-cotta trim. The two-story lobby features marble walls, elegant bronze grillwork, gold-and-white plaster and recessed lights of frosted glass.

★
★
★
★
★

10 a.m.-5 p.m., Saturday-Sunday 10 a.m.-6 p.m.; November-March: daily 10 a.m.-5 p.m.

Cadillac Palace Theatre
151 W. Randolph St., Chicago, 312-977-1700

This theater is a Chicago landmark whose design was inspired by the decadence of the palace at Versailles. It originally played first-run movies during the 1920s and 1930s and was converted to a live theater in the 1950s. In 2008, it will host Avenue Q, Dirty Dancing, Rent, My Fair Lady and more.

Chicago Architecture Foundation Tours
224 S. Michigan Ave., Chicago, 312-922-3432; www.architecture.org

This not-for-profit organization conducts one of the city's most popular tours, a 90-minute Architecture River Cruise that passes more than 50 architecturally significant sights on the Chicago River and Lake Michigan. Other offerings include walking tours of the Loop's historic skyscrapers, Art Deco buildings, the Theater District, modern skyscrapers and Loop sculpture, or individual city neighborhoods like Old Town, River North and Sheffield Historic District. You can purchase tickets and meet for tours at one of two tour centers on Michigan Avenue.

Chicago River Boat Tour
455 E. Illinois St., Chicago, 312-922-3432.

This 1 1/2-hour tour covers the north and south branches of the Chicago River, with views of the city's celebrated riverfront architecture; historic 19th-century railroad bridges and warehouses, 20th-century bridge houses and magnificent Loop skyscrapers. Reservations required. May-September: daily; October: Tuesday, Thursday, Saturday-Sunday; no tours Labor Day.

Graceland Cemetery Tour
4001 N. Clark St., Chicago,
773-525-1105
Walking through Graceland Cemetery on the city's north side is like taking a step back into Chicago's early history. Not only will you recognize the names of the movers and shakers who put Chicago on the map, but there are also memorials to the people who helped build it. Highlights include Louis Sullivan's tomb for Carrie Eliza Getty, a landmark described as the beginning of modern architecture in America; Daniel Burnham's island resting place in the middle of the lake; and Mies van der Rohe's elegantly understated grave marker. Daily 8 a.m.-4:30 p.m.

Chicago Cultural Center
78 E. Washington St., Chicago,
312-744-6630;
www.ci.chi.il.us/tourism/culturalcenter
The Chicago Cultural Center is housed in a landmark Michigan Avenue building (formerly a library) that features Tiffany glass domes, mosaics and marble walls and stairs. The center itself often offers exhibitions of groundbreaking art, as well as performances by renowned poets and musicians. On weekdays during the summer, you can catch "Lunchbreak," a program designed to offer good music in a great setting during the lunch hour. Monday-Thursday 10 a.m.-7 p.m., Friday until 6 p.m., Saturday until 5 p.m., Sunday 11 a.m.-5 p.m., archives closed Sunday.

Chicago Fire Academy
558 W. DeKoven St., Chicago,
312-747-8151
This academy is built on the site where the Great Chicago Fire of 1871 is believed to have started. Legend has it that a cow in Mrs. O'Leary's barn knocked over a lantern and began the fire, but recent investigations suggest this story may be fictitious. The fire academy pays tribute to the city's firefighters.

Chicago Historical Society
1601 N. Clark St., Chicago
312-642-4600; www.chicagohs.org
The society has rotating exhibits that focus on the history and development of Chicago. There are selected aspects of Illinois and U.S. history on display, including galleries devoted to costumes, decorative arts and architecture. There are pioneer craft demonstrations and a hands-on gallery. Free admission on Monday. Daily.

Chicago Temple
77 W. Washington St., Chicago,
312-236-4548; www.chicagotemple.org
Built in 1923, this is considered the first Methodist Episcopal Church. At 568 feet from street level to the tip of its Gothic tower, this is the highest church spire in the world. Tours. Monday-Saturday 2 p.m., Sunday after 8:30 a.m. and 11 a.m. services.

Chicago Theatre
175 N. State St., Chicago, 312-443-6300
The Chicago Theatre may be best known for the flashy, classic marquee sign, but visitors to the theater may be more impressed by its French baroque design. The extravagant and ornate interior features bronze light fixtures with Steuben glass shades, crystal chandeliers, polished marble and soaring murals hand-painted on the auditoriums ceiling. Opened in 1921 as the city's first movie palace, the theater now hosts live performances by musicians, comedians and actors. The theater's original Wurlitzer pipe organ has been restored and still produces a lush, powerful sound.

Chicago Tribune Tower
435 N. Michigan Ave., Chicago,
312-222-3994
This 36-story tower, headquarters for the Tribune Company, is a *moderne* building with a Gothic-detailed base and crown. It does exactly what publisher Joseph Medill intended: it "thames" the Chicago River.

17

ILLINOIS

Bits and pieces of historic structures from around the world are embedded in the exterior walls of the lower floors.

Chinatown

Cermak Rd. and Wentworth Ave., Chicago
312-326-5320; www.chicagochinatown.org
Chicago's Chinatown is a vibrant and lively cultural center that makes for a fascinating visit. Located south of the Loop at Cermak and Wentworth, Chinatown's boundary is marked by a tiled gateway. Within a 10-block radius are 10,000 community members, more than 40 restaurants, 20 gift shops, herbal and tea stores and bakeries. Neighborhood festivals include Chinese New Year, the Dragon Boat Festival and the midautumn Moon Festival.

Civic Opera Building

20 N. Wacker Dr., Chicago, 312-332-2244
On the lower levels, under 45 floors of commercial office space, is the Art Deco, 3,400-seat Civic Opera House, home of the Lyric Opera of Chicago. **Lyric Opera of Chicago** (312-419-0033) performs some of the biggest shows in operatic theater. Each season begins with a new 12-person repertory cast chosen in March and given additional professional training to make Chicago's performances among the finest anywhere.

DuSable Museum of African-American History

740 E. 56th Place, Chicago, 773-947-0600;
www.dusablemuseum.org
This museum houses African and African-American art objects along with displays of black history in Africa and the United States. There is an extensive collection of paintings, sculptures, artifacts, textiles, books and photographs. Tuesday-Sunday, January-May. Free admission Sunday.

Elks National Veterans Memorial

2750 N. Lakeview Ave., Chicago
773-755-4876; www.elks.org/memorial
The Elks Fraternal Order erected this memorial, designed by New York architect Egerton Swarthout, in 1926 to honor Amer-

ican soliders of World War I. The memorial has since become a tribute to Americans who lost their lives in World War II, the Korean War and the Vietnam War. The domed structure has a 100-foot rotunda made of marble and adorned with murals, art-glass windows and bronze sculptures. December-March: Monday-Friday 9 a.m.-5 p.m.; April-November: also Saturday-Sunday 10 a.m.-5 p.m.

Field Museum of Natural History

1400 S. Lake Shore Dr., Chicago
312-922-9410; www.fmnh.org
This more than 100-year-old natural history museum made headlines in 2000 when it unveiled Sue, the largest and most complete tyrannosaurus Rex skeleton. Sue joined a fine collection of artifacts from civilizations in Egypt and Mesopotamia and a vast assortment of taxidermy. Daily 9a.m.-5p.m. Discounted admission in January-February, mid-September-late December on Monday-Tuesday.

Ford Center for the Performing Arts Oriental Theatre

24 W. Randolph St., Chicago,
312-977-1700
The Oriental Theatre was originally a movie house that doubled as an entertainment venue for musicians like Duke Ellington during the early 20th century. The theater closed its doors to moviegoers in the 1980s but came back with a flourish. Reopening in 1998, it was converted into a place to see live shows. The theater is currently hosting a production of the musical Wicked.

Garfield Park Conservatory

300 N. Central Park Ave., Chicago
312-746-5100;
www.garfield-conservatory.org
The park has outdoor formal gardens while the Conservatory has eight houses and propagating houses on more than 5 acres. There are four major shows annually at Horticultural Hall and Show House. Friday-Wednesday 9 a.m.-5 p.m., Thursday to 8 p.m.

Goodman Theatre

170 N. Dearborn St., Chicago
312-443-3800; www.goodman-theatre.org
The Goodman Theatre can be considered a breeding ground for up-and-coming actors and productions. A good example is its production of Eugene O'Neill's *A Long Day's Journey into Night*, which took star Brian Dennehy with it to Broadway and captured several Tony Awards. Tickets can be pricey, but not as expensive as a Broadway show, and there are discounts for students and groups.

Grant Park

337 E. Randolph St., Chicago
312-742-7648;
www.chicagoparkdistrict.com
Grant Park was built on a landfill created by debris from the Great Chicago Fire of 1871. Now it's one of the great landmarks of the city, with **Buckingham Fountain** as its centerpiece. The fountain was given to the city by Kate Buckingham in 1927 in honor of her brother. Every minute, 133 jets spray approximately 14,000 gallons of water as high as 150 feet. Every hour on the hour, there is a 20-minute water display (accompanied at dusk by lights and music). Each year, the **Taste of Chicago** is held here, as are many picnics and smaller festivals. Recently, the park has been the host to **Lollapalooza,** the huge three-day outdoor music festival. You can enjoy concerts at the Petrillo Music Shell or relax on the lawn on summer evenings to watch outdoor movies during the yearly Chicago Outdoor Film Festival. Daily 6 a.m.-11 p.m.

Green Mill

4802 N. Broadway St., Chicago,
773-878-5552
The oldest jazz club in America, the Green Mill is located in the still-dicey Uptown neighborhood. With a vintage sign out front and a gorgeous carved bar inside, this is a former speakeasy of the Capone gang. The jazz, however, is strictly contemporary, showcasing some of the most acclaimed musicians working today. On

GO CUBS, GO

If there is one story every Chicagoan knows, it is the Curse of the Billy Goat. According to local legend, William Sianis, owner of the now famous Billy Goat Tavern, bought two tickets to the last game of the 1945 World Series, one for himself and one for his goat. Upon arriving at the park, Sianis was told that his animal would not be admitted because of its smell. Infuriated, he put a curse on the ball club: Never again would a World Series be played at Wrigley Field! And that prediction has held true: the Cubs haven't been to a World Series since 1945 (and haven't won since 1908), making their losing the streak the longest in baseball history.

Attending a Cubs game is an experience rich with tradition. The Cubs' home park, Wrigley Field, was built in 1914 and is one of the nation's oldest ballparks. Its ivy-covered outer wall and urban setting are unique in an era of bigger and better (and more revenue-generating) baseball stadiums. This park was the last in the country to install lights when it did so in 1981; until then, games were played during the day only. And the seventh inning stretch is a gameday highlight—visiting celebrities such as Bill Murray, Vince Vaughn and John Cusack take the mike to lead the crowd in the singing of "Take Me Out to the Ballgame."

Beyond curses, these perennial underdogs are hometown favorites and beloved around the world. Will they or won't they make it to the World Series this year? Ask a hard-core, albeit heartbroken, fan and the answer is always the same, "Of course, they're going all the way!"

★
★
★
★
★

weeknights, you might find swing or a big band; on weekend nights, several acts pack in crowds; and on Sundays, you can experience the Poetry Slam (the nation's first, hosted by Marc Smith, the godfather of poetry slams), where area poets test their mettle against audience reaction. Daily

Harborside International Golf Center
11001 S. Doty Ave E., Chicago,
312-782-7837; www.harborsidegolf.com
Located just south of downtown Chicago, Harborside was manufactured by architect Dick Nugent out of a converted landfill into one of the most renowned municipal courses in America. The center has two courses, the Starboard and the Port layouts, and features four tee boxes on each hole. The center's practice facility is also top-notch, with driving ranges of longer than 400 yards and many opportunities to practice middle irons and short games even at night, as the 58-acre practice facility is fully lit.

Holy Name Cathedral
735 N. State St., Chicago
312-787-8040;
www.holynamecathedral.org
The home to the Chicago archdiocese and Francis Cardinal George, Holy Name is a good example of Gothic Revival architecture in Chicago. Thousands of parishoners attend services at Holy Name each week, many of them to hear the cardinal say Mass on Sunday morning. The church is also affiliated with the Francis Xavier Warde School.

Illinois Institute of Technology (IIT)
3300 S. Federal St., Chicago
312-567-3000; www.iit.edu
Students from more than 100 countries converge on this campus to engage themselves in IIT's Interprofessional Project, which aims to teach students the skills they'll need to fit in wherever they choose in a job market that is constantly expanding technologically. Ninety-eight percent of the faculty (who teach almost all the classes) hold doctorate

or other advanced degrees. The campus was designed by architect Mies van de Rohe.

International Museum of Surgical Science
1524 N. Lake Shore Dr., Chicago
312-642-6502; www.imss.org
Covering the advancement of surgical medicine across more than four millennia of history, this four-story museum housed in an old mansion organizes its exhibits into categories like radiology, orthopedics and "A Day in the Life of a Turn-of-the-Century Apothecary." Located on Lake Shore Drive, the museum offers free admission on Tuesday. There are permanent exhibits, such as the optical history exhibit and displays of Victorian-era surgical implements, as well as rotating features covering subjects like art's depiction of anatomy. May-August: Tuesday-Sunday; September-April: Tuesday-Saturday, 10 a.m.-4 p.m.

Jane Addams Hull-House Museum
800 S. Halsted St., (The Campus of the University of Illinois at Chicago),
312-413-5353;
www.uic.edu/jaddams/hull/hull_house.html
Two original Hull-House buildings, the restored Hull Mansion built in 1856 and dining hall built in 1905, formed the nucleus of the 13-building settlement complex founded in 1889 by Jane Addams and Ellen Gates Starr, social welfare pioneers. There are exhibits and presentations on the history of Hull House, the surrounding neighborhood, ethnic groups and women's history. Tuesday-Friday 10 a.m.-4 p.m., Sunday noon-4 p.m.

John Hancock Center
875 N. Michigan Ave., Chicago
312-751-3681, 888-875-8439;
www.hancock-observatory.com
The John Hancock Center, standing at 1,127 feet and 100 floors, is the world's 13th tallest building. Since completion in 1969, this innovative office and residential building has won awards for its distinctive exterior X bracing, which eliminated the need for inner support beams and increased usable space. The 94th-floor observatory features an open-air skywalk, a history wall chronicling

Chicago's growth, multilingual sky tours and a 360-degree view that spans 80 miles and four states. Visitors can dine or have a drink at the 95th-floor Signature Room. Daily 9 a.m.-11 p.m.

Lake Michigan
312-742-7529, Chicago;
www.chicagoparkdistrict.com
Chicago's lakefront reflects the vision of architect Daniel Burnham, whose 1909 plan for Chicago specified that the shoreline remain publicly owned and enjoyed by all. It is also one of the things that makes this city unique. After all, how many major cities have beaches, 31 in total, within the city limits? In addition, the lakefront sports 18 miles of bicycle, jogging and in-line skating paths, skating rinks, tennis courts, field houses, theaters and more, all easily accessible and open to the public. Daily, Sunrise-11 p.m.

Lincoln Park
2400 N. Stockton Dr., Chicago, 312-742-7529
The largest in Chicago, Lincoln Park stretches almost the entire length of the north end of the city along the lake. It contains statues of Lincoln, Hans Christian Andersen, Shakespeare and others. There is a nine-hole golf course, driving range, miniature golf and bike and jogging paths and, of course, protected beaches. In the park is **Lincoln Park Conservatory** (2391 N. Stockton Dr. 312-742-7736) which has formal and rock gardens and an extensive collection of orchids. (Daily 9 a.m.-5 p.m.) The **Lincoln Park Zoo** (2200 N. Cannon Dr. 312-742-2000) may be small (just 35 acres), but it's free, open to the public 365 days a year and a leader in education and conservation. (Daily; hours vary by season.)

Merchandise Mart
222 Merchandise Mart Plaza, Chicago
312-527-7600;
www.merchandisemart.com
The world's largest commercial building, the Merchandise Mart was built in 1930

and now houses restaurants, shopping and the city's top interior design showrooms.

Michigan Avenue Bridge
At the Chicago River between
Michigan and Wabash Aves., Chicago
This well-known Chicago landmark offers stunning views of the city as it crosses the Chicago River. The bridge was completed in 1920, designed by Edward Burnnett and based on the Alexander III Bridge over the Seine River in Paris. Four 40-foot limestone bridge houses (two on either end) were added in 1928. Each contains a sculptured relief depicting historic Chicago events.

Millennium Park
Michigan Ave. and Randolph St., Chicago
312-742-1168; www.millenniumpark.org
The city's newest and most popular attraction, this 24.5-acre park is a center of world-class art, music, architecture and landscape design. Don't miss the 50-foot-high Crown Fountain, the Frank Gehry-designed Pritzker Pavillion or the giant silver reflective *Cloud Gate* sculpture. Daily 6 a.m.-11 p.m.

Monadnock Building
53 W. Jackson Blvd., Chicago
This Burnham and Root structure is the highest wall-bearing building in Chicago, and at the time of its construction (1889-1891), was the tallest and largest office building in the world. It is now considered one of the master works of the Chicago school of architecture.

Museum of Contemporary Art
220 E. Chicago Ave., Chicago,
312-280-2660; www.mcachicago.org
Just half a block east of Michigan Avenue lies the Museum of Contemporary Art, one of the nation's largest facilities dedicated to post-1945 works. With a large, rotating permanent collection and a reputation for cutting-edge exhibits, the museum showcases some of the finest artists working today. The museum has been in its current building since 1995, and positions itself as a cultural center. An annual highlight is the 24-hour summer solstice celebration. The

terraced sculpture garden with views of Lake Michigan serves as a peaceful urban sanctuary. Tuesday-Sunday. Free admission Tuesday.

Museum of Science and Industry
5700 S. Lake Shore Dr., 773-684-1414, 800-468-6674; www.msichicago.org
This museum includes a free tour of a German U-boat captured during World War II, a re-creation of a coal mine and a model train layout that encapsulates almost the entire country. The museum also includes an exhibit on genetics and the improvements made to medicine through the Human Genome Project, as well as several rooms dedicated to the telling of time, with more than 500 unique instruments. Free admission varies by season; see website for details. Daily; hours vary by season.

Music Box Theatre
3733 N. Southport Ave., Chicago
773-871-6604;
www.musicboxtheatre.com
This circa 1929 neighborhood art house attracts a loyal following not just because its one of the few places in town devoted to independent, foreign, cult, documentary and classic films, but because the Music Box is one of the last surviving old-time movie palaces. The theater is also home to screenings for the Chicago International Film Festival, held for three weeks each October. Daily.

Navy Pier
600 E. Grand Ave., Chicago,
312-595-7437;
www.navypier.com
Known as one of the city's top venues for families, Navy Pier is an old naval station renovated during the 1990s and converted into an urban playground. It's most visible attraction, the 150-foot-high Ferris wheel, offers spectacular views of the lake and skyline and is modeled after the world's first, which was built in Chicago in 1893. Take advantage of the city's free trolley service from downtown hotels and other locations.

Daily. Also here is the **Chicago Children's Museum.** Daily 10 a.m.-8 p.m.

Old Chicago Water Tower and Pumping Station
806 N. Michigan Ave.,
Near North Side, Chicago,
312-742-0808
These castle-like Gothic Revival buildings survived the Great Chicago Fire of 1871. Today, they house a visitor center and City Gallery, presenting photography exhibits with a Chicago theme, and are also the home of the acclaimed Lookingglass Theatre Company. Monday-Saturday 10 a.m.-6:30 p.m., Sunday 10 a.m.-5 p.m.

The Notebaert Nature Museum
2430 N. Cannon Dr., Chicago,
773-755-5100;
www.naturemuseum.org
Hands-on exploration of nature is the mission of the Notebaert Nature Museum, built in 1999 as an offshoot of the Chicago Academy of Sciences. Visitors can connect with the natural world via indoor exhibits and outdoor adventures. Permanent exhibits include a 28-foot-high butterfly haven, a city science interactive display and a wilderness walk, and children's gallery designed for kids ages 3 to 8. Free admission on Thursday. Monday-Friday 9 a.m.-4:30 p.m., Saturday-Sunday 10 a.m.-5 p.m.

Polish Museum of America
984 N. Milwaukee Ave., Chicago,
773-384-3352;
www.prcua.org
The museum has one of the best collections of Polish music and literature outside of Warsaw, catering to Chicago's large Polish population. There are exhibits on Polish culture, folklore and immigration. Founded in 1935, the museum is used by many Polish scholars to complete research on projects they produce. Friday-Wednesday 11 a.m.-4 p.m., closed holidays.

Prairie Avenue Historic District
1800 S. Prairie Ave., Chicago,

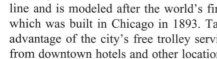

OUTDOOR ART

Batcolumn
Harold Washington Social Security
Administration Building Plaza,
600 W. Madison St., Chicago
Designed by artist Claes Oldenburg in
1977, this 100-foot-tall, 20-ton welded
steel sculpture resembles a baseball bat,
set in a concrete base.

Flamingo
Federal Center Plaza,
Adams and Dearborn Sts.
Sculptor Alexander Calder's famous red
stabile, a Chicago landmark, is 53 feet
high and weighs 50 tons; it was built in
1974.

The Four Seasons
First National Plaza,
Monroe and Dearborn Sts.
This 3,000-square-foot mosaic designed
by Marc Chagall in 1974 contains more
than 320 different shades of marble,
stone, granite and glass.

Untitled
50 W. Washington St., Chicago
Richard J. Daley Plaza

Miro's *Chicago*
Cook County Administration Building,
69 W. Washington
The structure built 1981, made of steel,
wire mesh, concrete, bronze, and ceramic
tile, is 39 feet tall.

Picasso Sculpture
129 N. Dearborn Ave.
No one's really sure what it is . . . perhaps
a horse, a bird or a woman . . . but since its
unveiling in 1967, this 50-foot-tall, 162-
ton steel work of art has become an unof-
ficial and an unlikely icon for the city.
Some consider it a miracle that the city's
famously conservative mayor, Richard J.
Daley (aka "the Boss"), would commission a work of cubist abstract expression-
ism, but with one of Chicago's leading
architectural firms as liaison, the project
happened and led the way for other major
public art projects.

Untitled Sounding Sculpture
AON Center, 200 E. Randolph St.
This unique "sounding sculpture" set in
a reflecting pool, was designed by Harry
Bertoia in 1975.

312-326-1480
This is the area where millionaires lived
during the 1800s. The Clarke House (circa
1835), the oldest house in the city, has been
restored and now stands at a site near its
original location. The Glessner House, 1800
S. Prairie Ave., is owned and maintained by
the Chicago Architecture Foundation and
was designed by architect Henry Hobson
Richardson. Two-hour guided tours of both
houses are offered Wednesday-Sunday.
Other houses on the cobblestone street are
the Kimball House (1890), 1801 S. Prairie
Ave., a replica of a French chateau; Cole-
man House (circa 1885), 1811 S. Prairie
Ave.; and Keith House (circa 1870), 1900
S. Prairie Ave. Architectural tours. Free
admission Wednesday.

Richard J. Daley Center and Plaza
50 W. Washington Blvd., Chicago,
312-603-7980
This 31-story, 648-foot building houses
county and city courts and administrative
offices. In the plaza is the Chicago Picasso
sculpture; across Washington Street is
Miro's *Chicago* sculpture.

River North Gallery District
With the highest concentration of art galleries outside Manhattan, Chicago's River
North Gallery District, just a short walk
from Michigan Avenue and the Loop, offers
world-class art in a stylish setting of renovated warehouses and upscale restaurants.
Find the majority of galleries on Superior
and Franklin Streets. If you happen to be
in town on the second Friday of the month,

wander over to the opening-night reception (5-7 p.m.) for a glass of wine and a glimpse of up-and-coming artists. Tuesday-Saturday.

Rookery
209 S. LaSalle St., Chicago
This is the oldest surviving steel-skeleton skyscraper in the world. Designed by Burnham & Root in 1886, the remarkable glass-encased lobby was remodeled in 1905 by Frank Lloyd Wright.

Royal George Theatre
1641 N. Halsted St., Chicago,
312-988-9000
Located in Chicago's Lincoln Park neighborhood, this theater features seats that are sparse in number but well spaced, enabling a relaxing theater experience. The stage has hosted such shows as Tony Kushner's acclaimed *Angels in America* and the review *Forever Plaid*.

Sears Tower
233 S. Wacker Dr., Chicago,
312-875-9696;
www.thesearstower.com;
www.theskydeck.com
It's fitting that the town that gave birth to the skyscraper should lay claim to North America's tallest building. Built in 1974 by Skidmore, Owings & Merrill, the 110-story Sears Tower soars 1/4 mile (1,450 feet) above the city, making it the most prominent building in the skyline. The building was constructed of black anodized aluminum in nine bundled square tubes, an innovation that provides both wind protection and the necessary support for its extraordinary height. The 103rd-floor observatory offers panoramic views of the city; on a clear day, you can easily see 35 miles away. During the height of the tourist season, expect long waits. May-September: daily 10 a.m.-10 p.m.; October-April: daily 10 a.m.-8 p.m.

Shedd Aquarium
1200 S. Lake Shore Dr., Chicago,
312-939-2438; www.sheddnet.org
This aquarium features more than 8,000 freshwater and marine animals displayed in 200 naturalistic habitats while divers hand-feed fish, sharks, eels and turtles several times daily in the 90,000-gallon Caribbean Reef exhibit. The beluga whale breeding progam has been particularly successful, with calves born in 2006 and 2007. In the summer, the aquarium hosts live jazz performances. Free admission Monday-Tuesday. September-February only. Summer: daily 9 a.m.-6 p.m.; Winter: daily 9 a.m.-5 p.m.

Soldier Field
1410 S. Museum Campus Dr., Chicago
312-235-7000; www.soldierfield.net
Soldier Field opened in 1924 as Municipal Grant Park Stadium. The first game played saw Notre Dame down Northwestern 13-6. The Chicago Bears didn't play home games at the stadium until 1971, when they moved from baseball's Wrigley Field. In 2003, the stadium underwent a massive renovation that maintained its look from the outside, but provided a modern venue inside.

Steppenwolf Theatre Company
1650 N. Halsted St., Chicago,
312-335-1650;
www.steppenwolf.org
One of the most acclaimed theater groups in the country, Steppenwolf not only helped put Chicago theater on the map, but also gave many famous actors, including John Malkovich, Joan Allen and Gary Sinise their start. Steppenwolf quickly became known for its risky choices and edgy performances, an approach critics aptly termed rock-and-roll theater. Today, the company has its own state-of-the-art building in the Lincoln Park neighborhood. Performances are almost uniformly excellent, with stunning sets, strong acting and plenty of original material.

Symphony Center
220 S. Michigan Ave., Chicago,
312-294-3000; www.cso.org
The historic Symphony Center is the home of the Chicago Symphony Orchestra and

the stage for the Civic Orchestra of Chicago, chamber music groups, diverse musical attractions and children's programs. The center includes Buntrock Hall, a ballroom, rehearsal space and restaurant.

Chicago Symphony Orchestra (CSO)
220 S. Michigan Ave., Chicago,
312-294-3333
Long considered one of the great orchestras of the world, the CSO has been a fixture on the Chicago cultural scene for more than 100 years. While the big-name shows may sell out in advance, it is often possible to get day-of-show or single-seat tickets at the box office especially for weeknight and Friday afternoon or Saturday afternoon at a reasonable price.

The Magnificent Mile
N. Michigan Ave., Chicago;
www.themagnificentmile.com
Although often compared to Rodeo Drive in Beverly Hills and Fifth Avenue in New York because of the quality and quantity of its stores, Michigan Avenue has a vibe all its own. Known as the Magnificent Mile, this one-mile flower-lined stretch between Oak Street and the Chicago River boasts 3.1 million square feet of retail space, 460 stores, 275 restaurants, 51 hotels, numerous art galleries and two museums, all set among some of Chicago's most architecturally significant buildings.

The Oprah Winfrey Show
1058 W. Washington Blvd., Chicago,
312-591-9222; www.oprah.com
One of the most coveted tickets in town is for *The Oprah Winfrey Show*, taped at Harpo Studios in Chicago's West Loop. The show generally tapes only on Tuesday, Wednesday and Thursday from September through early December and from January to June. The only way to get tickets is to call the studio's Audience Department in advance. Security for the show is tight, and you must be over 18 to attend (although teens ages 16 and 17 can attend with a parent or legal guardian if they bring a copy of their birth certificate for check-in).

The Second City
1616 N. Wells St., Chicago,
312-664-4032;
www.secondcity.com
Opened in 1959 by a group of University of Chicago students, this comedy troup has launched the careers of many successful comics, including John Belushi, Bill Murray, Steve Carrell, Stephen Colbert and Mike Myers. Resident troupes perform original comedy revues nightly on two stages: The Second City Mainstage, which seats 340, and The Second City e.t.c., which seats 180. The Second City also operates a comedy training center, with student productions held at Donny's Skybox Studio Theatre.

Theatre Building Chicago
1225 W. Belmont Ave., Chicago,
773-327-5252;
www.theatrebuildingchicago.org
The Theatre Building serves as the impromptu home for traveling companies to show their wares. More often than not, these shows are a little more "off the beaten path" and do not include names or plays that may be recognizable, but this does not take away from the enjoyment of the experience. Shows are generally cheaper than at other area theaters, but may not be for the entire family.

United Center
1901 W. Madison St., Chicago,
312-455-4500; www.unitedcenter.com
Affectionately known as the house that Michael built, the United Center replaced the cavernous Chicago Stadium in the mid-1990s as the home of Chicago Bulls. It's also home to the Blackhawks, Chicago's hockey team, and numerous concerts and special events are held here.

University of Chicago
5801 S. Ellis Ave., Chicago,
773-702-8374; www.uchicago.edu
On this campus, Enrico Fermi produced the first sustained nuclear reaction. The University of Chicago has also had one of the highest numbers of Nobel Prize winners

25

ILLINOIS

of any institution. The campus includes the **Oriental Institute,** which has an outstanding collection of archaeological material; the **Robie House,** designed by Frank Lloyd Wright in 1909 and the ultimate example of a Prairie house (Daily 10 a.m.-3 p.m.); and **Rockefeller Memorial Chapel,** designed by Bertram Grosvenor Goodhue Associates and noted for its Gothic construction, vaulted ceiling, 8,600-pipe organ and 72-bell carillon.

Victory Gardens Theater
2257 N. Lincoln Ave. Chicago,
773-549-5788; www.victorygardens.org
Although it often produces plays by lesser-known authors, the Victory Gardens did win the Regional Theatre Tony Award in 2001. Some better-known playwrights and plays have been produced here as well, such as Neil Simon's *Lost in Yonkers.*

Wrigley Building
410 N. Michigan Ave., Chicago,
312-923-8080; www.wrigley.com
Perched on the north bank of the Chicago River on Michigan Avenue, the sparkling white Wrigley Building has been one of Chicago's most recognized skyscrapers since its completion in 1924 by architects Graham, Anderson, Probst and White. The building's triangular shape is patterned after the Giralda Tower in Seville, Spain, and its ornamental design is an adaptation of French Renaissance style. The building is actually two towers linked by an open walkway at street level and two enclosed walkways on the third and 14th floors. Today, the building remains the headquarters of the Wrigley family of chewing gum fame.

Wrigley Field
1060 W. Addison St., Chicago,
773-404-2827;
www.cubs.com
America's second-oldest Major League ballpark is also one of its most unique, located within a vibrant city neighborhood where residents often watch games from their roof decks. While the Cubs' long-term losing streak is a perpetual heartbreak, it never keeps people away from the ballpark—games are consistently sold out.

SPECIAL EVENTS
57th Street Art Fair
57th St., Chicago, 773-493-3247;
www.57thstreetartfair.org
Every year, the 57th Street Art Fair takes over a city block between Kenwood and Dorchester to showcase more than 300 artists from around the country. Early June.

Air and Water Show
1600 N. Lake Shore Dr., Chicago,
312-744-2400; egov.cityofchicago.org
The nation's largest two-day air show attracts more than two million people every August and is a free event. There are daredevil pilots, parachute teams and jets flying in formation, as well as a water-skiing and boat-jumping component. Mid-August.

Art Chicago
Butler Field, Columbus Dr., Chicago,
312-587-3300
This festival attracts hundreds of dealers from around the globe. Before the show opens, serious collectors can attend the Vernissage party to preview the art before the general public is admitted the following day. Mid-May.

Chicago Auto Show
McCormick Place, 2301 S. Lake Shore Dr.
Chicago, 312-744-3370
The world's largest auto show takes up all of the south wing of Chicago's enormous McCormick Place. It is often here that domestic and international automakers first put their latest models on public display.

Chicago Blues Fest
Grant Park, 331 E. Randolph St., Chicago,
312-744-2400; egov.cityofchicago.org
In a city virtually synonymous with the blues, Chicago's annual Blues Fest features local stars as well as national names. This free outdoor festival attracts more than 600,000 visitors over its four-day run. Early-mid-June.

Chicago International Film Festival

32 W. Randolph St., Chicago,
312-683-0121;
www.chicagofilmfestival.com

This is the oldest international film festival in North America. For three weeks each October, Chicago is introduced to some of the best cinema from the United States and around the world. Over the years, the festival has helped introduce innovative filmmakers like Martin Scorsese and John Carpenter. October.

Chicago Jazz Fest

Grant Park, 331 E. Randolph St., Chicago, 312-744-2400; egov.cityofchicago.org

This event has become a giant outdoor jazz cafe with more than 300,000 people in attendance. Lesser-known and local artists perform during the day on the small stage, but world-class jazz musicians take over the main stage at the Petrillo Music Shell after 5 p.m. Labor Day weekend.

Chicago Outdoor Film Festival

Grant Park, 331 E. Randolph St., Chicago, 312-744-2400; egov.cityofchicago.org

Once a week in July and August, free classic movies are shown in Grant Park, from *Casablanca* and *Vertigo* to new classics like *Ferris Bueller's Day Off*. Movies start at dusk. Mid-July-late August.

Chicago to Mackinac Races

400 E. Monroe St., Chicago,
312-744-3370;
www.chicagomackinac.com

For more than a century, yacht racers have raced from the Windy City to Mackinac Island in Michigan's Upper Peninsula. Run by the Chicago Yacht Club, this race attracts around 300 vessels every year. Participation is by invitation only and usually takes between 40 and 60 hours to complete. July.

Grant Park July 3 Concert

Petrillo Music Shell, 235 S. Columbus Dr., Chicago, 312-744-3370

The lakefront blazes with cannon flashes and fireworks as the Grant Park Symphony welcomes Independence Day with Tchaikovsky's *1812 Overture*. July 3.

Grant Park Music Festival

Pritzker Pavilion, N. Columbus Dr., Chicago, 312-742-4763

Live music concerts Wednesday, Friday and Saturday in late June-September.

Magnificent Mile Lights Festival

N. Michigan Ave., Chicago,

SINGING THE BLUES

It all started in a small, lopsided former automobile parts factory at 2120 S. Michigan Ave. The building was purchased by the Chess brothers and, from 1957 to 1967, it operated as the home of Chess Records, the recording studio that gave the world the sad, edgy sound of the Chicago blues. Most of the greats recorded here and helped define Chicago's West Side scene.

What exactly are the Chicago blues? When people migrated from the Mississippi Delta, they came through Memphis and settled in Chicago, where their soulful music took on a tougher edge, influenced by the rhythms of the city and the noise of the clubs.

The city has scores of blues clubs with live performances every night. Some of the best include Lincoln Park's Kingston Mines (2548 N. Halsted St.), Buddy Guys' Legends (754 S. Wabash Ave.) and Blue Chicago (736 N. Clark St.). Blues legend Buddy Guy plays a series of shows every January at his club. Tickets sell out months in advance, but those who snag them see an incredible show in which Guy is often joined by surprise guests (last year John Mayer dropped by).

ILLINOIS

★
★
★
★
★

312-409-5560;
www.themagnificentmile.com
As a kickoff to the holiday season, the North Michigan Avenue Association has sponsored the Magnificent Lights Festival, during which the avenue's trademark tiny white lights get turned on to much fanfare. Late November.

St. Patrick's Day Parade
Columbus Dr., Chicago,
312-942-9188;
www.chicagostpatsparade.com
Chicago's St. Patrick's Day parade is famous around the world, not because of its size or its spirit, but because on the day of the parade, the city dyes the Chicago River green, a tradition started during the early 1960s. The parade features dozens of bands, Irish step dancers, floats and representatives of unions and local organizations and politicians. Weekend closest to St. Patrick's Day.

Taste of Chicago
Grant Park, Chicago,
312-744-2400;
egov.cityofchicago.org
What began in 1980 as a way to sample cuisines from some of the city's best-known restaurants has become an all-out food fest that attracts more than 3.5 million visitors a year. This 10-day event features booths from more than 50 area vendors, free live music by big-name headliners and amusement park rides Late June-early July.

Venetian Night
Monroe Harbor, 100 S. Lake Shore Dr., Chicago, 773-267-9131
This Chicago tradition has a Venetian-themed aquatic parade and fireworks. Late July.

HOTELS
★★★Affinia
166 E. Superior St., Chicago,
312-787-6000; www.affinia.com
Close to Michigan Avenue and Chicago's top shopping, this contemporary hotel recently underwent a complete renovation, primarily to make room for upgraded, plush beds in each of the guest rooms. To top those thick, fluffy mattresses, the hotel offers a pillow menu with everything from goose down to foam available. Other thoughtful touches include a full range of complimentary toiletries (contact lens solution, toothpaste, hairspray) to replace anything you weren't allowed to bring through airport security in your carry-on. Even pets are pampered here with everything from sitter services to pet psychics.

★★Courtyard by Marriott
30 E. Hubbard St., Chicago,
312-329-2500, 800-321-2211;
www.courtyard.com
337 rooms. High-speed Internet access. Restaurant, bar. Fitness room. Indoor pool, whirlpool. Airport transportation available. Business center. $$

★Fairfield Inn
216 E. Ontario St., Chicago,
312-787-3777, 800-228-2800;
www.fairfieldsuiteschicago.com
185 rooms. Complimentary continental breakfast. High-speed Internet access. Fitness room. Airport transportation available. Business center. $$

★★Hampton Inn Chicago and Suites
33 W. Illinois St., Chicago,
312-832-0330, 800-426-7866;
www.hamptoninnchicago.com
230 rooms. Complimentary full breakfast. Pets accepted. High-speed Internet access. Two restaurants, two bars. Fitness room. Indoor pool, whirlpool. Airport transportation available. Business center. $$

★★★ Hotel Blake
500 S. Dearborn St., Chicago,
312-663-3200; www.hotelblake.com
Though it's off the beaten tourist path, this Printer's Row hotel is in the middle of the city's newly buzzing South loop neighborhood, and within walking distance of Lake Michigan and Grant Park. The décor here

is contemporary, with rooms stocked with Egyptian cotton linens, luxury bath products and CD players. The onsite Custom House restaurant is a favorite with locals for its sophisticated take on American classics.

★★Tremont Hotel
100 E. Chestnut St., Chicago,
312-751-1900, 800-621-8133;
www.tremontchicago.com
130 rooms. Restaurant, bar. Fitness room. Airport transportation available. $$

★★★Amalfi Hotel Chicago
20 W. Kinzie St., Chicago,
312-395-9000;
www.amalfihotelchicago.com
Ultramodern, luxurious and unique, the Amalfi is a hotel like no other. Guest rooms are referred to as Spaces and doormen are called Impressionists, the Amalfi is a hotel like no other. In your Space, you'll find a pillow-top mattress and 316-thread-count Egyptian cotton linens, a CD library and a multihead shower.
215 rooms. Pets accepted. Complimentary continental breakfast. High-speed, wireless Internet access. Restaurant, bar. Fitness room. Airport transportation available. Business center. $$$

★★★Burnham Hotel
1 W. Washington Blvd., Chicago,
312-782-1111, 877-294-9712;
www.burnhamhotel.com
Reviving the historic Reliance Building (predecessor of the modern skyscraper and early 1900s home of department store Carson Pirie Scott), the Burnham retains the integrity of the landmark architecture, integrating it with a whimsically elegant ambience. Rooms and suites offer dramatic views of the Chicago cityscape. The in-house Atwood Cafe serves upscale American comfort food (including breakfast, lunch, dinner, Sunday brunch, and prctheater options).
122 rooms. High-speed Internet access. Restaurant, bar. Fitness room. Airport transportation available. $$

★★★Chicago Marriott at Medical District/UIC
625 S. Ashland Ave., Chicago,
312-491-1234, 800-228-9290;
www.marriottchicago.com
This comfortable hotel has a business center, a car rental desk and airline desk. You'll be within five miles of a large number of the city's best sights, but you won't have to stay amid the congestion of the major tourist areas. Enjoy a fireside dinner at Rook's Corner and then a nightcap at Rook's Lounge, both located in the hotel.
113 rooms. High-speed Internet access, wireless Internet access. Restaurant, bar. Fitness room. Airport transportation available. Business center. $$

★★★Conrad Chicago
521 N. Rush St., Chicago,
312-645-1500;
www.conradchicago.com
Perched atop the Shops at North Bridge and Nordstrom, with a main entrance on Rush Street and one on Michigan Avenue, this hotel has an ideal location close to the Loop, the Merchandise Mart and Navy Pier. Cerise restaurant offers exceptional cuisine in a casual setting, while Le Rendezvous bar provides an intimate place to sample the signature chocolate martini. Rooms offer high-tech accoutrements such as CD player/clock radios, cordless phones and electronic safes with charging capabilities.
311 rooms. Pets accepted, some restrictions; fee. High-speed, wireless Internet access. Restaurant, bar. Fitness room. Airport transportation available. Business center. $$$

★★★Embassy Suites
600 N. State St., Chicago,
312-943-3800, 800-362-2779;
www.embassysuiteschicago.com
This all-suite hotel has rooms with kitchens and sleeper sofas. Other amenities include VIP rooms, complimentary breakfast, on-site car rental, and fitness facilities with a pool.

CURTAIN CALL

Chicago is second city to none when it comes to theater. A place of multiple companies, it has mainstream stages and storefront theaters, front-page attention-getters and neighborhood productions. Actor John Malkovich got his start here alongside Gary Sinese when they launched the Steppenwolf theater company—both still come back to perform from time to time. Long before he became a "Friend," David Schwimmer cofounded Lookingglass Theatre (821 N. Michigan Ave.), a company known for its sometimes acrobatic, always colorful and highly creative performances.

Pegasus Players (1145 W. Wilson Ave.) often gets the rights to Stephen Sondheim's works. And there are plenty of venues for both the famous and the almost-famous. Chicago-style entertainment comes in dozens of styles and sizes. The adventurous Bailiwick Repertory Theatre (1229 W. Belmont Ave.) frequently puts on performances for the deaf. ETA Creative Arts Foundation (7558 S. Chicago Ave.) produces original or seldom-seen dramatic works by African-American writers. Noble Fool Theater (16 W. Randolph St.) presents full-length plays on its main stage, while the Roadworks (1239 N. Ashland Ave.) always has a strong ensemble cast that focuses on Midwest and world premieres.

Each week from June through August, a different independent theater company puts on a production at Theatre on the Lake, a screened-in Prairie school style building in Lincoln Park on the shore of Lake Michigan.

366 rooms, all suites. Complimentary full breakfast. High-speed Internet access. Restaurant, bar. Fitness room. Indoor pool, whirlpool. Airport transportation available. Business center. **$$**

★★★Embassy Suites Downtown/Lakefront
511 N. Columbus Dr., Chicago, 312-836-5900;
www.chicagoembassy.com
Navy Pier and Michigan Avenue are a short walk from this modern hotel. Suites feature refrigerators and microwaves. A host of amenities and services for both business and leisure travelers is provided by a friendly staff.

455 rooms, all suites. Complimentary full breakfast. High-speed Internet access. Restaurant, bar. Fitness room. Indoor pool, whirlpool. Airport transportation available. Business center. **$$**

★★★★★Four Seasons Hotel Chicago
120 E. Delaware Place, Chicago, 312-280-8800
www.fourseasons.com/chicagofs
Located in a 66-story building on Michigan Avenue, the Four Seasons Hotel Chicago is a shopper's paradise. More than 100 stores, including Gucci and Bloomingdales, are located downstairs from the hotel. The recently renovated rooms, decorated with contemporary furniture and soothing, neutral fabrics, are stylish and comfortable. With amenities like DVD players and flat-screen TVs, it may be hard to leave the luxury of your room. If you do, there's a Roman-columned indoor pool, well-stocked fitness center and full-service spa. Edible indulgences include American and French dishes at Seasons restaurant and continental favorites at the Café. The Seasons Lounge, with its working fireplace and live piano, is a favorite gathering spot for cocktails or tea.

343 rooms. Pets accepted, some restrictions. High-speed, wireless Internet access. Two restaurants, bar. Fitness room, spa. Indoor pool, children's pool, whirlpool.

Airport transportation available. Business center. **$$$$**

★★★Hard Rock Hotel Chicago
230 N. Michigan Ave., Chicago,
312-345-1000, 877-762-5468;
www.hardrockhotelchicago.com
This hip hotel is located in Chicago's historic Carbon and Carbide building, a 1929 Art Deco skyscraper on the Chicago River. The lobby is decorated with rock-and-roll memorabilia and special exhibits (such as the famous Space Suit, Space Boots and guitar of Styx's James Young). Rooms have high-speed Internet access, entertainment centers with flat-screen TVs and DVD/CD players.
381 rooms. Pets accepted, some restrictions; fee. High-speed Internet access. Restaurant, bar. Fitness room. Airport transportation available. Business center. **$$$**

★★★Hilton Chicago
720 S. Michigan Ave., Chicago,
312-922-4400, 800-774-1500;
www.hilton.com
Built in 1927 as the world's largest hotel, this grande dame overlooks Grant Park and Lake Michigan. Tower rooms on the top floors offer slightly more luxurious accommodations.
1,544 rooms. Pets accepted, some restrictions. High-speed, wireless Internet access. Four restaurants, four bars. Fitness room, fitness classes available. Indoor pool, whirlpool. Airport transportation available. Business center. **$$**

★★★Hotel Indigo
1244 N. Dearborn St., Chicago,
312-787-4980, 800-972-2494;
www.ichotelsgroup.com
This Gold Coast boutique hotel has a beach theme (think plenty of cool blue tones and white-washed furnishings), which is fitting with its close proximity to Chicago's beaches (yes, the city has some) along the Lake Michigan coast. The onsite fitness center comes complete with personal trainers, while the free WiFi throughout the hotel makes it easy to stay connected.

165 rooms. Pets accepted, some restrictions; fee. WiFi. Restaurants, bar. Fitness room. Business center. **$$$**

★★★Hotel InterContinental Chicago
505 N. Michigan Ave., Chicago,
312-944-4100;
www.chicago.intercontinental.com
Built in 1929 as a luxury men's club, the InterContinental has since undergone extensive renovations but retained the original Spanish-tiled swimming pool in the fitness center. Room service is available 24 hours, and the hotel's restaurant, Zest, serves contemporary Mediterranean fare. High tea is also offered in the Salon.
792 rooms. Pets accepted, some restrictions; fee. High-speed, wireless Internet access. Two restaurants, two bars. Fitness room. Indoor pool. Airport transportation available. Business center. **$$$**

★★★Hotel Sax
333 N. Dearborn St., Chicago,
312-245-033, 877-569-3742;
www.hotelsaxchicago.com
Located in trendy River North next to the House of Blues, this sexy, sophisticated hotel is close to the city's best nightlife and restaurants. Rooms are loaded with luxuries like Egyptian cotton linens and flat-screen TVs. The Crimson Lounge has the look of a Victorian living room, with tufted velvet couches and intimate seating areas, and serves snacks like truffle-scented popcorn and an extensive menu of cocktails.
High-speed, wireless Internet access. Restaurants, bar. Valet parking **$$$**

★★★Hotel Monaco Chicago
225 N. Wabash Ave., Chicago,
312-960-8500, 888-775-9223;
www.monaco-chicago.com
The Monaco's stylishly eclectic, Euro aesthetic is equally suited to business or pleasure travel. Colorful rooms have plush furnishings, Fuji tubs and even a companion goldfish on request. Order round-the-clock room service or visit the South

ILLINOIS

Water Kitchen, the hotel's restaurant, for breakfast, lunch, or dinner.
192 rooms. High-speed, wireless Internet access. Restaurant, bar. Fitness room. Airport transportation available. Business center. **$$**

★★★Hyatt Regency McCormick Place
2233 S. Martin Luther King Dr., Chicago, 312-567-1234, 800-633-7313; www.hyattregencymccormickplace.com
Connected by an enclosed walkway to three exposition buildings, this hotel is a favorite of visiting conventioneers. Rooms are spacious and well-furnished.
800 rooms. High-speed Internet access. Restaurant, bar. Fitness room. Indoor pool. Airport transportation available. Business center. **$$**

★★★James Hotel
55 E. Ontario St., Chicago, 312-337-1000, 877-526-3755; www.jameshotels.com
Those who want to stay in style (and by that we mean not only comfort and luxury, but in the company of like-minded, well-heeled travelers) check into the James. This River North boutique hotel has sleek, uncluttered rooms decked out with plasma TVs, stereos with iPod docks and baths stocked with Kiehl's bath products. David Burke's Primehouse, the hotel's restaurant, serves some of the city's best steaks, while the Jbar mixes potent cocktails. A fitness center and spa provide excuses to leave the comfort of your guest room.
297 rooms. Pets accepted. High-speed, wireless Internet access. Restaurant, bar. Fitness room. Business center. **$$$**

★★★Marriott Chicago Downtown
540 N. Michigan Ave., Chicago, 312-836-0100, 800-228-9290; www.marriott.com
Business and leisure travelers appreciate this hotel's convenient location on Michigan Avenue. Guest rooms are designed for working travelers, with data ports, work areas and wireless Internet access.
1,192 rooms. High-speed Internet access. Restaurant, two bars. Fitness room. Indoor

pool, whirlpool. Airport transportation available. Business center. **$$**

★★★Omni Ambassador East
1301 N. State Pkwy., Chicago, 312-787-7200, 800-377-6664; www.omnihotels.com
A prime Gold Coast location and the world-famous Pump Room restaurant are two reasons to stay at this grand hotel, designated a Historic Hotel of America. The 14 Celebrity Suites honor some of the many notable guests who have stayed or eaten on-site.
285 rooms. Pets accepted, some restrictions; fee. High-speed, wireless Internet access. Restaurant, bar. Fitness room. Airport transportation available. Business center. **$$**

★★★Omni Chicago Hotel
676 N. Michigan Ave., Chicago, 312-944-6664, 800-377-6664; www.omnihotels.com
This hotel, host to many famous guests of *The Oprah Winfrey Show,* is located on Michigan Avenue and has spacious bedrooms. The fourth floor Cielo restaurant provides fantastic views of the street below. Spa services are offered in-room or at the treatment room inside the health club.
347 rooms, all suites. Pets accepted, some restrictions; fee. High-speed, wireless Internet access. Restaurant, bar. Fitness room, spa. Indoor pool, whirlpool. Airport transportation available. Business center. **$$**

★★★Palmer House Hilton
17 E. Monroe St., Chicago, 312-726-7500, 800-774-1500; www.hilton.com
This Loop landmark has been renovated to restore designer-builder Potter Palmer's original French Empire opulence, including the Beaux Arts ceiling in the lobby. Located in the center of the Loop, the hotel is just steps away from popular Chicago attractions such the Art Institute, Grant Park and Michigan Avenue shopping.
1,639 rooms. Pets accepted, some restrictions. High-speed Internet access. Two restaurants, two bars. Fitness room. Indoor

pool, whirlpool. Airport transportation available. Business center. **$$**

★★★Park Hyatt Chicago
800 N. Michigan Ave., Chicago,
312-335-1234, 800-233-1234;
www.parkchicago.hyatt.com
From its stylish interiors to its historic Water Tower Square location, the Park Hyatt is intrinsically tied to the history of Chicago. The public and private spaces feature Mies van der Rohe, Eames and Noguchi furnishings, as well as photography commissioned by the Art Institute of Chicago. The nouvelle cuisine at NoMI is a standout, as are the seventh-floor views of the city below.
198 rooms. Pets accepted, some restrictions; fee. High-speed, wireless Internet access. Restaurant, bar. Fitness room, spa. Indoor pool, whirlpool. Airport transportation available. Business center. **$$$$**

★★★Renaissance Chicago Hotel
1 W. Wacker Dr., Chicago,
312-372-7200, 888-236-2427;
www.renaissancehotels.com
This Loop high-rise is an urban sanctuary. Comfortable rooms have views of the city. Additional amenities include 24-hour room service, expanded club-level rooms, a fitness club and pool, a lobby bar and a 24-hour FedEx Kinkos business center.
553 rooms. Pets accepted, some restrictions; fee. High-speed Internet access. Restaurant, bar. Fitness room, fitness classes available. Indoor pool, whirlpool. Airport transportation available. Business center. **$$$**

★★★Sheraton Chicago Hotel and Towers
301 E. North Water St., Chicago,
312-464-1000, 800-233-4100;
www.sheratonchicago.com
Contemporary yet comfortable, every room of this hotel has a view of the cityscape, the Chicago River or Lake Michigan. The spacious lobby has imported marble and rich woods. The luxurious fitness facilities feature a pool and sauna. The five in-house dining options include Shula's Steak House and an indoor-outdoor cafe overlooking the river.

1,209 rooms. Pets accepted; fee. High-speed Internet access. Five restaurants, three bars. Fitness room. Indoor pool. Airport transportation available. Business center. **$$**

★★★Sofitel Chicago Water Tower
20 E. Chestnut St., Chicago,
312-324-4000, 800-763-4835;
www.sofitel.com
A stunning design created by French architect Jean-Paul Viguier gives this hotel an unmistakable presence on the Gold Coast, just off the Magnificent Mile. Le Bar is a popular after-work meeting place, while Cafe des Architectes serves up French cuisine in a contemporary setting.
415 rooms. Pets accepted, some restrictions. High-speed, wireless Internet access. Restaurant, bar. Fitness room. Airport transportation available. Business center. **$$$**

★★★Swissotel Chicago
323 E. Wacker Dr., Chicago,
312-565-0565, 800-637-9477;
www.swissotel.com
This tastefully decorated hotel has views of Lake Michigan and Grant Park and over sized rooms. The Palm restaurant, a classic steakhouse, is located inside the hotel.
632 rooms. High-speed Internet access. Two restaurants, bar. Children's activity center. Fitness room (fee). Indoor pool, whirlpool. Airport transportation available. Business center. **$$**

★★★The Allerton Hotel—Michigan Avenue
701 N. Michigan Ave., Chicago,
312-440-1500, 800-621-8311;
www.theallertonhotel.com
This hotel has both Historic Landmark Hotel status and a recent $60 million renovation. It was built in 1924 and at the time of its construction, was the tallest building on Michigan Avenue. The 25th-floor health club has views of the city. No two guest rooms have the same layout or design.
443 rooms. Pets accepted, some restrictions; fee. High-speed Internet access. Restaurant, bar. Fitness room. Airport transportation available. Business center. **$$**

33

ILLINOIS

★
★
★
★
★

★★★The Drake Hotel Chicago

140 E. Walton Place, Chicago,
312-787-2200; 800-774-1500;
www.thedrakehotel.com

A favorite Chicago landmark, this hotel was built in 1920 as a summer resort. Extensive renovations have preserved the ornate, elegant charm of this venerable classic. Amenities include executive floors, luxurious bathrooms, a shopping arcade and multiple dining options. The clubby Cape Cod Room is famous for its oyster bar and seafood. Afternoon tea in the lobby's Palm Court and 24-hour room service are also offered.
532 rooms. High-speed Internet access. Restaurant, bar. Fitness room. Airport transportation available. Business center. $$

★★★The Fairmont Chicago

200 N. Columbus Dr., Chicago,
312-565-8000, 800-866-5577;
www.fairmont.com

This sleek tower rests on the edge of leafy Grant and Millennium parks. The interiors are refined, with rich colors and antique reproductions. There is praise for the American dishes at Aria restaurant and afternoon tea is a special event at the Lobby Lounge. Guests can use the adjoining Lakeshore Athletic Club and Waves day spa. Noteworthy for its indoor rock-climbing wall, this establishment is considered one of the city's top exercise facilities.
687 rooms. Pets accepted, some restrictions; fee. High-speed Internet access. Restaurant, bar. Fitness room, fitness classes available. Indoor pool, outdoor pool, whirlpool. Airport transportation available. Business center. $$

★★Old Town Chicago Bed and Breakfast

1442 N. North Park Ave., Chicago,
312-440-9268;
www.oldtownchicago.com

Guests staying in this modern, four-room bed-and-breakfast housed in an Art Deco mansion have access to amenities such as a complimentary washer and dryer, a private bathroom and walk-in closet. There is also a communal kitchen where guests can do their own cooking.
4 rooms. Complimentary continental breakfast. High-speed Internet access, wireless Internet access. Fitness room. Airport transportation available. Business center. $$

★★★★★The Peninsula Chicago

108 E. Superior St., Chicago,
312-337-2888, 866-288-8889;
www.peninsula.com

The unparalleled level of service and meticulous attention to detail make this hotel a standout. Rooms, with classic and elegant décor, are outfitted with bedside electronic control panels and flat-screen televisions. The sprawling spa and fitness center (and beautiful sky-high indoor pool) feature the most up-to-date equipment and cutting edge treatments. Pets at the Peninsula are pampered as much as their masters with special beds, their own room service menus and doggie massages. The hotel's restaurants, including the fine-dining room Avenues and more casual Shanghai Terrace, are some of the city's most acclaimed.
339 rooms. Pets accepted, some restrictions. High-speed, wireless Internet access. Four restaurants, bar. Fitness room, fitness classes available, spa. Indoor pool, whirlpool. Airport transportation available. Business center. $$$$

★★★★★The Ritz-Carlton, A Four Seasons Hotel

160 E. Pearson St., Chicago,
312-266-1000, 800-621-6906;
www.fourseasons.com

Located on the upper levels of Water Tower Place, guest rooms have views of Lake Michigan or the city. Take advantage of those views by booking an in-room massage, or visit the hotel's full-service spa. Pets can feast on filet mignon and salmon from room service.
435 rooms. Pets accepted, some restrictions. High-speed Internet access. Two restaurants, two bars. Fitness room, fitness classes available, spa. Indoor pool,

34

ILLINOIS

whirlpool. Airport transportation available. Business center. **$$$$**

★★★The Sutton Place Hotel—Chicago
21 E. Bellevue Place, Chicago,
312-266-2100; 866-378-8866;
www.suttonplace.com
Stylish understatement is the mantra at this luxurious 23-story hotel, an Art Deco-inspired building with a handsome, modern interior. Soundproofed rooms feature deep-soaking tubs, separate glass-enclosed showers, plush robes and lavish bath accessories. Room service is offered around the clock, while dining (and people-watching) is available at the Whiskey Bar & Grill.
246 rooms. Pets accepted, some restrictions; fee. High-speed, wireless Internet access. Restaurant, bar. Fitness room. Airport transportation available. Business center. **$$**

★★★The Westin Chicago River North
320 Dearborn St., Chicago,
312-744-1900, 800-937-8461;
www.westin.com/rivernorth
This hotel overlooks the Chicago River and offers a welcoming home for business or leisure travelers visiting the city. The Kamehachi Sushi Bar delights fish lovers, the Celebrity Cafe features all-day dining with a focus on American dishes, and the Hana Lounge entertains nightly with hors d'oeuvres and live music.
424 rooms. Pets accepted. High-speed Internet access, wireless Internet access. Restaurant, bar. Fitness room. Airport transportation available. Business center. **$$$**

★★★The Westin Chicago North Shore
601 N. Milwaukee Ave., Wheeling, IL,
847-777-6500, 800-937-8461
This north suburban Chicago Westin outpost is contemporary and sleek in design and amenities. Rooms have luxury bedding, flat screen TVs and wireless high-speed internet access. The fitness center features an indoor lap pool and a gym stocked with Reebok equipment. Local chef Rick Tramonto is the force behind the hotel's restaurants, which include a steakhouse and an Italian-themed eatery.
412 rooms. Restaurant, bar. Indoor pool. Fitness room. Business center. High speed, wireless Internet access. Pets Accepted. **$$**

★★★The Whitehall Hotel
105 E. Delaware Place, Chicago,
312-944-6300, 800-948-4255;
www.thewhitehallhotel.com
Built in 1927 and extensively renovated since then, the independent Whitehall retains its stature as a small sanctuary with personal service and old-world charm. Rooms combine traditional decor (including some four-poster beds) and modern technology. The California-Mediterranean restaurant, Molive, offers an excellent wine service, a bar and outdoor dining.
221 rooms. Pets accepted, some restrictions; fee. High-speed Internet access. Restaurant, bar. Fitness room. Airport transportation available. Business center. **$$**

★★★W Chicago City Center
172 W. Adams St., Chicago,
312-332-1200, 888-625-5144;
www.whotels.com
Located in the city's financial district, this hotel provides a much-needed dash of style to the Loop. The old architecture of the former Midland Hotel mixes with modern accents in the W Living Room, where an after-work crowd mingles beneath the vaulted ceiling while listening to tunes spun by a DJ from a balcony above. Guest rooms are modern but comfortable.
369 rooms. Pets accepted; fee. High-speed Internet access. Restaurant, two bars. Fitness room. Airport transportation available. Business center. **$$$**

★★★Westin Michigan Avenue
909 N. Michigan Ave., Chicago,
312-943-7200, 800-937-8461;
www.westin.com/michiganave
Friendly service makes everyone from business travelers to families feel welcome at this hotel. Even pets are made to feel special here—they receive their own "Heavenly Bed," a treat bag and bowl.

751 rooms. Pets accepted, some restrictions. High-speed Internet access. Restaurant, bar. Fitness room. Airport transportation available. Business center. **$$$**

★★★Wyndham Chicago Downtown Hotel

633 N. St. Clair St., Chicago,
312-573-0300; 800-996-3426;
www.wyndham.com

The lobby of this downtown hotel is inviting with fresh fruit, beautiful marble floors and an abundance of natural light streaming in from the many windows. Caliterra Bar & Grill offers a convenient dining option, serving California and Italian cuisine, with live jazz in the evenings. The comfortable guest rooms feature pillowtop mattresses, Herman Miller desk chairs and Golden Door bath products.

417 rooms. High-speed Internet access, wireless Internet access. Restaurant, bar. Fitness room. Indoor pool, whirlpool. Airport transportation available. Business center. **$$**

SPECIALTY LODGINGS

Gold Coast Guest House

113 W. Elm St., Chicago,
312-337-0361;
www.bbchicago.com

Tucked into the heart of the lively Gold Coast neighborhood, within walking distance of the Magnificent Mile, this bed-and-breakfast provides an oasis of calm. Guests stay in one of four cozily furnished rooms, all individually air-conditioned and with private baths. This 1873 brick home features a 20-foot glass window off the living room, overlooking a small two-level garden out back. Guests enjoy health club privileges (for a fee) at a nearby multiplex as well as access to the house kitchen for snacks.

4 rooms. Children over 12 years only. Complimentary continental breakfast. Check-in by arrangement, check-out 11 a.m. High-speed Internet access, wireless Internet access. **$**

The Wheeler Mansion

2020 S. Calumet Ave., Chicago,
312-945-2020;

www.wheelermansion.com

Housed in a historic 1870 mansion in the city's South Loop, the building has been lovingly restored to provide guests with a unique European-style experience. No two rooms are alike, but all are charming.

11 rooms. Pets accepted, some restrictions. Complimentary full breakfast. High-speed Internet access. Airport transportation available. Business center. **$$$**

RESTAURANTS

★★312 Chicago

136 N. La Salle St., Chicago,
312-696-2420;
www.312chicago.com

American, Italian menu. Breakfast, lunch, dinner, Sunday brunch. Bar. Children's menu. Business casual attire. Reservations recommended. Valet parking. Outdoor seating. **$$**

★★A La Turka

3134 N. Lincoln Ave., Chicago,
773-935-6101;
www.alaturkachicago.com

Mediterranean, Turkish menu. Lunch, dinner. Bar. Casual attire. Reservations recommended. Valet parking. Outdoor seating. **$$**

★★Adobo Grill

1610 N. Wells St., Chicago,
312-266-7999;
www.adobogrill.com

Mexican menu. Dinner, brunch. Two bars. Children's menu. Casual attire. Reservations recommended. Valet parking. Outdoor seating. **$$**

★★★★★Alinea

1723 N. Halsted St., Chicago,
312-867-0110;
www.alinearestaurant.com

A dimly lit corridor provides the dramatic entrance to Chef/Owner Grant Achatz's stunning restaurant. Once inside, you can catch a glimpse of the spotless open kitchen and watch a team of chefs cook with scientific precision. The four intimate dining rooms, appointed with dark mahogany tables, provide the perfect setting for the adventurous cuisine. The restaurant offers two types of menus: a 12- or 24-course degustation feast. Steaming eucalyptus leaves, smoking cinnamon sticks or lavender air-filled pillows are just some of the unusual elements that may be incorporated in the presentation of some dishes. The knowledgeable and affable waitstaff are passionate about every guest's experience and deflate any sense of pretension. American menu. Dinner. Closed Monday-Tuesday; July 4. Business casual attire. Reservations recommended. Valet parking. $$$$

★Amarind's
6822 W. North Ave., Chicago, 773-889-9999
Thai menu. Lunch, dinner. Closed Monday. Casual attire. Reservations recommended. $$

★Ann Sather
929 W. Belmont Ave., Chicago, 773-348-2378; www.annsather.com
Four additional locations can be found on the city's North Side: 5207 N. Clark, 1448 N. Milwaukee, 3416 N. Southport and 3411 N. Broadway. Continental menu. Breakfast, lunch, dinner. Casual attire. $$

★★Arco de Cuchilleros
3445 N. Halsted St., Chicago, 773-296-6046
Spanish, tapas menu. Dinner. Closed Monday. Bar. Casual attire. Reservations recommended. Valet parking. Outdoor seating. $$

★★★Aria
200 N. Columbus Dr., Chicago, 312-444-9494; www.ariachicago.com
Although it's lodged in the Fairmont Chicago, Aria distances itself from the bland stereotype of hotel restaurants by maintaining a street entrance to encourage local patrons to visit. Nan with four dipping sauces is served at all tables, and the bar offers sushi, Asian appetizers and noodles to the cocktail crowd.

International menu. Breakfast, lunch, dinner. Bar. Children's menu. Business casual attire. Reservations recommended. Valet parking. $$$

★★★Arun's
4156 N. Kedzie Ave., Chicago, 773-539-1909; www.arunsthai.com
Regarded as the best Thai interpreter in the city, if not the country, Arun's takes a fine-dining turn with the complex cooking of Thailand, but without the snobbery of many serious restaurants. An original prix fixe menu with 12 courses is offered nightly, half of them small appetizers, served family-style. You won't know what is on the menu until you arrive, but the kitchen easily adapts to food and spice sensitivities.
Thai menu. Dinner. Closed Monday; also the first two weeks in January. Bar. Business casual attire. Reservations recommended. Valet parking. $$$$

★★★Atwood Cafe
1 W. Washington Blvd., Chicago, 312-368-1900; www.atwoodcafe.com
The whimsical ground-floor occupant of the Burnham Hotel, Atwood Cafe draws a cross-section of travelers, theater-goers and shoppers. Modern dishes like grilled calamari and tuna carpaccio balance comfort food classics like grilled pork chops with spaetzle.
American menu. Breakfast, lunch, dinner, brunch. Bar. Children's menu. Business casual attire. Reservations recommended. Valet parking. Outdoor seating. $$$

★★Avec
615 W. Randolph St., Chicago, 312-377-2002; www.avecrestaurant.com
Mediterranean menu. Dinner, late-night. Bar. Casual attire. Valet parking. $$

★★★★Avenues
108 E. Superior St., Chicago, 312-573-6754; www.peninsula.com

Cutting edge, contemporary cuisine awaits diners at Avenues, located within Chicago's Peninsula Hotel. Foodies will jump at the chance to order the chef's palate, a multi-course tasting menu that showcases chef Graham Elliot Bowles' considerable talents. The tasting menu is offered with a wine pairing for each course. Reservations are required, but plan ahead if you'd like to be seated at the Chef's Bar, which overlooks the exhibition kitchen. American menu. Dinner. Closed Sunday-Monday. Bar. Business casual attire. Reservations recommended. Valet parking. **$$$$**

★★Bandera
535 N. Michigan Ave., Chicago,
312-644-3524;
www.banderarestaurants.com
American menu. Lunch, dinner. Bar. Children's menu. Business casual attire. **$$**

★★★Bice
158 E. Ontario St., Chicago,
312-664-1474;
www.bicechicago.com
A chain that grew out of Milan, Bice stays true to its northern Italian roots. While the menu changes monthly, expect hits such as veal Milanese and beef carpaccio. For a cheaper, more casual version of the menu, try the next-door sibling, Bice Cafe, a lunchtime favorite of Michigan Avenue shoppers.
Italian menu. Lunch, dinner. Bar. Business casual attire. Reservations recommended. Valet parking. Outdoor seating. **$$$**

★★Bin 36
339 N. Dearborn St., Chicago,
312-755-9463;
www.bin36.com
American menu. Breakfast, lunch, dinner, brunch. Bar. Children's menu. Business casual attire. Reservations recommended. Valet parking. **$$**

★★★Blackbird
619 W. Randolph St., Chicago,
312-715-0708;
www.blackbirdrestaurant.com

The minimalist Blackbird girds style with substance. Like the decor, the food is spare, hitting just the right contemporary notes without drowning in too many flavors. The market-driven menu changes frequently, with seasonal favorites such as homemade charcuterie and braised veal cheeks. Noise levels are high but the elegantly attired fans who flock here consider it simply good buzz.
American menu. Lunch, dinner. Closed Sunday. Bar. Business casual attire. Valet parking. Outdoor seating. **$$$**

★★Blue Fin Sushi
1952 W. North Ave., Chicago,
773-394-7373;
www.bluefinsushibar.com
Japanese, sushi menu. Dinner. Closed Sunday. Casual attire. Outdoor seating. **$$**

★★★Bob San
1805-07 W. Division, Chicago,
773-235-8888;
www.bob-san.com
Sushi-savvy urban diners will love this Wicker Park Japanese spot, which offers a long list of fresh fish. Sushi chefs will go off the menu and create special selections if they're not too busy.
Japanese, sushi menu. Dinner. Bar. Casual attire. Reservations recommended. Valet parking. Outdoor seating. **$$**

★★Bongo Room
1470 N. Milwaukee Ave., Chicago,
773-489-0690.
American menu. Breakfast, lunch, brunch. Bar. Children's menu. Casual attire. **$$**

★★Brasserie Jo
59 W. Hubbard St., Chicago,
312-595-0800;
www.brasseriejo.com
French bistro menu. Dinner. Bar. Children's menu. Business casual attire. Reservations recommended. Valet parking. Outdoor seating. **$$$**

★★Bricks
1909 N. Lincoln Ave., Chicago,

★
★
★
★
★

312-255-0851
Pizza. Dinner. Bar. Casual attire. Reservations recommended. **$$**

★★Cafe Absinthe
1954 W. North Ave., Chicago,
773-278-4488
American menu. Dinner. Bar. Casual attire. Reservations recommended. Valet parking. **$$**

★★Cafe Ba-Ba-Reeba!
2024 N. Halsted St., Chicago,
773-935-5000, 888-538-8823;
www.cafebabareeba.com
Spanish, tapas menu. Lunch, dinner. Bar. Children's menu. Business casual attire. Reservations recommended. Valet parking. Outdoor seating. **$$**

★★Cafe Bernard
2100 N. Halsted St., Chicago,
773-871-2100;
www.cafebernard.com
French menu. Dinner. Bar. Casual attire. Valet parking. Outdoor seating. **$$$**

★★Cafe Iberico
739 N. LaSalle Dr., Chicago,
312-573-1510;
www.cafe-iberico.com
Spanish, tapas menu. Lunch, dinner. Bar. Casual attire. Reservations recommended. Valet parking. **$$**

★★★Caliterra
633 N. St. Clair St., Chicago,
312-274-4444;
www.wyndham.com
Aptly named considering its Cal-Ital culinary concept (Tuscany meets northern California), this handsome and somewhat hidden spot in the Wyndham Chicago hotel draws a well-heeled Gold Coast business and shopping crowd. Innovative seasonal fare emphasizes organic produce and meats. The noteworthy cheese cart and Italian-American wine list are additional highlights.
California, Italian menu. Breakfast, lunch, dinner. Bar. Children's menu. Business

casual attire. Reservations recommended. Valet parking. **$$$**

★★Cape Cod Room
140 E. Walton Place, Chicago,
312-932-4625, 800-553-7253;
www.thedrakehotel.com
Seafood menu. Lunch, dinner. Bar. Children's menu. Business casual attire. Reservations recommended. Valet parking. **$$$**

★★Carmine's
1043 N. Rush St., Chicago,
312-988-7676;
www.rosebudrestaurants.com
Italian, seafood menu. Lunch, dinner. Bar. Business casual attire. Reservations recommended. Valet parking. Outdoor seating. **$$$**

★★★★★Charlie Trotter's
816 W. Armitage Ave., Chicago,
773-248-6228;
www.charlietrotters.com
Charlie Trotter's is a place for people who prefer food to be treated like a work of art. It's also a restaurant for those who value a chef's masterful ability to transform sustenance into culinary wonder. Set inside a two-story brick brownstone, this Lincoln Park legend is an intimate, peaceful place. The menu features French and Italian influences and seasonal ingredients. Trotter prefers saucing with vegetable juice-based vinaigrettes, light emulsified stocks and purees as well as delicate broths and herb-infused meat and fish essences. The result is flavors that are remarkably intense, yet light. And staying true to its accommodating reputation, the staff will adjust, adapt and substitute to match personal preferences.
American menu. Dinner. Closed Sunday-Monday. Bar. Jacket required. Reservations recommended. Valet parking. **$$$$**

★★★Chez Joel
1119 W. Taylor St., Chicago,
312-226-6479
Just a few minutes from the Loop, tiny Chez Joel dares to be French within the

39

ILLINOIS

friendly confines of Little Italy. Classic bistro fare is seasoned with more adventurous specials and an appealing sandwich selection at lunch.
French bistro menu. Lunch, dinner. Bar. Business casual attire. Reservations recommended. Valet parking. Outdoor seating. $$$

★★★Chicago Chop House
60 W. Ontario St., Chicago,
312-787-7100, 800-229-2356;
www.chicagochophouse.com
Choosing a steakhouse amoung the many in Chicago is no easy task, but independently owned Chicago Chop House stands out for its affinity for the city. Papered in 1,400 photos of Chicago, the Chop House provides a history lesson as a side dish to meals centered on steaks and chops.
Steak menu. Lunch, dinner. Bar. Business casual attire. Reservations recommended. Valet parking. Outdoor seating. $$$

★Chicago Diner
3411 N. Halsted St., Chicago,
773-935-6696;
www.veggiediner.com
Vegetarian menu. Lunch, dinner. Bar. Casual attire. $

★★Club Lucky
1824 W. Wabansia Ave., Chicago,
773-227-2300
Italian menu. Lunch, dinner. Bar. Business casual attire. Valet parking. Outdoor seating. $$

★★Coco Pazzo
300 W. Hubbard St., Chicago,
312-836-0900
Italian menu. Lunch, dinner. Bar. Casual attire. Valet parking. Outdoor seating. $$

★★Coobah
3423 N. Southport Ave., Chicago,
773-528-2220;
www.coobah.com
Latin American menu. Lunch, dinner, late-night, brunch. Bar. Children's menu. Casual

attire. Reservations recommended. Outdoor seating. $$

★★★Crofton on Wells
535 N. Wells St., Chicago,
312-755-1790;
www.croftononwells.com
Chef Suzy Crofton turns out elegant meals in an understated candlelit River North setting, a region rife with look-at-me eateries. The French-trained Crofton specializes in refined American cooking that marries style and substance with attention to detail and presentation. Flavor combinations are both harmonious and exciting as typified by the sweet and savory grilled New Zealand venison medallions with baby arugula and apricot jam. Her signature smoked apple chutney, also sold by the bottle, tops barbecued pork tenderloin and roast quail. Crofton thoughtfully caters to special interests with both a vegetarian menu and an extensive list of loose-leaf teas.
American menu. Lunch, dinner. Closed Sunday. Bar. Business casual attire. Reservations recommended. Valet parking. $$$

★★★Custom House
500 S. Dearborn St., Chicago,
312-523-0200; www.customhouse.cc
Chef Shawn McClain is such a rising star in Chicago (his vegetarian restaurant Green Zebra is a local hipster favorite, and his Asian-influenced Spring is packed nightly) that he was awarded the coveted regional best chef James Beard award in 2006. At Custom House, McClain showcases his talent for preparing meat and seafood dishes with a Mediterranean flair. Entrees include roasted flat iron steak with salt and vinegar fries or salmon with baby beets and parsley emulsion. Lunch, served on weekdays, is a favorite with Loop powerbrokers.

★★Cyrano's Bistrot and Wine Bar
546 N. Wells St., Chicago,
312-467-0546;
www.cyranosbistrot.com
French bistro menu. Lunch, dinner. Bar. Business casual attire. Reservations recommended. Valet parking. Outdoor seating. $$

★★Dinotto Ristorante
215 W. North Ave., Chicago,
312-202-0302;
www.dinotto.com
Italian menu. Lunch, dinner. Bar. Business casual attire. Reservations recommended. Outdoor seating. **$$$**

★Ed Debevic's
640 N. Wells St., Chicago,
312-664-1707;
www.eddebevics.com
American menu. Breakfast, lunch, dinner. Bar. Children's menu. Casual attire. Valet parking. **$**

★★Erwin
2925 N. Halsted St., Chicago,
773-528-7200;
www.erwincafe.com
Contemporary American menu. Dinner, Sunday brunch. Closed Monday. Bar. Casual attire. Reservations recommended. Valet parking. **$$**

★★★★Everest
440 S. LaSalle St., Chicago,
312-663-8920;
www.leye.com
Perched high atop the city on the 40th floor of the Chicago Stock Exchange building, Everest affords spectacular views and equally fabulous contemporary French cuisine. Chef and owner Jean Joho blends European influences with local, seasonal American ingredients. He's not afraid to pair noble ingredient like caviar with humbler fruits of American soil such as potatoes and turnips. Everest's dining room is luxuriously decorated with vaulted draped ceilings, mirrored walls, reflective paintings by Adam Seigel and floor-to-ceiling windows.
French menu. Dinner. Bar. Business casual attire. Reservations recommended. Valet parking. **$$$$**

★★Fogo de Chao
661 N. LaSalle St., Chicago,
312-932-9330;
www.fogodechao.com
Steak menu. Lunch, dinner. Bar. Children's menu. Casual attire. Reservations recommended. Valet parking. **$$$**

★★★Frontera Grill
445 N. Clark St., Chicago,
312-661-1434;
www.fronterakitchens.com
The casual, more accessible of chef Rick Bayless' side-by-side Mexican duo (see also **Topolobampo**), Frontera introduces a wealth of deceptively simple Mexican dishes and a world of flavors that you won't find at your neighborhood taco stand. An exhaustive tequila list for sipping or for shaken-to-order margaritas and a fine wine list stand up to the food. A seat here is a coveted one, as reservations are for parties of five to 10 only.
Mexican menu. Lunch, dinner, Saturday brunch. Closed Sunday-Monday. Bar. Children's menu. Casual attire. Business casual attire. Valet parking. Outdoor seating. **$$$**

★★Geja's Cafe
340 W. Armitage Ave., Chicago,
773-281-9101;
www.gejascafe.com
Fondue menu. Dinner. Closed holidays. Casual attire. Reservations recommended. Valet parking. **$$$**

★★★Gene & Georgetti
500 N. Franklin St., Chicago,
312-527-3718;
www.geneandgeorgetti.com
A veteran steakhouse with a masculine, insider's ambience and a past—it opened in 1941, long before River North was a hip 'hood—Gene & Georgetti is an old-school Chicago haunt. Prime steaks, gigantic "garbage salads," and gruff service are among the draws.
Italian, American menu. Lunch, dinner. Closed Sunday; also the first week in July. Bar. Casual attire. Valet parking. **$$$**

★★★Gibsons Steakhouse
1028 N. Rush St., Chicago,
312-266-8999;
www.gibsonssteakhouse.com

★
★
★
★
★

The theme at Gibsons is outsized, from the massive steaks to the stogie-puffing personalities who dine here, a blend of politicians, sports figures, celebrities and conventioneers. Some crave the generous porterhouses, but the kitchen also manages to issue some of the sea's biggest lobster tails and desserts that could easily feed a four-top.

Steak menu. Lunch, dinner. Bar. Business casual attire. Reservations recommended. Valet parking. Outdoor seating. **$$$**

★★**Gioco**
1312 S. Wabash Ave., Chicago,
312-939-3870;
www.gioco-chicago.com
Italian menu. Lunch, dinner. Bar. Children's menu. Reservations recommended. Valet parking. Outdoor seating. **$$$**

★★**Greek Islands**
200 S. Halsted St., Chicago,
312-782-9855;
www.greekislands.net
Greek menu. Lunch, dinner. Bar. Children's menu. Business casual attire. Reservations recommended. Valet parking. Outdoor seating. **$$**

★★★**Green Zebra**
1460 W. Chicago Ave., Chicago,
312-243-7100;
www.greenzebrachicago.com
This is chef/owner Shawn McClain's temple to vegetarian cooking. Seasonally modified, the restaurant offers a multitude of small-plates that would convert any carnivore. The globally-inspired menu includes such dishes as avocado panna cotta with pickled sweet peppers and crimson lentil cake with red pepper jam. A few fish and light meat options are also available. The ever-changing menu is especially popular, so plan on making reservations far in advance.
American, vegetarian menu. Dinner. Closed Monday. Bar. Casual attire. Reservations recommended. Valet parking. **$$**

★★**Harry Caray's**
33 W. Kinzie St., Chicago,
312-828-0966; www.harrycarays.com

Steak menu. Lunch, dinner. Bar. Children's menu. Business casual attire. Reservations recommended. Valet parking. **$$$**

★★**Heaven On Seven On Rush**
600 N. Michigan Ave., Chicago,
312-280-7774;
www.heavenonseven.com
Cajun/Creole menu. Lunch, dinner. Bar. Casual attire. **$$**

★**Hema's Kitchen**
2111 N. Clark St., Chicago,
773-338-1627
Indian menu. Lunch, dinner. Casual attire. **$**

★**Itto Sushi**
2616 N. Halsted St., Chicago,
773-871-1800
Japanese, sushi menu. Lunch, dinner, late-night. Closed Sunday. Casual attire. **$$**

★★**Jane's**
1655 W. Cortland St., Chicago,
773-862-5263;
www.janesresaurant.com
American menu. Breakfast, lunch, dinner, brunch. Bar. Casual attire. Outdoor seating. **$$**

★★★**Japonais**
600 W. Chicago Ave., Chicago,
312-822-9600;
www.japonaischicago.com
This spacious River North restaurant is a sensuous, hip setting for contemporary Japanese fare that includes, but goes far beyond, traditional sushi. The creative menu inspires sharing and ordering in phases while enjoying the exotic cocktails or selections from the extensive sake and wine lists.
Japanese, sushi menu. Lunch, dinner. Bar. Business casual attire. Reservations recommended. Valet parking. Outdoor seating. **$$$**

★★**Jin Ju**
5203 N. Clark St., Chicago,
773-334-6377

42

ILLINOIS

★
★
★
★
★

Korean menu. Dinner. Closed Monday. Bar. Casual attire. **$$**

★Joe's Be-Bop Cafe
600 E. Grand Ave., Chicago,
312-595-5299;
www.joesbebop.com
American menu. Lunch, dinner. Bar. Children's menu. Casual attire. Outdoor seating. **$$**

★John's Place
1200 W. Webster Ave., Chicago,
773-525-6670.
American menu. Lunch, dinner, brunch. Closed Monday. Bar. Children's menu. Casual attire. Outdoor seating. **$$**

★★★Keefer's
20 W. Kinzie., Chicago,
312-467-9525;
www.keefersrestaurant.com
In busy River North, stylish Keefer's offers prime steaks, chops, seafood and some bistro dishes served in a handsome circular dining room with a contemporary Arts and Crafts feel. Steakhouse classics like lobster bisque, Caesar salad and creamed spinach, as well as some updated but not fussy alternatives, are also featured. There's also a pared-down lunch menu, and the adjacent Keefer's Kaffé offers a menu of soups, salads, and simple sandwiches.
Steak, seafood menu. Lunch, dinner. Closed Sunday. Bar. Business casual attire. Reservations recommended. Valet parking. Outdoor seating. **$$$**

★★★Kevin
9 W. Hubbard St., Chicago,
312-595-0055;
www.kevinrestaurant.com
Chicago fans of chef Kevin Shikami have chased him from kitchen to kitchen for years. But in Kevin, his eponymous restaurant, they finally know where to find the talented chef each night. From delicate fish to juicy meats, Shikami brings an Asian flair to contemporary dishes that include tuna tartare, sesame-crusted opakapaka (a Hawaiian fish) and sautéed buffalo strip steak.

American, French, Asian menu. Lunch, dinner. Closed Sunday, also two weeks in August. Bar. Business casual attire. Valet parking. **$$$**

★★★Kiki's Bistro
900 N. Franklin St., Chicago,
312-335-5454;
www.kikisbistro.com
Long before bistros were blossoming all over town, this little spot on an out-of-the-way corner in River North was charming diners with its traditional bistro fare and regional specials. A somewhat older crowd frequents cozy, casual Kiki's for its romantic, country inn ambience, with its reliable kitchen and free valet parking.
French bistro menu. Lunch, dinner. Closed Sunday. Bar. Business casual attire. Reservations recommended. Valet parking. **$$**

★★Klay Oven
414 N. Orleans St., Chicago,
312-527-3999
Indian menu. Lunch, dinner. Closed holidays. Bar. Business casual attire. Reservations recommended. Valet parking. **$$**

★★La Bocca Della Verita
4618 N. Lincoln Ave., Chicago,
773-784-6222;
www.laboccachicago.com
Italian menu. Dinner. Closed Monday. Casual attire. Reservations recommended. Outdoor seating. **$$**

★La Creperie
2845 N. Clark St., Chicago,
773-528-9050;
www.lacreperie.com
French menu. Breakfast, lunch, dinner. Closed Monday. Bar. Casual attire. Outdoor seating. **$$**

★★★La Sardine
111 N. Carpenter St., Chicago,
312-421-2800;
www.lasardine.com
Perhaps a bit large for a bistro, La Sardine nevertheless delivers wonderful aromas, creature comforts and menu classics. This

43

ILLINOIS

★
★
★
★
★

restaurant draws both hip and mature urbanites who come for the escargots, brandade, bouillabaisse, roast chicken and profiteroles. Those scents waft from an open kitchen and rotisserie. The impressive wine list includes some hard-to-find French selections.
French menu. Lunch, dinner. Closed Sunday. Bar. Casual attire. Reservations recommended. Valet parking. **$$**

★★La Tache
1475 W. Balmoral Ave., Chicago,
773-334-7168
French bistro menu. Dinner, brunch. Bar. Casual attire. Outdoor seating. **$$**

★★Lawry's The Prime Rib
100 E. Ontario St., Chicago,
312-787-5000;
www.lawrysonline.com
Steak menu. Lunch, dinner. Bar. Business casual attire. Reservations recommended. Valet parking. **$$$**

★★Le Bouchon
1958 N. Damen Ave., Chicago,
773-862-6600;
www.lebouchonofchicago.com
French bistro menu. Dinner. Closed Sunday. Bar. Casual attire. Reservations recommended. Valet parking. **$$**

★★Le Colonial
937 N. Rush St., Chicago,
312-255-0088;
www.lecolonialchicago.com
Vietnamese menu. Lunch, dinner. Bar. Outdoor seating. **$$**

★★★★Les Nomades
222 E. Ontario St., Chicago,
312-649-9010;
www.lesnomades.net
Les Nomades is a serene spot tucked away off Michigan Avenue in an elegant turn-of-the-century townhouse. Romantic and intimate with a fireplace, hardwood floors, deep, cozy banquettes and gorgeous flowers, Les Nomades was originally opened as a private club. Chef Chris Nugent has crafted a traditional French menu that features dishes such

as white asparagus soup with wild mushrooms and truffle froth.
French menu. Dinner. Closed Sunday-Monday. Bar. Jacket required. Reservations recommended. Valet parking. **$$$$**

★Maggiano's
516 N. Clark St., Chicago,
312-644-7700;
www.maggianos.com
Italian menu. Lunch, dinner. Bar. Casual attire. Reservations recommended. Valet parking. Outdoor seating. **$$**

★★★Marché
833 W. Randolph St., Chicago,
312-226-8399;
www.marche-chicago.com
Located along restaurant row in the West Loop, Marché serves imaginative versions of brasserie-style French fare in a nightclub-like setting. Numerous chef changes over the years have done nothing to diminish the popularity of this Randolph Market District mainstay.
French menu. Lunch, dinner. Bar. Children's menu. Casual attire. Reservations recommended. Valet parking. Outdoor seating. **$$$**

★★Mas
1670 W. Division St., Chicago,
773-276-8700;
www.masrestaurant.com
Latin American menu. Dinner. Bar. Casual attire. Reservations recommended. Valet parking. Outdoor seating. **$$$**

★★Maza
2748 N. Lincoln Ave., Chicago,
773-929-9600
Lebanese menu. Dinner. Bar. Business casual attire. Reservations recommended. Valet parking. **$$**

★★★Meritage
2118 N. Damen Ave., Chicago,
773-235-6434;
www.meritagecafe.com
Meritage aims high, serving seafood-focused fare inspired by the cuisine and

44

ILLINOIS

wines of the Pacific Northwest. Entrees include seared salmon with taro pancakes and Japanese spiced roast scallops. The interior of this Bucktown eatery is cozy, with exposed brick walls and a pressed tin ceiling. Though the spacious outdoor patio is enclosed and heated in winter, only a canopy cloisters the space in summer, making Meritage one of the city's best open-air eateries.

American menu. Dinner, Sunday brunch. Bar. Business casual attire. Reservations recommended. Valet parking. Outdoor seating. $$$

★★**Mia Francesca**
3311 N. Clark St., Chicago,
773-281-3310;
www.miafrancesca.com
Italian menu. Dinner. Bar. Children's menu. Casual attire. Reservations recommended. Valet parking. Outdoor seating. $$

★★**Mike Ditka's**
100 E. Chestnut St., Chicago,
312-587-8989;
www.mikeditkaschicago.com
American menu. Lunch, dinner. Bar. Children's menu. Business casual attire. Reservations recommended. Valet parking. Outdoor seating. $$$

★★★**Mirai Sushi**
2020 W. Division St., Chicago,
773-862-8500;
www.miraisushi.com
This Wicker Park spot is serious about sushi. Offering more than just your everyday maki and nigiri, Mirai ups the ante with incredibly fresh sushi and a generous sake list. The bi-level restaurant boasts a bright main floor dining area and a sushi bar—your best bet for experiencing the sushi chef's specials. The upstairs sake bar is dark and seductive, with a choice of barstools, tables or sleek lounge furniture, with DJ music on weekends.

Japanese, sushi menu. Dinner. Bar. Casual attire. Reservations recommended. Valet parking. Outdoor seating. $$$

★★★**mk**
868 N. Franklin St., Chicago,
312-482-9179;
www.mkchicago.com
Style meets substance at Michael Kornick's mk, where refined yet real contemporary cuisine is offered in a perfect setting. The seasonal American food is clean and uncontrived, the multitiered architectural space linear and neutral without severity. Tasting menus are available, and the chic lounge area is perfect for a before or after dinner drink.

American menu. Dinner. Bar. Reservations recommended. Valet parking. $$$

★★★**Mon Ami Gabi**
2300 N. Lincoln Park W., Chicago,
773-348-8886;
www.monamigabi.com
The charming setting in Lincoln Park's Belden-Stratford, a 1922 landmark building, is so French you may start speaking with an accent. Solid bistro fare, including a selection of steak preparations and fresh seafood, is a big draw, as are the cozy ambience and rolling wine cart. There is also a large outdoor seating area for warm evenings.

French bistro menu. Dinner. Bar. Children's menu. Business casual attire. Reservations recommended. Valet parking. Outdoor seating. $$$

★★★**Morton's, The Steakhouse**
1050 N. State St., Chicago,
312-266-4820;
www.mortons.com
This steakhouse chain, which originated in Chicago in 1978, appeals to serious meat lovers. With a selection of belt-busting dishes—like the house specialty, a 24-ounce porterhouse—as well as fresh fish, lobster, and chicken entrees, Morton's rarely disappoints. Here, main course selections are placed on a cart that is rolled to your table, where servers describe each item in detail.

Steak menu. Dinner. Bar. Business casual attire. Reservations recommended. $$$

★
★
★
★
★

★★★Moto
945 W. Fulton Market, Chicago,
312-491-0058;
www.motorestaurant.com

Hidden away in Chicago's meatpacking district of the West Loop, Moto can be easy to miss. But after a visit here, you'll certainly never forget it. The elegant and minimalist decor is the perfect backdrop for the eclectic, Asian-influenced tasting menu, available in 5, 10 or 16 courses. Food is the ultimate in freshness, presentations are distinctive and service is warm at this unique restaurant, where dinner isn't just a meal—it's an experience.

International menu. Dinner. Closed Sunday-Monday. Bar. Business casual attire. Reservations recommended. Valet parking. **$$$$**

★★★Nacional 27
325 W. Huron, Chicago,
312-664-2727;
www.nacional27.net

The name hints at the 27 Latin countries that influence the menu at this stylish River North restaurant. Exotic ingredients, creative preparations and some refreshingly different desserts lend a unique feel to a meal here. Things heat up on weekends with late-night DJ dancing (with a cover charge for nondiners).

Latin American menu. Dinner, late-night. Closed Sunday. Bar. Casual attire. Outdoor seating. **$$$**

★★★NAHA
500 N. Clark St., Chicago,
312-321-6242;
www.naha-chicago.com

Chef Carrie Nahabadian cooked at the Four Seasons Beverly Hills before opening her own River North spot, NAHA, where she merges her Armenian background with her California training. The result is a luscious Mediterranean-like blend of flavors in creative dishes such as sea scallops with grapefruit, bass with olive oil-poached tomatoes and roast pheasant with grilled asparagus.

American menu. Lunch, dinner. Closed Sunday. Bar. Business casual attire. Reservations recommended. Valet parking. Outdoor seating. **$$$**

★★Naniwa
607 N. Wells St., Chicago,
312-255-8555;
www.sushinaniwa.com

Japanese menu. Lunch, dinner. Bar. Casual attire. Reservations recommended. Valet parking. Outdoor seating. **$$**

★★★Nick's Fishmarket
51 S. Clark St., Chicago,
312-621-0200;
www.nicksfishmarketchicago.com

Although Nick's specializes in seafood, it acts in every other way like a steakhouse. Consider the dark, subterranean room with low ceilings, colorful celebrity pictures and traditional dishes like lobster bisque

DOG DAYS

The humble weiner, although German in origin, has been an American culinary classic since its first serving at the turn of the 20th century. For a completely different take on the common hot dog, come to Chicago, where a perfect hot dog is an art form unto itself. Although the rest of the world can't seem to understand why anyone would want a salad on their hot dog, Chicagoans take the expansive ingredient list very seriously and put much care into crafting the perfect hot dog. Poppy seed buns are the name of the game, and the dogs themselves had better be steamed and hot. Hot chili peppers, chunks of tomato, relish, onions, mustard, celery salt and, last but not least, a sharp dill pickle spear completes the dog.

and lobster thermador. Appetizers feature shellfish, sashimi and caviar, followed by sole, salmon and lobster entrees. The street-level bar serves casual versions of the main menu.

Seafood menu. Lunch, dinner. Closed Sunday. Bar. Business casual attire. Reservations recommended. Valet parking. $$$

★★★Nine
440 W. Randolph St., Chicago,
312-575-9900;
www.n9ne.com

A scene-setter in the West Loop, this spot serves serious steakhouse fare, and has a central champagne and caviar bar that's great for people-watching. Upstairs is the late-night lounge, the Ghost Bar.

Steak menu. Lunch, dinner. Closed Sunday. Bar. Business casual attire. Reservations recommended. Valet parking. $$$

★★Nix
163 E. Walton Place, Chicago,
312-867-7575, 866-866-8086;
www.milleniumhotels.com

American menu. Breakfast, lunch, dinner. Bar. Business casual attire. Reservations recommended. Valet parking. $$$

★★★NoMi
800 N. Michigan Ave., Chicago,
312-239-4030;
www.nomirestaurant.com

NoMI is the Park Hyatt's stylish destination for contemporary French cuisine by chef Christophe David. Asian influences are evident in sushi and sashimi selections on the menu. Luxurious materials such as white marble, Italian mosaic tile and leather are combined in the streamlined décor. The wine list is extensive, with 3,000 or so bottles. NoMI also serves breakfast and lunch and offers outdoor terrace dining in fair weather.

French menu. Breakfast, lunch, dinner, Sunday brunch. Bar. Business casual attire. Reservations recommended. Valet parking. Outdoor seating. $$$

★★★North Pond
2610 N. Cannon Dr., Chicago,
773-477-5845;
www.northpondrestaurant.com

North Pond delivers a dining experience like no other. Seasonal, contemporary American food with French influences can be paired with an all-American wine list, served in a one-of-a-kind location on the Lincoln Park lagoon. The handsome Arts and Crafts decor and open floor-to-ceiling windows add to the contemporary feel. Sunday brunch is a refined indulgence, and outdoor dining is a special treat in seasonable weather.

American menu. Lunch, dinner, Sunday brunch. Closed Mondays. Bar. Children's menu. Business casual attire. Reservations recommended. Valet parking. Outdoor seating. $$$

★Northside Cafe
1635 N. Damen Ave., Chicago,
773-384-3555;
www.northsidechicago.com

American menu. Lunch, dinner, late-night, Saturday-Sunday brunch. Bar. Casual attire. Valet parking. Outdoor seating. $$

★Oak Tree
900 N. Michigan Ave., Chicago,
312-751-1988

American menu. Breakfast, lunch, dinner, brunch. Casual attire. $

★★★One Sixtyblue
1400 W. Randolph, Chicago,
312-850-0303;
www.onesixtyblue.com

Award-winning, haute contemporary cuisine and sleek, high-styled decor by designer Adam Tihany define this adult, urban dining experience in the West Loop. Bold American fare with French roots is served in the dining room. The open kitchen and dramatic wine storage are focal points. A cocoa bar offers sinful chocolate creations while the chic lounge is a popular spot.

American menu. Dinner. Closed Sunday. Bar. Business casual attire. Reservations recommended. Valet parking. $$$

ILLINOIS

★★★Opera
1301 S. Wabash Ave., Chicago,
312-461-0161;
www.opera-chicago.com

Helping to position the South Loop as a foodie destination, Opera updates Chinese fare by banning gummy sauces and upping the presentation appeal. Top picks include five-spice squid and slow-roasted pork shoulder. The lively, art-filled interior encourages lingering over cocktails.

Chinese menu. Dinner. Bar. Business casual attire. Reservations recommended. Valet parking. **$$$**

★Orange
3231 N. Clark St., Chicago,
773-549-4400

American menu. Breakfast, lunch, brunch. Children's menu. Casual attire. **$**

★★Osteria Via Stato
620 N. State St., Chicago,
312-642-8450;
www.leye.com

Italian menu. Lunch, dinner. Bar. Children's menu. Business casual attire. Reservations recommended. Valet parking. Outdoor seating. **$$$**

★P J Clarke's
302 E. Illinois St., Chicago,
312-670-7500;
www.pjclarkeschicago.com

American menu. Lunch, dinner, late-night, brunch. Closed December 24. Bar. Casual attire. Outdoor seating. **$$**

★★★Pane Caldo
72 E. Walton St., Chicago,
312-649-0055;
www.pane-caldo.com

This little spot off the Magnificent Mile is home to some of the best Italian food this side of Piedmont. It's easy to miss this tiny restaurant so look for the shoppers enjoying risotto Milanese. An extensive wine list complements the kitchen's lovely creations, made with organic meats and locally grown organic produce.

Italian menu. Lunch, dinner. Bar. Business casual attire. Reservations recommended. Valet parking. Outdoor seating. **$$$**

★Parthenon
314 S. Halsted St., Chicago,
312-726-2407;
www.theparthenon.com

Greek menu. Lunch, dinner. Bar. Casual attire. Reservations recommended. Valet parking. **$$**

★Penny's Noodle Shop
3400 N. Sheffield Ave., Chicago,
773-281-8222

Thai menu. Lunch, dinner. Closed Monday; holidays. Casual attire. Outdoor seating. **$**

★★Petterino's
150 N. Dearborn., Chicago,
312-422-0150;
www.leye.com

American menu. Lunch, dinner. Bar. Business casual attire. Reservations recommended. Valet parking. Outdoor seating. **$$$**

★Piece
1927 W. North Ave., Chicago,
773-772-4422;
www.piecechicago.com

Pizza. Lunch, dinner. Bar. Casual attire. Valet parking. **$**

★★Pizza D. O. C
2251 W. Lawrence., Chicago,
773-784-8777;
www.pizza-doc.com

Italian, pizza menu. Lunch, dinner. Bar. Casual attire. **$$**

★Pizzeria Uno
29 E. Ohio St., Chicago,
312-321-1000;
www.unos.com

Pizza. Lunch, dinner, late-night. Bar. Children's menu. Casual attire. Outdoor seating. **$$**

★★★Pump Room
1301 N. State Pkwy., Chicago,

312-266-0360;
www.pumproom.com

This revered Chicago classic combines grand hotel dining with contemporary French-American fare. The Pump Room remains popular with tourists and special-occasion celebrants. Booth One comes complete with a vintage telephone, and the bar could have been transported from a *Thin Man* set. Highlights include live music with a small dance floor and a Sunday champagne brunch.

American menu. Breakfast, lunch, dinner, Sunday brunch. Bar. Children's menu. Business casual attire. Reservations recommended. Valet parking. **$$$**

★★Quartino
626 N. State St., Chicago,
312-698-5000;
www.quartinochicago.com

Italian menu. Lunch, dinner. Bar. Casual attire. Valet parking. Outdoor seating. **$$**

★★Ras Dashen
5846 N. Broadway., Chicago,
773-506-9601;
www.rasdashenchicago.com

Ethiopian menu. Lunch, dinner. Bar. Casual attire. Reservations recommended. **$$**

★★Red Light
820 W. Randolph St., Chicago,
312-733-8880;
www.redlight-chicago.com

Pan-Asian menu. Lunch, dinner. Bar. Business casual attire. Reservations recommended. Valet parking. Outdoor seating. **$$$**

★Redfish
400 N. State St., Chicago,
312-467-1600;
www.redfishamerica.com

Cajun/Creole menu. Lunch, dinner, late-night. Bar. Children's menu. Casual attire. Valet parking. **$$**

★★Riva
700 E. Grand Ave., Chicago,
312-644-7482;

www.stefanirestaurants.com

Seafood menu. Lunch, dinner. Bar. Children's menu. Business casual attire. Reservations recommended. Valet parking. Outdoor seating. **$$$**

★★★RL Restaurant
115 E. Chicago Ave., Chicago,
312-475-1100

Located in Ralph Lauren's flagship Chicago store on Michigan Avenue, RL restaurant focuses its efforts on American classics. Menu items such as Crab Louie, Green Goddess salad or Steak Diane are updated, presented with flair and worthy of a splurge. The restaurant exudes the warmth and elegance of a city club, with herringbone hardwood floors and mahogany ceilings.

American menu. Lunch, dinner, Sunday brunch. Bar. Children's menu. Casual attire. Reservations recommended. Valet parking. Outdoor seating. **$$$**

★★★Rodan
1530 N. Milwaukee Ave., Chicago,
773-276-7036;
www.rodan.ws

A funky Wicker Parker spot, Rodan unites the foods of South America and Asia on its menu. Graze from gingered swordfish and shrimp rolls back West to adobo Cornish hen and fish tacos with mango salsa. Somewhere in between lie the tasty wasabi tempura fries. Go casual to Rodan, and go late-night if you're looking for a hip lounge. As the night progresses, audio and visual artists show digital images and mix music.

Pan-Asian, South American menu. Dinner, late-night. Bar. Casual attire. Reservations recommended. **$$**

★★Rosebud
1500 W. Taylor St., Chicago,
312-942-1117;
www.rosebudrestaurants.com

Italian menu. Lunch, dinner. Bar. Business casual attire. Reservations recommended. Valet parking. Outdoor seating. **$$**

★★★Roy's
720 N. State St., Chicago,

49

ILLINOIS

★
★
★
★
★
★

312-787-7599;
roysrestaurant.com

Don't expect luau fare at this sleek, contemporary Hawaiian restaurant. Lots of creative seafood dishes populate the menu, with several unusual fish varieties and French and Asian fusion dishes evident throughout. Menu selections are listed with suggested wine pairings.

Pacific-Rim/Pan-Asian menu. Dinner. Bar. Children's menu. Business casual attire. Reservations recommended. Valet parking. Outdoor seating. **$$$**

★★Rumba
351 W. Hubbard St., Chicago,
312-222-1226;
www.rumba351.com

Latin American menu. Dinner. Bar. Casual attire. Business casual attire. Valet parking. **$$$**

★★Russian Tea Time
77 E. Adams St., Chicago,
312-360-0000;
www.russianteatime.com

Continental, Russian menu. Lunch, dinner. Bar. Children's menu. Casual attire. Reservations recommended. **$$**

★★Sai Cafe
2010 N. Sheffield Ave., Chicago,
773-472-8080;
www.saicafe.com

Sushi menu. Dinner. Bar. Casual attire. Reservations recommended. **$$**

★★Saloon Steakhouse
200 E. Chestnut St., Chicago,
312-280-5454;
www.saloonsteakhouse.com

Steak menu. Lunch, dinner. Bar. Casual attire. **$$$**

★★★Salpicon
1252 N. Wells St., Chicago,
312-988-7811;
www.salpicon.com

Chef Priscilla Satkoff grew up in Mexico City and honors her native cuisine here with rich moles, tender-roasted meats and upscale twists like an ancho chile quail. The extensive wine list, managed by the chef's husband, has won numerous awards, but it's hard to get past the 50-some tequilas on offer to mix in margaritas.

Mexican menu. Lunch, dinner. Bar. Casual attire. Reservations recommended. Valet parking. Outdoor seating. **$$**

★★Santorini
800 W. Adams St., Chicago,
312-829-8820;
www.santorinichicago.com

Greek menu. Lunch, dinner. Bar. Casual attire. Reservations recommended. Valet parking. Outdoor seating. **$$**

★★Sayat Nova
157 E. Ohio St., Chicago,
312-644-9159;
www.sayatnovachicago.org

Armenian menu. Lunch, dinner. Closed holidays. Bar. Casual attire. **$$**

★★Scoozi
410 W. Huron, Chicago,
312-943-5900;
www.leye.com

Italian menu. Dinner. Bar. Children's menu. Business casual attire. Reservations recommended. Valet parking. Outdoor seating. **$$**

★★★★Seasons
120 E. Delaware Place, Chicago,
312-280-8800;
www.fourseasons.com/chicagofs

Seasons restaurant has a diverse menu that changes depending upon the availability of fresh ingredients such as a surf and turf tartare, which features American Kobe beef with violet mustard, or ahi tuna with wasabi sorbet and tamarind-soy gelee. Groups that number six or more can request the Chef's Table and receive a personally guided eight-course meal with wine pairings.

American menu. Breakfast, lunch, dinner, Sunday brunch. Bar. Children's menu. Business casual attire. Reservations recommended. Valet parking. **$$$**

★★★Sepia
123 N. Jefferson St., Chicago,
312-441-1920;
www.sepiachicago.com
With a cozy and rustic dining room, this is the kind of eatery that makes you want to linger. Owner Emmanuel Nony and executive chef Kendal Duque have crafted a menu that spotlights fresh, seasonal ingredients. Creations include roasted duck with swiss chard and sweet corn or skate wing with broccoflower and raisin-caper sauce. Polish off your experience with a rich, hearty dessert like bittersweet chocolate crepes with fresh figs and pistachio ice cream.
American. Dinner, lunch, brunch. Valet parking.

★★★Shanghai Terrace
108 E. Superior, Chicago,
312-573-6744;
chicago.peninsula.com
Intimate and trimmed in rich hues of ruby red and black lacquer, Shanghai Terrace is housed in the stylish Peninsula Hotel. Start with the refined three-bite dim sum. Save room for flavorful entrees like spicy Szechuan beef and wok-fried lobster. The restaurant adjoins an expansive terrace offering alfresco dining in the summer six stories above Michigan Avenue.
Chinese menu. Lunch, dinner. Closed Sunday. Bar. Casual attire. Outdoor seating. $$$

★★Shaw's Crab House
21 E. Hubbard St., Chicago,
312-527-2722;
www.shawscrabhouse.com
Seafood menu. Lunch, dinner. Bar. Business casual attire. Reservations recommended. Valet parking. $$$

★★Signature Room at the 95th
875 N. Michigan Ave., Chicago,
312-787-9596;
www.signatureroom.com
American menu. Lunch, dinner, Sunday brunch. Bar. Children's menu. Casual attire. $$

PIE IN THE SKY

Chicagoans have never been satisfied with the ordinary, nor with doing things in a small way, which is illustrated nicely by their deep dish pizza. It must be noted that Chicago-style pizza *is* related to the East Coast-style, thin-crust pizza, by virtue that both have some type of tomato sauce and cheese. But all similarities end there.

Contrary to popular belief, the crust on a classic Chicago pizza isn't thick at all. It's actually a normal pizza crust that is put into a special pizza pan with deep sides to form the familiar deep dish shape.

Since it's bad form for the crust around the edge to perch over the pizza, this space must be filled with three to four times the quantity of ingredients on a thin-crust pizza. Sausage is a solid option, and is cited as the most frequently requested ingredient on pizzas in the city. Peppers, onions, pepperoni, olives and all of the best-loved standbys of the classic pizza are piled high to fill that waiting crust. Good things come to those who wait, and Chicago-style pizza is no exception; average baking times hover around the 45-minute mark at Chicago's most famous pizzerias.

When the pizza finally comes out of the oven, one piece is a meal unto itself. Two will prevent the need for breakfast. And three slices will make you famous in this city of big shoulders.

★★★Spiaggia

980 N. Michigan Ave., Chicago,
312-280-2750;
www.spiaggiarestaurant.com

Spiaggia offers contemporary, sophisticated Italian cuisine under the direction of chef Tony Mantuano's light, refined touch, working with artisanal and exotic ingredients like Piemontese beef and seasonal white truffles. Expect frequent menu changes, but typical dishes include wood-roasted scallops with porcini mushrooms and Parmesan shavings and lamb chops with slow-cooked lamb shoulder. The opulent trilevel dining room has views over Michigan Avenue.
Italian menu. Lunch, dinner. Bar. Jacket required. Reservations recommended. Valet parking. $$$

★★★Spring

2039 W. North Ave., Chicago,
773-395-7100;
www.springrestaurant.net

Although you can't always count on the fickle Chicago weather, you can always expect Spring to deliver freshness in food, service and style. The upscale restaurant showcases chef Shawn McClain's talent with seafood, a light approach often inflected with an Asian accent. Though they change to reflect the seasons, dishes such as tuna tartare with quail egg, cod in crab and sweet pea sauce, and diver scallops with braised oxtail are artistic but unfussy.
American, seafood menu. Dinner. Closed Monday. Bar. Business casual attire. Reservations recommended. Valet parking. $$$

★Su Casa

49 E. Ontario St., Chicago,
312-943-4041

Mexican menu. Lunch, dinner. Bar. Children's menu. Casual attire. Outdoor seating. $$

★★Sushi Samba Rio

504 N. Wells St., Chicago,
312-595-2300; www.sushisamba.com

Japanese, sushi menu. Lunch, dinner. Bar. Business casual attire. Reservations recom-

mended. Valet parking. Outdoor seating. $$

★★Sushi Wabi

842 W. Randolph St., Chicago,
312-563-1224;
www.sushiwabi.com

Japanese, sushi menu. Lunch, dinner. Bar. Casual attire. Reservations recommended. Valet parking. Outdoor seating. $$

★★★The Capital Grille

633 N. St. Clair St., Chicago,
312-337-9400;
www.thecapitalgrille.com

This steakhouse chain deliberately cultivates the old boys' network vibe. The clubby, masculine decor features dark woods and original oil paintings of fox hunts, cattle drives and the like. Sizable à la carte entrees like porterhouse steak, filet mignon and broiled fresh lobster, along with traditional sides that serve three, tempt the taste buds. Beef is dry-aged on the premises for 14 days and hand-cut daily.
Steak menu. Lunch, dinner. Bar. Business casual attire. Reservations recommended. Valet parking. $$$

★★★The Grill on the Alley

909 N. Michigan Ave., Chicago,
312-255-9009;
www.thegrill.com

An offshoot of the Beverly Hills eatery known for its power lunches, the Grill offers a vast selection of larger-than-life portions, including broiled steaks, seafood, pastas and specials that may feature comfort food like chicken pot pie, meat loaf or braised short ribs. The restaurant is located on the ground level of the Westin Michigan Avenue, steps away from world-class shopping.
American menu. Breakfast, lunch, dinner, brunch. Bar. Children's menu. Casual attire. Reservations recommended. Valet parking. Outdoor seating. $$$

★★The Indian Garden

2546 W. Devon Ave., Chicago,
773-338-2929;

★
★
★
★
★

www.theindiangarden.org
Indian menu. Lunch, dinner. Casual attire. Reservations recommended. Valet parking. $$

★★★The Palm
323 E. Wacker Dr., Chicago
312-616-1000;
www.thepalm.com
The Palm, located inside the Swissotel delivers on its promise of giant steaks and lobsters in a steakhouse atmosphere. Caricatures of famous people who have dined here are featured on the walls. Seasonal outdoor seating offers great views of Lake Michigan and Navy Pier.
American, steak menu. Lunch, dinner. Bar. Business casual attire. Reservations recommended. Valet parking. Outdoor seating. $$$

★★Tizi Melloul
531 N. Wells St., Chicago,
312-670-4338;
www.tizimelloul.com
Mediterranean menu. Dinner. Bar. Business casual attire. Reservations recommended. Valet parking. Outdoor seating. $$$

★Toast
2046 N. Damen Ave., Chicago,
773-772-5600
American menu. Breakfast, lunch. Children's menu. Casual attire. Outdoor seating. $

★★Topo Gigio Ristorante
1516 N. Wells St., Chicago,
312-266-9355;
www.topogigiochicago.com
Italian menu. Lunch, dinner. Bar. Casual attire. Reservations recommended. Valet parking. Outdoor seating. $$

★★★Topolobampo
445 N. Clark St., Chicago,
312-661-1434;
www.fronterakitchens.com
Pioneering chef/owner Rick Bayless is a cookbook author, television personality and perennial culinary award winner with a devoted following. His celebration of the regional cuisines of Mexico is realized at Topolobampo, the upscale counterpart to his famed Frontera Grill (which is next door). The seasonal menu, based on locally produced items, is paired with a tome of premium tequilas and an excellent wine list.
Mexican menu. Lunch, dinner. Closed Sunday-Monday. Bar. Children's menu. Business casual attire. Reservations recommended. Valet parking. Outdoor seating. $$$

★★Trattoria No. 10
10 N. Dearborn St., Chicago,
312-984-1718;
www.trattoriaten.com
Italian menu. Lunch, dinner. Closed Sunday. Bar. Business casual attire. Reservations recommended. Valet parking. $$

★Tre Kronor
3258 W. Foster Ave., Chicago,
773-267-9888
Scandinavian menu. Breakfast, lunch, dinner. Casual attire. $$

★★★★Tru
676 N. St. Clair St., Chicago
312-202-0001;
www.trurestaurant.com
Tru's modern, airy dining room is a stunning stage for chef and co-owner Rick Tramonto's progressive French creations and co-owner pastry chef Gale Gand's incredible, one-of-a-kind sweet and savory endings. Tramonto offers plates filled with ingredients that are treated to his unmatched creativity and artistic flair. The wine list, with more than 1,800 selections, is overseen by sommelier Scott Tyree. Museum quality artwork is on display, including pieces by Andy Warhol, Maya Lin and Gerhard Richter. A lounge area offers a somewhat less formal but no less memorable dining experience.
French menu. Dinner. Closed Sunday. Bar. Jacket required. Reservations recommended. Valet parking. $$$$

★★Tsunami
1160 N. Dearborn St., Chicago,
312-642-9911;

53

ILLINOIS

★
★
★
★
★

www.tsunamichicago.com
Japanese, sushi menu. Dinner. Bar. Children's menu. Reservations recommended. Valet parking. Outdoor seating. **$$$**

★★Tuscany
1014 W. Taylor St., Chicago,
312-829-1990;
www.stefanirestaurants.com
Italian menu. Lunch, dinner. Bar. Business casual attire. Reservations recommended. Valet parking. **$$**

★Twin Anchors Restaurant and Tavern
1655 N. Sedgwick St., Chicago,
312-266-1616;
www.twinanchorsribs.com
American menu. Lunch, dinner. Bar. Children's menu. Casual attire. Valet parking. Outdoor seating. **$$**

★★★Vivere
71 W. Monroe St., Chicago,
312-332-7005;
www.italianvillage-chicago.com
The high end of a trio of restaurants that comprises the Loop's long-standing Italian Village, Vivere plays it cool with showy decor and luxurious meals. The food stands its ground with new takes on the familiar, such as squid ink tortellini stuffed with bass. The Italian wine list rates among the country's best, making this a solid choice for a special occasion. Live jazz is performed on Wednesday evenings.
Italian menu. Lunch, dinner. Closed Sunday. Bar. Children's menu. Business casual attire. Reservations recommended. Valet parking. **$$$**

★★Vivo
838 W. Randolph St., Chicago,
312-733-3379;
www.vivo-chicago.com
Italian menu. Lunch, dinner. Bar. Business casual attire. Reservations recommended. Valet parking. Outdoor seating. **$$$**

★★Vong's Thai Kitchen
6 W. Hubbard St., Chicago,

312-644-8664;
www.vongsthaikitchen.com
Thai menu. Lunch, dinner. Bar. Casual attire. Reservations recommended. Valet parking. Outdoor seating. **$$**

★★Wave
644 N. Lake Shore Dr., Chicago,
312-255-4460;
www.waverestaurant.com
American, Mediterranean menu. Breakfast, lunch, dinner. Bar. Children's menu. Casual attire. Reservations recommended. Valet parking. Outdoor seating. **$$$**

★★★West Town Tavern
1329 W. Chicago Ave., Chicago,
312-666-6175;
www.westtowntavern.com
Chicago chef Susan Goss and her oenophile husband Drew Goss run West Town Tavern, an upscale comfort-food spot in a handsome brick-walled storefront. Entrees include chicken with zinfandel-chaterelle risotto. The wine list has interesting and affordable bottles while desserts, like bourbon pecan pie, are comfortaing and homemade. American menu. Dinner. Closed Sunday. Bar. Casual attire. Outdoor seating. **$$**

★Wishbone
1001 W. Washington Blvd., Chicago,
312-850-2663
3300 N. Lincoln, Chicago,
773-549-2663;
www.wishbonechicago.com
American menu. Breakfast, lunch, dinner, brunch. Bar. Children's menu. Casual attire. Reservations recommended. Valet parking. Outdoor seating. **$$**

★★★Yoshi's Cafe
3257 N. Halsted St., Chicago,
773-248-6160; www.yoshiscafe.com
Namesake chef Yoshi Katsumura comes from a fine-dining background, which accounts for the quality and sophistication of his French-Japanese fusion cuisine. His long-standing Lakeview cafe offers a relaxed atmosphere and good service. The menu changes monthly, and meanders from

shrimp cappuccino soup to sirloin steak. The relaxed, minimal decor features floor-to-ceiling windows, natural wood, tile floors and a covered patio, which is a popular spot in the warm weather.

Fusion/International menu. Lunch, dinner. Closed Monday. Bar. Casual attire. Outdoor seating. **$$**

★★★Zealous
419 W. Superior St., Chicago
312-475-9112;
www.zealousrestaurant.com

Charlie Trotter's protégé Michael Taus runs Zealous with a Trotter-like attention to detail and innovation. Menus change constantly, but you can expect them to be daring, with dishes such as veal paprikas with potato gnocchi and trumpet mushrooms. Put yourself in the chef's hands with a five- or seven-course tasting menu. This is event dining amplified by the thoughtful Asian-influenced decor.

American menu. Dinner. Closed Sunday-Monday. Bar. Business casual attire. Reservations recommended. Valet parking. **$$$**

SPAS

★★★★The Peninsula Spa, Chicago
108 E. Superior St., Chicago,
312-573-6860, 866-288-8889;
www.peninsula.com

This downtown spa combines Asian-inspired techniques with a full menu of traditional massages, body envelopments, skin care and salon services. Some massages incorporate reflexology to increase energy flow, while facials feature target shiatsu pressure points to counter stress. In the ESPA body envelopment treatment, the skin is brushed, exfoliated and oiled, then the whole body is encased in algae, marine mud or Oshadi clay, depending upon the goal—detoxificiation, de-stressing or an immune system boost. The crowning touch is an acupressure head massage.

★★★★The Spa at Four Seasons Chicago
120 E. Delaware Place, Chicago, 312-280-8800, 800-819-5053; www.fourseasons.com

This spa, located off Chicago's Michigan Avenue, features five soundproofed treatment rooms, ideal for escaping the noise of the city. Melt away with a Swedish, hot stone, sports conditioning or scalp rejuvenating massage. The elixir paraffin wrap combines olive stones, lavender, juniper berries and grapefruit to produce baby-soft skin. A variety of therapies, including manicures and pedicures, pamper and primp hands and feet. The facility also features a fitness center and indoor swimming pool.

★★★The Spa at the Carlton Club, Ritz-Carlton Chicago
160 E. Pearson St., Chicago, 312-266-1000; www.fourseasons.com/chicagorc

This spa, located at the Ritz-Carlton Chicago, has five elegant treatment rooms where massages, facials and body treatments are delivered by a professional, polite staff. Deep tissue, Swedish, healing stone and aromatherapy massages are wonderful ways to reward yourself. The adjacent state-of-the-art fitness center has treadmills, stair climbers, elliptical trainers and stationary bicycles equipped with televisions and VCRs to entertain you while you work up a sweat.

ILLINOIS

CHICAGO O'HARE AIRPORT

One of the world's busiest airports, O'Hare and neighboring Rosemont is surrounded by hotels, restaurants and entertainment facilities—a city unto itself, crossing municipal boundaries. The 18,500-seat Allstate Arena hosts professional sports and big-name musical acts, while the Rosemont Theater offers live entertainment in a more intimate environment.

Information: Des Plaines Chamber of Commerce, 1401 Oakton St., 847-824-4200; www.ohare.com

WHAT TO SEE AND DO

Cernan Earth and Space Center
2000 N. Fifth Ave., River Grove,
708-583-3100
A unique domed theater offering multimedia programs on astronomy, geography and other topics; the center also has free exhibits on space exploration. Friday-Saturday evenings, matinee Sunday.

Allstate Arena
6920 Mannheim Rd., Rosemont;
www.allstatearena.com
This auditorium seats 18,500 and hosts concerts, sports and other events.

Chicago Wolves
Allstate Arena, 6920 Mannheim Rd., Rosemont,
800-843-9658
The Wolves are an American Hockey League farm team for the Atlanta Thrashers. The team plays its home games in the Allstate Arena, a great venue for watching hockey at prices inexpensive enough that the entire family can attend.

HOTELS

★★Chicago Marriott Suites O'Hare
6155 N. River Rd., Rosemont,
847-696-4400, 800-228-9290;
www.marriott.com
256 rooms, all suites. High-speed Internet access. Restaurant, bar. Fitness room. Indoor pool, whirlpool. Airport transportation available. Business center. $$

★★★Westin O'Hare
6100 N. River Rd.,
Rosemont,
847-698-6000;
www.westin.com

This hotel is located near O'Hare International Airport and provides free shuttle service. There are several golf courses nearby. 525 rooms. Pets accepted, some restrictions; fee. High-speed Internet access. Restaurant, bar. Fitness room. Indoor pool, whirlpool. Business center. $$

★★★Hyatt Rosemont
6350 N. River Rd., Rosemont,
800-633-7313, 800-233-1234;
www.hyatt.com
A short drive away from O'Hare airport, this contemporary, small hotel caters to business travelers. Rooms have WiFi and spacious work areas. A complimentary airport shuttle is available 24 hours a day. 206 rooms. High-speed Internet access. Restaurant. Fitness room. Airport transportation available. $$

RESTAURANTS

★★Carlucci
6111 N. River Rd., Rosemont,
847-518-0990;
www.carluccirestaurant.com
Italian menu. Lunch, dinner. Bar. Business casual attire. Valet parking. $$

★★★Morton's, The Steakhouse
9525 W. Bryn Mawr Ave.,
Rosemont,
847-678-5155;
www.mortons.com
This steakhouse chain originated in Chicago in 1978, and appeals to serious meat lovers. With a selection of steaks as well as fresh fish, lobster and chicken entrees, Morton's rarely disappoints.
Steak menu. Dinner. Bar. Business casual attire. Reservations recommended. Valet parking. $$$

★★★Nick's Fishmarket
10275 W. Higgins Rd., Rosemont,
847-298-8200;
www.nicksfishmarketchicago.com
This location of the Hawaiian-born seafood restaurant is one of three in the Chicago area, and features three enormous aquariums.
Seafood menu. Dinner. Bar. Children's menu. Business casual attire. Reservations recommended. Valet parking. **$$$**

COLLINSVILLE

This western Illinois town was established in 1872. The town's great claim to fame is the world's largest catsup bottle, located just off Main Street.
Information: Chamber of Commerce, 221 W. Main St, 618-344-2884; www. discovercollinsville.com

WHAT TO SEE AND DO
Gateway Classic Cars
5401 Collinsville Rd., Fairmont City,
618-271-3000, 800-231-3616
If watching screaming stock cars ignites a little automobile lust within your soul, this place can satisfy your craving. Gateway Classic Cars deals in everything from fully restored American muscle cars and street rods to genuine racers. Monday-Friday 10 a.m.-5 p.m., Saturday 9 a.m.-5 p.m., Sunday noon-5 p.m.

HOTELS
★★Holiday Inn
1000 Eastport Plaza Dr.,
Collinsville,
618-345-2800, 800-465-4329;
www.holiday-inn.com
244 rooms. Pets accepted, some restrictions; fee. High-speed, wireless Internet access. Laundry services. Restaurant, bar. Fitness room. Indoor pool, whirlpool. Airport transportation available. Business center. **$**

DECATUR

In 1830, 21-year-old Abraham Lincoln drove through what would later become Decatur with his family to settle on the Sangamon River, a few miles west. He worked as a farmer and rail-splitter and made his first political speech in what is now Decatur's Lincoln Square. Today, the town is home to Richland Community College and Millikin University.
Information: Decatur Area Convention and Visitors Bureau, 202 E. North St., 217-423-7000, 800-331-4479; www.decaturcvb.com

WHAT TO SEE AND DO

Fairview Park
Hwys. 36 and 48, Decatur,
217-422-5911
This park has is a swimming pool, tennis, biking trail, picnicking, playground, baseball and horseshoe pits.

Millikin Place
Pine and Main Streets, Decatur.
This housing development was laid out and landscaped by Walter Burley Griffin in 1909, who designed Australia's capital, Canberra. The street features a Prairie school entrance, naturalized landscaping and houses by Marion Mahony, Griffin's wife, and Frank Lloyd Wright. Both Griffin and Mahony worked at Wright's famous Oak Park Studio. Numbers 1 and 3 Millikin Place are by Mahony; 2 Millikin Place is attributed to Wright.

Rock Springs Center for Environmental Discovery
Rocksprings Rd., Decatur,
217-423-7708
There are approximately 1,320 acres with hiking and self-guided interpretive trails in the center with a picnic area, shelter and asphalt bike trail. The ecocenter has hands-on educational exhibits. A visitor center holds scheduled events and programs throughout year. Daily.

Children's Museum
55 S. Country Club Rd., Decatur
217-423-5437
This museum features hands-on exhibits of arts, science, and technology. Daily.

Scovill Park and Zoo
71 S. Country Club Rd., Decatur
217-421-7435
The zoo has more than 500 animals. Picnicking and a playground are available. April-October, daily 10 a.m.-7 p.m.

HOTELS

★Baymont Inn
5100 Hickory Point Frontage Rd., Decatur,
217-875-5800;
www.baymontinns.com
102 rooms. Pets accepted, some restrictions; fee. Complimentary continental breakfast. $

★★Holiday Inn
4191 Hwy. 36, Decatur,
217-422-8800, 800-465-4329;
www.holiday-inn.com
370 rooms. Restaurant, bar. Fitness room. Indoor pool, children's pool, whirlpool. Tennis. Airport transportation available. Business center. $

DEKALB
DeKalb, founded in 1837, was home to model Cindy Crawford and actor Richard Jenkins.
Information: DeKalb Chamber of Commerce, 164 E. Lincoln Hwy.,
815-756-6306- www.dekalb.org

WHAT TO SEE AND DO

Northern Illinois University
W. Lincoln Hwy., DeKalb,
815-753-0446;
www.niu.edu
The University was founded in 1895 and currently has 22,000 students.

SPECIAL EVENTS

Corn Fest
First and Locust Streets, DeKalb,
815-748-2676.
This three-day street festival is devoted to corn. Last full weekend in August.

Stage Coach Players
126 S. Fifth St., DeKalb,
815-758-1940;
www.stagecoachers.com
This community theater puts on six performances a season. Reservations suggested. Mid-June-mid-September.

RESTAURANT

★★The Hillside Restaurant
121 N. 2nd St., DeKalb,
815-756-4749;

www.hillsiderestaurant.com
American menu. Lunch, dinner. Closed
Monday.

DIXON

At the southernmost point of the Black Hawk Trail, Dixon sits on the banks of the Rock River. Established as a trading post and tavern by John Dixon, it now is a center for light industry. Ronald Reagan was born in nearby Tampico and grew up in Dixon.
Information: Dixon Area Chamber of Commerce, 101 W. Second St.,
815-284-3361; www.dixonil.com

WHAT TO SEE AND DO

John Deere Historic Site
8393 S. Main, Grand Detour,
815-652-4551.
The first self-scouring steel plow was made here in 1837. The site has a reconstructed blacksmith shop, restored house and gardens and natural prairie. Early April-late November; daily.

Lincoln Statue Park
100 Lincoln Statue Dr., Dixon,
815-288-3404
This park includes the site of Fort Dixon, around which the town was built, and a statue of Lincoln as a young captain in the Black Hawk War of 1832. A plaque summarizes Lincoln's military career; at the statue's base is a bas-relief of John Dixon. Also in the park is **Ronald Reagan's boyhood home,** a three-bedroom house with

1920s furnishings. April-November: daily; rest of year: Saturday-Sunday.

SPECIAL EVENT

Petunia Festival
Dixon, 815-284-3361;
www.petuniafestival.org
This festival features a carnival, parade, arts and crafts, bicycle race, tennis tournament, festival garden and fireworks. July 4 week.

HOTELS

★★Best Western Reagan Hotel
443 Hwy. 2., Dixon,
815-284-1890, 800-780-7234;
www.bestwestern.com
91 rooms. Pets accepted; fee. Complimentary continental breakfast. Restaurant, bar. Fitness room. Outdoor pool, whirlpool. **$**

59

ILLINOIS

DOWNERS GROVE

A western Chicago suburb, this town has several houses thought to have been stops on the Underground Railroad.
Information: Visitors Bureau, 5202 Washington St., 800-934-0615;
www.vil.downers-grove.il.us

WHAT TO SEE AND DO

Historical Museum
831 Maple Ave., Downers Grove,
630-963-1309
This Victorian house, built in 1892, contains eight rooms of period furnishings, antiques and artifacts. Sunday-Friday 1-3 p.m.

Morton Arboretum
4100 Hwy. 53, Lisle,
630-968-0074;
www.mortonarb.org
The Morton Arboretum, located 25 miles west of the city in Lisle, was founded in 1923 by Joy Morton of the Morton salt family. This facility is renowned for its lush

collection of trees and plants from around the world. Daily.

HOTELS
★★Doubletree Guest Suites and Conference Center
2111 Butterfield Rd., Downers Grove,
630-971-2000, 800-222-8733;
www.doubletreedownersgrove.com
247 rooms, all suites. High-speed Internet access. Restaurant, bar. Fitness room, fitness classes available. Indoor pool, whirlpool. Business center. $

DUNDEE
Two Potawatomi villages were nearby when settlers first arrived in 1835. A Scotsman won a lottery and was permitted to name the settlement Dundee after his hometown.

WHAT TO SEE AND DO
Haeger Pottery Factory
7 Maiden Lane, Dundee,
847-783-5420
Located here is a pottery and artware outlet and a ceramic museum. Monday, Thursday-Sunday.

RESTAURANT
★★Milk Pail
14N630 Hwy. 25., Dundee,
847-742-5040;
www.themilkpail.com
American menu. Lunch, dinner, Sunday brunch. Closed Monday. Bar. Children's menu. $$

EFFINGHAM
This town is the seat of Effingham County. Outdoor recreation is popular here, with Lake Sara offering fishing, boating and golfing.
Information: Convention and Visitors Bureau, 201 E. Jefferson Ave., 217-342-5305, 800-772-0750; www.effinghamil.com

HOTELS
★★Best Western Raintree Inn
1809 W. Fayette Ave., Effingham,
217-342-4121, 800-780-7234;
www.bestwestern.com
65 rooms. Pets accepted, some restrictions. Complimentary continental breakfast. High-speed, wireless Internet access. Restaurant, bar. Outdoor pool. Business center. $

★Comfort Inn
1310 W. Fayette Rd., Effingham,
217-342-3151, 800-228-5150;
www.comfortsuites.com
65 rooms, all suites. Pets accepted, some restrictions. Complimentary continental breakfast. High-speed, wireless Internet access. Fitness room. Indoor pool. $

★Holiday Inn Express
1103 Avenue of Mid-America, Effingham,
217-540-1111, 888-465-4329;
www.holiday-inn.com
118 rooms. Pets accepted, some restrictions; fee. Complimentary continental breakfast. Wireless Internet access. Fitness room. Indoor pool. $

SPECIALTY LODGING
The Daisy Inn Bed & Breakfast
315 E. Illinois St.,
Greenup,
217-923-3050
This bed and breakfast is housed in a restored Victorian inn with comfortable rooms and private baths. 5 rooms. Check-in 3 p.m., check-out noon. $

RESTAURANT
★Niemerg's Steak House
1410 W. Fayette Ave., Effingham,
217-342-3921
American menu. Breakfast, lunch, dinner. Bar. Children's menu. $$

EVANSTON

Evanston sits immediately north of Chicago, occupying an enviable expanse of land along Lake Michigan. The home to Northwestern University, Evanston boasts a multitude of art galleries, theaters, shops and restaurants. The community is serviced by the Purple Line of Chicago's "L" system.

Information: Convention and Visitors Bureau, 1 Rotary Center, 1560 Sherman Ave., 847-328-1500; www.cityofevanston.org

WHAT TO SEE AND DO

Charles Gates Dawes House
225 Greenwood St., Evanston,
847-475-3410;
www.evanstonhistoricalsociety.org
The 28-room house of General Charles G. Dawes, Nobel Peace Prize winner (1926) and vice president under Calvin Coolidge. Tours. Tuesday-Saturday afternoons.

Grosse Point Lighthouse
Sheridan Rd. and Central St., Evanston,
847-328-6961
Constructed after a Lake Michigan wreck near Evanston claimed 300 lives, offered here are guided tours of the keeper's quarters, a museum and tower. No children under age 8 permitted. June-September, Saturday-Sunday.

Ladd Arboretum
2024 McCormick Blvd., Evanston,
847-448-8256;
www.laddarboretum.org
This arboretum has jogging and biking trails, canoeing, fishing, bird-watching and camping. There is an International Friendship Garden. Monday-Friday.

Mitchell Museum of the American Indian
3001 Central Park., Evanston,
847-475-1030;
www.mitchellmuseum.org
This collection of more than 3,000 items of Native American art and artifacts includes baskets, pottery, jewelry, Navajo rugs, beadwork, stoneware and more. Tuesday-Saturday 10 a.m.-5 p.m., Sunday noon-4 p.m.

Northwestern University
633 Clark St., Evanston,
847-491-3741;
www.northwestern.edu
Founded in 1851, this private university consistently ranks as one of the top in the nation. The Dearborn Observatory, built in 1888, has free public viewings. Other places of interest include the Shakespeare Garden, University Library, Norris University Center, Alice Millar Religious Center, Theatre and Interpretation Center, Mary and Leigh Block Museum of Art, Pick-Staiger Concert Hall, Ryan Field (Big Ten football), and Welsh-Ryan Arena (basketball). Guided walking tours of the lakefront campus leave 1801 Hinman Avenue. Academic year: one departure Monday-Saturday; July-August: two departures Monday-Friday; reservations, 847-491-7271.

HOTELS

★★★Hotel Orrington
1710 Orrington Ave., Evanston,
847-866-8700, 800-434-6835;
www.hotelorrington.com
Located across from Northwestern University, this elegant hotel combines historic character with modern touches. The hotel features amenities such as an on-site fitness center and access to the Evanston Athletic Club and Henry Crown Sports Pavilion/Norris Aquatics Center.

269 rooms. Pets accepted, some restrictions; fee. High-speed Internet access. Restaurant, bar. Fitness room. Airport transportation available. Business center. $

RESTAURANTS

★★Jilly's Cafe
2614 Green Bay Rd., Evanston,
847-869-7636;
www.jillyscafe.com
American, French menu. Lunch, dinner, Sunday brunch. Closed Monday. $$

★
★
★
★
★

★Las Palmas
817 University Place, Evanston,
847-328-2555
Mexican menu. Lunch, dinner. Bar. **$$**

★Lucky Platter
514 Main St., Evanston,
847-869-4064
International menu. Breakfast, lunch, dinner.
$$

★Merle's #1 Barbecue
1727 Benson St., Evanston,
847-475-7766
American menu. Dinner. Bar. Children's
menu. **$$**

★★★Oceanique
505 Main St., Evanston,
847-864-3435;
www.oceanique.com
As the name suggests, the focus of this res-
taurant is seafood. Dishes include a bouil-
labaisse of squid, salmon and shrimp in a
saffron-scented broth.
French, American menu. Dinner. Closed
Sunday. **$$$**

★★Pete Miller's Steakhouse
1557 Sherman Ave., Evanston,
847-328-0399
Steak menu. Dinner. Bar. Valet parking. **$$**

★Prairie Moon
1502 Sherman Ave., Evanston
847-864-8328;
www.prairiemoonrestaurant.com
International menu. Lunch, dinner, late-
night, Sunday brunch. Bar. Children's
menu. Casual attire. Outdoor seating. **$$**

★★Va Pensiero
1566 Oak Ave., Evanston,
847-475-7779;
www.va-p.com
Italian menu. Dinner. Bar. Outdoor seating.
$$

FREEPORT

According to legend, Freeport is named for the generosity of its pioneer settler, William Baker,
who was chided by his wife for running a "free port" for everyone coming along the trail.
It was the scene of the second Lincoln-Douglas debate—the site is marked by a memorial
boulder and a life-size statue of Lincoln and Douglas in debate.
Information: Stephenson County Convention and Visitors Bureau, 2047 AYP Rd., 815-
233-1357; 800-369-2955. www.stephenson-county-il.org

WHAT TO SEE AND DO
Freeport Arts Center
121 N. Harlem Ave., Freeport,
815-235-9755
The center has a collection that includes
Asian and Native American art, Euro-
pean paintings and sculptures, Egyptian,
Greek and Roman antiquities along with
contemporary exhibits. Tuesday-Sunday.

Silver Creek and Stephenson Railroad
2954 S. Walnut St., Freeport,
815-232-2306
Trips are offered here on a 1912, 36-
ton steam locomotive with three antique
cabooses and a flat car. Memorial Day-
Labor Day, periodic weekends.

Stephenson County Historical Museum
1440 S. Carroll Ave., Freeport,
815-232-8419
In the 1857 Oscar Taylor house, this
museum features 19th-century furnishings
and exhibits. Wednesday-Sunday.

HOTELS
★Country Inn & Suites
1710 S. Dirk Dr., Freeport,
815-233-3300, 800-456-4000;
www.countryinns.com

66 rooms. Complimentary full breakfast. Fitness room. Indoor pool, whirlpool.

★**Ramada Inn**
1300 E. South St., Freeport,
815-297-9700, 800-272-6232;
www.ramada.com
90 rooms. Pets accepted; fee. Restaurant, bar. Fitness room. Indoor pool. **$**

FORT KASKASKIA STATE HISTORIC SITE

This 275-acre park includes the earthworks of an old fort, first built in 1733, rebuilt in 1736 by the French, and finally destroyed to prevent British occupation after the Treaty of Paris. As a result of post Revolutionary War anarchy (1784), the ruins of the fort, while in the hands of Connecticut renegade John Dodge, were the scene of murders and revelry. Nearby is Garrison Hill Cemetery. The Pierre Menard Mansion, at the base of bluffs along the Mississippi, was built in 1802 in the style of a French colonial house. The home has been called the "Mount Vernon of the West." Some original furnishings have been reclaimed and reinstalled by the state. The park provides hiking, picnicking, tent and trailer camping. For information, contact the park manager, 4372 Park Rd., Ellis Grove, 618-859-3741; 618-859-3031.

GALENA

A quiet town of historical and architectural interest set on terraces cut by the old Fever River, Galena was once a major crossroads for French exploration of the New World and the commercial and cultural capital of the Northwest Territory. The grand mansions standing today were built on lead and steamboat fortunes and ninety percent of the town's buildings are listed on the National Register of Historic Places.
Information: Galena/Jo Daviess County Convention and Visitors Bureau, 720 Park Ave.,800-747-9377; www.galena.org

WHAT TO SEE AND DO

Belvedere Mansion
1008 Park Ave., Galena,
815-777-0747
This Italianate/Steamboat Gothic mansion built in 1857, has been restored and furnished with antiques, including pieces used on set of *Gone With the Wind*. Combination ticket with Dowling House. Memorial Day-October; daily.

Dowling House
220 N. Diagonal St., Galena,
815-777-1250
A restored stone house, the oldest in Galena, this house is authentically furnished as a trading post with primitive living quarters. Guided tours. Combination ticket with Bel-

vedere Mansion. May-December: daily; rest of year: limited hours.

Grace Episcopal Church
309 Hill St., Galena,
817-777-2590
A Gothic Revival church built in 1848, this building was later remodeled by William LeBaron Jenney, father of the skyscraper. Sunday; also by appointment

Ulysses S. Grant Home State Historic Site
500 Bouthillier St., Galena,
815-777-3310;
www.granthome.com
This Italianate house was given to General Grant on his return from the Civil War in 1865. It features original furnishings and Grant family items. Wednesday-Sunday 9 a.m.-5 p.m.

HOTELS
★Best Western Quiet House & Suites
9923 Hwy. 20 E., Galena,
815-777-2577, 800-937-8376;
www.quiethouse.com
42 rooms. Pets accepted, some restrictions; fee. Fitness room. Indoor pool, outdoor pool, whirlpool. $

★Country Inn & Suites
11134 Oldenburg Lane, Galena,
815-777-2400, 888-201-1746;
www.countryinns.com
75 rooms. Complimentary full breakfast. Fitness room. Indoor pool, children's pool, whirlpool. $

★★Desoto House Hotel
230 S. Main St., Galena,
815-777-0090, 800-343-6562;
www.desotohouse.com
55 rooms. Two restaurants, bar. $

★Ramada Galena
11383 Hwy. 20 W., Galena,
815-777-2043
96 rooms. Complimentary continental breakfast. Fitness room. Indoor pool, whirlpool. $

★★★Eagle Ridge Resort and Spa
444 Eagle Ridge Dr., Galena,
815-777-2444, 800-892-2269,
www.eagleridge.com
Located in the Galena Territories, a 6,800-acre recreational planned community adjacent to the river town of Galena, this resort has golf courses, horseback riding, hiking, bike and boat rentals. Villas and three- to eight-bedroom homes are available.
80 rooms. Pets accepted, some restrictions; fee. Three restaurants, bar. Children's activity center. Fitness room, spa. Indoor pool, whirlpool. Golf, 63 holes. Tennis. Airport transportation available. Business center. $$

SPECIALTY LODGINGS
Aldrich Guest House
900 3rd St., Galena,
815-777-3323;

www.galena.com/aldrich
Abraham Lincoln didn't sleep here but he sat in the front parlor for many a discussion with owner Robert H. McClellan, an Illinois state senator, lawyer and prominent Galena citizen in the 1880s. Rooms feature antique beds, handmade quilts and tapestries.
5 rooms. Children over 15 years only. Complimentary full breakfast. $

Hellman Guest House
318 Hill St., Galena,
815-777-3638;
www.hellmanguesthouse.com
Perched on a bluff overlooking downtown Galena, this 1895 Queen Anne home has four bedrooms, each with private bath.
4 rooms. Children over 12 years only. Complimentary full breakfast. $

Park Avenue Guest House
208 Park Ave., Galena,
815-777-1075, 800-359-0743;
www.galena.com/parkave
This historic guest house has rooms decorated with antiques.
4 rooms. Children over 12 years only. Complimentary full breakfast. $

Pine Hollow Inn Bed & Breakfast
4700 N. Council Hill Rd., Galena,
815-777-1071;
www.pinehollowinn.com
Tucked into a secluded valley on 120 acres of wooded land, this bed and breakfast has five suites with wood-burning fireplaces.
5 rooms. Children over 12 years only. Complimentary full breakfast. $

RESTAURANTS
★Backstreet Steak & Chophouse
216 S. Commerce St., Galena,
815-777-4800;
www.backstreetgalena.com
Traditional steakhouse, Steak menu. Dinner. $$$

★Log Cabin
201 N. Main St., Galena,
815-777-0393

ILLINOIS

Seafood, steak menu. Lunch, dinner. Bar.
Children's menu. **$$**

★★Woodlands Restaurant
444 Territory Dr., Galena,
815-777-5050, 800-998-6338;
www.eagleridge.com
American menu. Breakfast, lunch, dinner.
$$

GALESBURG
Eastern pioneers came to this area on the prairie to establish a school for the training of ministers, Knox College. The town was named for their leader, G. W. Gale. Galesburg was an important station on the Underground Railroad. It is also the birth and burial place of poet Carl Sandburg.
Information: Galesburg Area Convention and Visitors Bureau, 2163 E. Main St.,
309-343-2485; www.visitgalesburg.com

WHAT TO SEE AND DO
Carl Sandburg State Historic Site
331 E. Third St., Galesburg,
309-342-2361
Located here is the restored birthplace cottage of the famous poet. Remembrance Rock, named for Sandburg's historical novel, is a granite boulder under which his ashes were placed. Wednesday-Sunday.

Lake Storey Recreational Area
1033 S. Lake Storey Rd., Galesburg,
309-345-3683
This water park offers boat rentals, an 18-hole golf course, tennis, picnicking, a playground, gardens, concessions and camping. Daily.

HOTELS
★★Ramada Inn
29 Public Square, Galesburg,
309-343-9161, 800-272-6232;
www.ramada.com
96 rooms. Pets accepted; fee. Restaurant, bar. Indoor pool, whirlpool. **$**

★★Best Western Prairie Inn
300 S. Soangetaha Rd., Galesburg,
309-343-7151, 866-343-7151;
www.bestwestern.com
109 rooms. Pets accepted, some restrictions; fee. High-speed Internet access. Restaurant, bar. Fitness room. Indoor pool, whirlpool. Airport transportation available. **$**

RESTAURANTS
★Landmark Cafe & Creperie
62 S. Seminary St., Galesburg,
309-343-5376
American, French menu. Breakfast, lunch, dinner. Outdoor seating. **$$**

★Packinghouse
441 Mulberry, Galesburg,
309-342-6868
Steak, seafood menu. Lunch, dinner. Children's menu. **$$**

★
★
★
★
★

GENEVA
This quaint town has more than 100 specialty stores and a restored historic district, which has more than 200 buildings listed on the National Register of Historic Places. Cyclists and hikers enjoy the trails that wind through the parks adjacent to the Fox River.
Information: Chamber of Commerce, 8 S. Third St., 630-232-6060;
www.genevachamber.com

WHAT TO SEE AND DO

Garfield Farm and Inn Museum
Rte. 38., Geneva,
630-584-8485;
www.garfieldfarm.org
This 281-acre living history farm includes an 1846 brick tavern, an 1842 hay barn and an 1849 horse barn; gardens and prairie.

Wheeler Park
822 N. First St., Geneva,
630-232-4542
This 57-acre park features flower and nature gardens, hiking, tennis, ball fields, access to a riverside bicycle trail, picnicking and miniature golf. The Geneva Historical Society Museum is located in the park.

SPECIAL EVENTS

Festival of the Vine
Third St. and Hwy. 38., Geneva,
630-232-6060
An autumn harvest celebration, this festival features food and wine tastings, music, craft shows and antique carriage rides. Second weekend in September.

HOTELS

★★★Herrington Inn
15 S. River Lane, Geneva,
630-208-7433, 800-216-2466;

www.herringtoninn.com
Located in an old creamery building on the Fox River, the Herrington dates back to 1835. This lovingly restored limestone building has 61 rooms, each with its own fireplace, terrace, private bar and oversized whirlpool bath with heated marble floor.
61 rooms. Complimentary continental breakfast. High-speed Internet access. Restaurant, bar. Fitness room. Airport transportation available. Business center.

RESTAURANTS

★★Atwater's
15 S. River Lane, Geneva,
630-208-8920;
www.herringtoninn.com
American menu. Breakfast, lunch, dinner, Sunday brunch. Bar. Casual attire. Outdoor seating. $$

★★Mill Race Inn
4 E. State St., Geneva,
630-232-2030;
www.themillraceinn.com
American menu. Lunch, dinner, Sunday brunch. Bar. Children's menu. Casual attire. Valet parking. Outdoor seating. $$

GLENVIEW

Glenview is located 20 miles north of downtown Chicago and boasts numerous shops and restaurants, desirable residential neighborhoods and exceptional public schools.
Information: Chamber of Commerce, 2320 Glenview Rd., 847-724-0900;
www.glenviewchamber.com

WHAT TO SEE AND DO

Grove National Historic Landmark
1421 N. Milwaukee Ave., Glenview,
847-299-6096
This 124-acre nature preserve includes miles of hiking trails and three structures. On the grounds is the restored 1856 Kennicott House (tours February-September, Sunday); the Interpretative Center (daily), a nature center museum; and a house designed by George G. Elmslie, who studied under and worked with Louis Sullivan. Daily.

Hartung's Automotive Museum
3623 W. Lake Ave., Glenview,
847-724-4354
This museum has displays of more than 100 antique autos, trucks, tractors and motorcycles. Saturday-Sunday; Monday-Friday, by appointment.

SPECIAL EVENTS

Civil War Living History Days
Grove National Historic Landmark,
Glenview, 1421 Glenview Rd.,
847-299-6096
Features realistic battle reenactment with hospital tent and camps of the period and participants in authentic clothing and uniforms. Exhibits, lectures, house tours. Last weekend in July

Summer Festival
Glenview Rd., Glenview,
847-724-0900
The festival has entertainment, vendors and food. Last Saturday in June.

RESTAURANT

★Periyali Greek Taverna
9860 Milwaukee Ave., Glenview,
847-296-2232
Greek menu. Lunch, dinner. Bar. Casual attire. Outdoor seating. **$$**

HIGHLAND PARK

This lakefront suburban community is located 23 miles north of Chicago. Browse the city's pricey upscale boutiques, enjoy free summer music concerts in Port Clinton Square or dine in one of the local restaurants. Warm-weather concerts under the stars take place at Ravinia Festival, which runs from June through mid-September.
Information: Chamber of Commerce, 508 Central Ave., Suite 206., 847-432-0284; www.highland-park.com

WHAT TO SEE AND DO

Francis Stupey Log Cabin
326 Central Ave., Highland Park
This 1847 cabin is the oldest structure in town. May-October; Saturday-Sunday; also by appointment.

Ravinia Festival
200 Ravinia Park Rd., Highland Park, 847-266-5100;
www.ravinia.org
Located on the North Shore, this is the summer home of the Chicago Symphony Orchestra. Special programs include Jazz in June, the Young Artists series and Kids Concerts. While there is a 3,200-seat, open-air pavilion and two indoor venues for chamber music and smaller concerts, the majority of festival-goers prefer the lawn, ideal for picnicking. The park offers five restaurants, a picnic catering facility, chair rentals and wine kiosks. June-mid-September.

RESTAURANTS

★★Cafe Central
455 Central Ave., Highland Park
847-266-7878;
www.cafecentral.com
French menu. Lunch, dinner. Closed Monday; holidays. Bar. Children's menu. Casual attire. Outdoor seating. **$$**

★★★Carlos
429 Temple Ave., Highland Park
847-432-0770;
www.carlos-restaurant.com
Owned by husband-and-wife team Carlos and Debbie Nieto, this is an elegant and intimate restaurant. Carlos is known for its stellar haute cuisine served in classic French style: entrees arrive topped with silver domes. The wine list has more than 3,500 international selections.
French menu. Dinner. Closed Tuesday. Bar. Jacket required. Reservations recommended. Valet parking. **$$$**

67

ILLINOIS

HIGHWOOD

Sandwiched between Highland Park and Lake Forest, this suburban community along Chicago's North Shore is known both for its many restaurants and its close association to Fort Sheridan, a former army base. Local attractions include Everts Park, the Robert McClory Bicycle Path and the 18-hole Lake County Forest Preserve golf course at the Fort Sheridan Club.

www.cityofhighwood.com

RESTAURANTS

★★Del Rio
228 Green Bay Rd., Highwood,
847-432-4608
Italian menu. Dinner. Closed Sunday. Business casual attire. Reservations recommended. Valet parking. **$$**

★★★Froggy's
306 Green Bay Rd., Highwood
847-433-7080;
www.froggyscatering.com
This cheery bistro offers country French cuisine at reasonable prices, with specialties like onion soup, coq au vin and rabbit casserole. The wine list features a number of red and white Burgundies, Bordeaux and champagnes, while decadent cakes and carry-out items can be purchased from the adjacent bakery.

French menu. Lunch, dinner. Closed Sunday. Bar. Casual attire. **$$**

★★★Gabriel's
310 Green Bay Rd., Highwood,
847-433-0031;
www.egabriels.com
Chef/owner Gabriel Viti, formerly of Carlos' in Highland Park, turns out complex French-Italian dishes. Entrees range from grilled veal porterhouse to roasted Maine lobster with baby bok choy and ginger butter sauce. Seasonal specials and a tasting menu are also available.
French, Italian menu. Dinner. Closed Sunday-Monday. Bar. Business casual attire. Reservations recommended. Valet parking. Outdoor seating. **$$$**

HOMEWOOD

Located 24 miles south of Chicago's Loop, Homewood boasts two city blocks of fascinating art. New York muralist Richard Haas refurbished older business buildings with trompe l'oeil artwork on the backs of the structures.
Information: www.village.homewood.il.us

RESTAURANT

★Aurelio's Pizza
18162 Harwood Ave., Homewood,
708-798-8050;
www.aureliospizza.com
Italian menu. Lunch, dinner. Bar. Children's menu. Casual attire. Outdoor seating. **$$**

JOLIET

The Des Plaines River, the Chicago Sanitary and Ship Canal and railroad freight lines triggered Joliet's growth as a center of industry. The canal's Brandon Road Locks, to the south of Joliet, are among the largest in the world, and the canal continues to carry millions of tons of barge traffic annually through the city. Although Joliet was named in honor of Louis

Jolliet, the French-Canadian explorer who visited the area in 1673, it was incorporated in 1837 as Juliet, companion to the nearby town of Romeo (now renamed Romeoville). Information: Heritage Corridor Convention and Visitors Bureau, 81 N. Chicago St., 815-727-2323, 800-926-2262; www.heritagecorridorcvb.com

WHAT TO SEE AND DO

Bicentennial Park Theater/Band Shell Complex
201 W. Jefferson St., Joliet
815-724-3760;
www.bicentennialpark.org
Joliet Drama Guild and other productions perform here. See outdoor concerts in the band shell during the summer on Thursday evenings.

Challenge Park Xtreme
2903 Schweitzer Rd., Joliet,
815-726-2800;
www.challengepark.com
This 150-acre complex contains a skate park, miles of mountain biking trails and 25 paintball fields. Wednesday-Thursday 10 a.m.-6 p.m., Friday 10 a.m.-9 p.m., Saturday 9 a.m.-9 p.m., Sunday 9 a.m.-6 p.m.; winter hours vary.

Chicagoland Speedway
500 Speedway Blvd., Joliet,
815-727-7223;
www.chicagolandspeedway.com
This 75,000-seat track hosts NASCAR and Indy Racing League events in mid-July and mid-September. Come on the Friday before a race for qualifying/practice day, when the admission fee is cheaper and good seats are easier to come by.

Harrah's Joliet Casino
151 N. Joliet St., Joliet,
815-740-7800, 800-427-7247;
www.harrahs.com
Harrah's features two riverboats, one a 210-foot mega-yacht and the other a re-creation of a Mississippi paddle wheeler. Illinois gaming boats are no longer required to cruise, so there is open boarding between 8:30 a.m. and 6:15 a.m. daily.

Joliet Jackhammers
Silver Cross Field,
1 Major Art Schultz Dr., Joliet,
815-726-2255;
www.jackhammerbaseball.com
The Joliet Jackhammers play in the Northern League with nine other independent teams. As is the tradition in minor league baseball, the Jackhammers' season is peppered with unusual promotions like a hospital scrubs giveaway and a Christmas in July Ornament Giveaway. Mid-May-early September.

Rialto Square Theatre
102 N. Chicago St., Joliet,
815-726-7171;
www.rialtosquare.com
This performing arts center, designed by the Rapp brothers in 1926, is considered one of the most elaborate and beautiful of old 1920s movie palaces. Tours Tuesday and by appointment.

HOTELS
★Comfort Inn
2600 W. Main St., Marion,
618-993-6221, 800-228-5150;
www.choicehotels.com
122 rooms. Pets accepted, some restrictions. Complimentary continental breakfast. High-speed Internet access. Fitness room. Outdoor pool. Airport transportation available. $

★★Holiday Inn
200 Gore Rd., Morris,
815-942-6600, 800-465-4329;
www.holiday-inn.com
120 rooms. Pets accepted, some restrictions. High-speed Internet access, wireless Internet access. Restaurant, bar. Fitness room. Indoor pool, whirlpool. $

69

ILLINOIS

★
★
★
★
★

RESTAURANTS

★Merichka's Restaurant
604 Theodore St., Crest Hill,
815-723-9371
American menu. Lunch, dinner. Casual attire. $

★R-Place Family Eatery
21 Romines Dr., Morris,
815-942-3690;
www.rplaceromines.com
American menu. Breakfast, lunch, dinner, late-night. Children's menu. Casual attire. $

★★Rockwell Inn
2400 W. Hwy. 6, Morris,
815-942-6224;
www.rockwellinn.50megs.com
American menu. Lunch, dinner, Sunday brunch. Bar. Children's menu. Casual attire. Reservations recommended. $$

★★Syl's Restaurant
829 Moen Ave.,
Rockdale,
815-725-1977
www.sylsrestaurant.com
American menu. Dinner. Casual attire. $$

★★Truth Restaurant
808 W. Jefferson St., Joilet,
815-744-5901
American menu. Dinner. Closed Sunday-Monday. Bar. Children's menu. Business casual attire. Reservations recommended. $$

LAKE FOREST

Lake Forest, a North Shore Chicago suburb, has long been regarded as an enclave of affluence and prestige. Sprawling estates spread out on bluffs overlooking Lake Michigan. It's home to Lake Forest College as well as Halas Hall, the headquarters of the Chicago Bears. Actor Vince Vaughn is its most famous resident. Lake Forest's central business district, Market Square, was listed on the National Register of Historic Places in 1979. www.cityoflakeforest.com

HOTELS

★★★Deer Path Inn
255 E. Illinois Rd., Lake Forest,
847-234-2280, 800-788-9480;
www.dpihotel.com
Patterned after a 1453 manor house in England, this half-timbered mansion has the look of a stately residence and the feel of a weekend estate. It was built in the 1920s by architect William C. Jones, who was instrumental in the design of the Chicago World's Fair. Each room, named after a National Trust property in England, is individually decorated and furnished, and many have views of the well-manicured English garden.
55 rooms. High-speed wireless Internet access. Restaurant, bar. Airport transportation available. Business center. $$

RESTAURANTS

★★Bank Lane Bistro
670 Bank Lane, Lake Forest,
847-234-8802
www.banklanebistro.com
Contemporary American, French menu. Lunch, dinner. Closed Sunday. Bar. Business casual attire. Reservations recommended. Outdoor seating. $$$

★★South Gate Cafe
655 Forest Ave., Lake Forest,
847-234-8800;
www.southgatecafe.com
American menu. Lunch, dinner, brunch. Bar. Children's menu. Casual attire. Reservations recommended. Outdoor seating. $$

★★★The English Room
255 E. Illinois St.,
Lake Forest,
847-234-2280;
www.dpihotel.com
Set inside the historic Deer Path Inn, a popular destination for weekend getaways and fine dining since 1929, the English Room

is an elegant dining room with a traditional dinner menu that includes options like lobster bisque, roasted rack of lamb and Dover sole. The Sunday champagne brunch is especially good here.

International menu. Breakfast, lunch, dinner, Sunday brunch. Bar. Business casual attire. Reservations recommended. Outdoor seating. **$$$**

LEMONT

Located in northeast Illinois, Lemont was settled in 1836 and incorporated in 1873. Limestone was the reason for the town's growth—an example of Lamont limestone can be seen today at Chicago's Water Tower.
Information: www.lemont.il.us

WHAT TO SEE AND DO

Cog Hill Golf & Country Club
12294 Archer Ave., Lemont,
866-264-4455;
www.coghillgolf.com
Easily the best course in Chicago and home to the PGA Tour's BMW Championship, the Dubsdread Course features so many bunkers that average players might think they're playing on a beach. The course is beautifully maintained and is open to the public.

Ruffled Feathers Golf Club
1 Pete Dye Dr., Lemont,
630-257-1000
Home to the Illinois Professional Golf Association, Ruffled Feathers has been open since 1991 and was designed Pete Dye. Like Lemont neighbor Cog Hill, the course has more than 100 sand bunkers but has wide fairways to compensate.

SPECIAL EVENTS

BMW Championship (*formerly the Western Open Golf Tournament*)
12294 S. Archer Ave., Lemont,
866-264-4455;
www.coghillgolf.com/bmw_championship
The third of four PGA tour tournaments that lead to the FedEx championship, the BMW Championship is a three-day, four-round event that hosts the top players in the field of golf. Tickets are available in daily, practice packs and weekly bundles.

RESTAURANT

★White Fence Farm
11700 Joliet Rd., Lemont,
630-739-1720;
www.whitefencefarm.com/chicago
American menu. Dinner. Closed Monday; also January. Children's menu. Casual attire. **$$**

71

ILLINOIS

★
★
★
★
★

LIBERTYVILLE

Marlon Brando, Helen Hayes and Adlai Stevenson are a few of the famous personalities who have lived in Libertyville. The Roman Catholic St. Mary of the Lake Theological Seminary borders the town. There are four lakes near the village limits.
Information: Chamber of Commerce, 731 N. Milwaukee Ave., 847-680-0750;
www.libertyville.com

WHAT TO SEE AND DO

Cuneo Museum and Gardens
1350 N. Milwaukee Ave., Vernon Hills,
847-362-3042;
www.lake-online.com/cuneo
This museum is a Venetian-style mansion that features a Great Hall with arcade balconies, a chapel with stained glass and a fresco ceiling and a collection of master paintings. The grounds include fountains, gardens, sculptures and a conservatory. Tuesday-Sunday.

David Adler Cultural Center
1700 N. Milwaukee Ave., Libertyville,
847-367-0707;
www.adlercenter.org
This was the summer residence of the distinguished neoclassical architect David Adler. It's now an art and music center. There are folk concerts and children's events.

Lambs Farm
14245 W. Rockland Rd., Libertyville,
847-362-4636
The farm has grown from a small pet store to a nonprofit residential and vocational community that benefits adults with developmental disabilities. It includes a children's farmyard, small animal nursery, miniature golf and a thrift shop. Daily.

RESTAURANTS
★Country Inn Restaurant at Lambs Farm
14245 W. Rockland Rd., Libertyville,
847-362-5050;
www.lambsfarm.org
American menu. Breakfast, lunch. Closed Monday. Children's menu. Casual attire. Outdoor seating. **$**

★★Tavern in the Town
519 N. Milwaukee Ave., Libertyville,
847-367-5755
American menu. Dinner. Closed Sunday. Bar. **$$$**

LOCKPORT
Lockport was founded as the headquarters of the Illinois and Michigan Canal. In its heyday, the town boasted five different locks. The Old Canal Town National Historic District preserves several buildings from this era.
Information: Chamber of Commerce, 222 E. 9th., 815-838-0549; www.lockport.org

★
★
★
★
★

WHAT TO SEE AND DO
Illinois and Michigan Canal Museum
803 S. State St., Lockport,
815-838-5080
This building was originally used as the Canal Commissioner's office. Museum includes artifacts, pictures and documents relating to the construction and operation of the canal. Guided tours by costumed docents. Daily, afternoons.

SPECIAL EVENTS
Old Canal Days
222 E. 9th St., Lockport,
815-838-5080
This four-day festival celebrates Lockport with pioneer craft demonstrations, horse-drawn wagon tours, Illinois and Michigan Canal walking tours and Lockport prairie tours along with entertainment and food. Third weekend in June.

RESTAURANTS
★★Public Landing
200 W. 8th St., Lockport,
815-838-6500;
www.publiclandingrestaurant.com
American menu. Lunch, dinner. Closed Monday. Bar. Children's menu. Casual attire. **$$**

★★★Tallgrass
1006 S. State, Lockport,
815-838-5566;
www.tallgrassrestaurant.com
Master chef Robert Burcenski offers a well-balanced, contemporary menu. Diners can choose from three or five courses, including entrees such as grilled beef tenderloin with garlic potato puree.
French menu. Dinner. Closed Monday-Tuesday. Bar. Reservations recommended. **$$$**

MACOMB

Originally known as Washington, the town was renamed to honor General Alexander Macomb, an officer in the War of 1812. Macomb is best known as the home of Western Illinois University.

Information: Macomb Area Convention and Visitors Bureau, 201 S. Lafayette St., 309-833-1315; www.macomb.com

WHAT TO SEE AND DO

Argyle Lake State Park
640 Argyle Park Rd., Macomb, 309-776-3422
The park has 1,700 acres with a 95-acre lake. Fishing, boating, hiking, cross-country skiing, snowmobiling, picnicking and playground are available. Daily.

Western Illinois University
1 University Circle, Macomb, 309-298-1414; www.wiu.edu
The 1,050-acre campus, founded in 1899, includes an art gallery, agricultural experiment station and a nine-hole public golf course.

HOTELS

★★Days Inn
1400 N. Lafayette St., Macomb, 309-833-5511, 800-329-7466; www.daysinn.com
144 rooms. Restaurant, bar. Outdoor pool. $

RESTAURANT

★★Cellar
137 S. State St., Geneseo, 309-944-2177
Steak menu. Dinner. Closed Monday. Bar. Children's menu. $$$

MATTOON

Named for a railroad official who built the Big Four Railroad from St. Louis to Indianapolis, Mattoon is an industrial town and a retail center for the surrounding farm area. In 1861, General Ulysses S. Grant mustered the 25th Illinois Infantry into service in Mattoon.

Information: Mattoon Chamber of Commerce, 500 Broadway Ave., 217-235-5661; www.mattoonchamber.com

WHAT TO SEE AND DO

Lake Mattoon
Hwy. 45, Mattoon
This lake offers fishing, boating, launching facilities, picnicking and camping.

HOTELS

★★Ramada Inn
300 Broadway Ave. E., Mattoon, 217-235-5695, 888-628-8666; www.ramada.com
124 rooms. Pets accepted, some restrictions. Restaurant, bar. Indoor pool, outdoor pool, whirlpool. $

★

★

★

★

★

MCHENRY

This city is located 50 miles northwest of Chicago, and was named after Major William McHenry.

Information: Chamber of Commerce, 1257 N. Green St., 815-385-4300

WHAT TO SEE AND DO

Moraine Hills State Park
914 S. River Rd., McHenry, 815-385-1624
The park consists of three small lakes on 1,690 acres.

HOTELS

★★Holiday Inn Crystal Lake
Hwy. 31., Crystal Lake,
815-477-7000, 800-465-4329;
www.hicrystallake.com
197 rooms. High-speed Internet access. Restaurant, bar. Fitness room, fitness classes available. Indoor pool, whirlpool. Airport transportation available. Business center. **$**

RESTAURANTS

★★★Le Vichyssois
220 W. Hwy. 120, Lakemoor,
815-385-8221;
www.levichyssois.com

Situated across from a lake in northwest suburban Lakemoor, this inn is a retreat for classic French cuisine lovers. The chef and owner, Bernard Cretier, trained under Paul Bocuse and was an executive chef at Chicago's Maxim. The menu includes a smaller bistro menu or the larger regular menu, and either can be pared easily with selections from the wine list. Le Vichyssois is also an art gallery, so most of the oil paintings lining the walls are for sale.
French bistro menu. Dinner. Closed Monday-Tuesday. Reservations recommended. **$$$**

NAPERVILLE

Though it's one of the fastest growing suburbs in the nation, Naperville retains the atmosphere of a small town with its core of large Victorian houses and a beautiful historic district. The downtown shopping area features more than 100 shops and restaurants in historic buildings and adjoins the Riverwalk, a 3 1/2-mile winding brick pathway along the DuPage River.
Information: Visitors Bureau, 131 W. Jefferson Ave., 630-355-4141; www.napervilleil.com

WHAT TO SEE AND DO

DuPage Children's Museum
301 N. Washington St., Naperville,
630-637-8000;
www.dupagechildrensmuseum.org
This museum has three floors of kid-friendly, hands-on exhibits. Tuesday-Wednesday, Friday-Saturday 9 a.m.-5 p.m., Monday to 1 p.m., Thursday to 8 p.m., Sunday noon-5 p.m., closed late August-mid-September.

Naper Settlement
523 S. Webster St., Naperville,
630-420-6010
A 13-acre living history museum, this site has 25 buildings in a village setting that depict a 19th-century northern Illinois town. Tours are led by costumed guides April-October: Tuesday-Sunday; rest of year: Monday-Friday.

HOTELS

★Courtyard By Marriott
1155 E. Diehl Rd., Naperville,
630-505-0550, 888-854-9667;

www.courtyard.com
147 rooms. High-speed Internet access. Restaurant. Fitness room. Indoor pool, whirlpool. Airport transportation available. **$**

★Hampton Inn
1087 E. Diehl Rd., Naperville,
630-505-1400, 800-426-7866;
www.hamptoninn.com
128 rooms. Complimentary full breakfast. High-speed Internet access, wireless Internet access. Fitness room. Outdoor pool. Airport transportation available. Business center. **$**

★★★Hyatt Lisle
1400 Corporetum Dr., Lisle,
630-852-1234;
www.lisle.hyatt.com
Venture out for a round of golf at one of three courses within an eight -mile radius of this hotel.
312 rooms. Restaurant, bar. Fitness room. Indoor pool, whirlpool. **$$**

★★★Wyndham Lisle/Naperville
3000 Warrenville Rd., Lisle,
630-505-1000, 800-996-3426;
www.wyndham.com
This suburban hotel has spacious rooms and a 17,000 square foot fitness center. 242 rooms. High-speed Internet access. Restaurant, bar. Fitness room. Indoor pool, whirlpool. $

RESTAURANTS
★★Meson Sabika
1025 Aurora Ave., Naperville,
630-983-3000;
www.mesonsabika.com
Spanish, tapas menu. Lunch, dinner, Sunday brunch. Bar. Children's menu. Casual attire. Outdoor seating. $$

★★Raffi's on 5th
200 E. Fifth Ave., Naperville,
630-961-8203;
www.raffison5th.com
Mediterranean menu. Lunch, dinner. Closed Sunday. Bar. Casual attire. Business casual attire. Reservations recommended. $$

NAUVOO

Once the largest cities in Illinois, Nauvoo has a colorful history. When the Mormon prophet Joseph Smith was driven out of Missouri, he came with his Latter-day Saints to a tiny village called Commerce on a headland overlooking the Mississippi River and established what was virtually an autonomous state. A city of 8,000 houses was created and, in 1841, construction began on a great temple. A schism in the church led to riots and the persecution of the Mormons. Joseph Smith and his brother were arrested and murdered by a mob while in the Carthage jail. Brigham Young became leader of the Nauvoo Mormons. When the city charter was repealed and armed clashes broke out, Young led much of the population westward in 1846 to its final settlement in Utah. Nauvoo became a ghost town, and the almost-completed temple was burned by an arsonist. In 1849, the Icarians, a band of French communalists, migrated to Nauvoo from Texas and attempted to rebuild the temple, but a storm swept the building back into ruin. The Icarians failed to prosper and in 1856 moved on. The city was gradually resettled by a group of Germans, who developed the wine culture begun by the French group.
Information: Tourist Center, 1295 Mulholland, 217-453-6648

WHAT TO SEE AND DO
Baxter's Vineyards
2010 E. Parley St., Nauvoo,
217-453-2528
The vineyards were established in 1857 and host tours and wine tastings. Daily.

Joseph Smith Historic Center
149 Water St., Nauvoo,
217-453-2246
A 50-minute tour begins in the visitor center and includes a visit to Smith's grave. Daily.

Joseph Smith Homestead
This 1803 structure was the Log cabin the prophet occupied after coming to Nauvoo in 1839 and is the town's oldest structure. Daily.

Smith's Mansion
A refined, Federal-style frame house, this was occupied by Smith from 1843 to 1844. Monday-Saturday, 9 a.m.-5 p.m., Sunday from 1 p.m.

Nauvoo Restoration, Inc, Visitor Center
Young and N. Main Streets, Nauvoo,
217-453-2237
This center has a 20-minute movie on Nauvoo history and information on points of interest. Daily.

HOTELS
★★★Hotel Nauvoo
1290 Mulholland St., Nauvoo,
217-453-2211;
www.hotelnauvoo.com

★
★
★
★
★

This restored historic inn was originally a private residence. 8 rooms. Restaurant, bar. $

RESTAURANTS
★Grandpa John's
1255 Mulholland St., Nauvoo,
217-453-2310
American menu. Breakfast, lunch. Closed January-February. Children's menu. $

★★★Hotel Nauvoo
1290 Mulholland St, Nauvoo,
217-453-2211;
www.hotelnauvoo.com
From mid-April through mid-November, visitors can sample the prix fixe all-American buffet here, which includes such favorites as fried chicken and apple pie. American menu. Dinner, Sunday brunch. Closed mid-November-mid-March. Bar. $$

NORTHBROOK
Brickyards played a major role in the prosperity and growth of this north Chicago suburb. After the Great Chicago Fire of 1871, about bricks per day were produced here between 1915 and 1920. It's now home to many corporate headquarters, including national home goods retailer Crate & Barrel.
Information: Chamber of Commerce, 2002 Walters Ave., 847-498-5555

WHAT TO SEE AND DO
Chicago Botanic Garden
1000 Lake Cook Rd., Glencoe,
847-835-5440
www.chicagobotanic.org
Managed by the Chicago Horticultural Society, this garden includes 300 acres of formal plantings, lakes, lagoons and wooded naturalistic areas. Daily.

River Trail Nature Center
3120 Milwaukee Ave., Northbrook,
847-824-8360.
This park is a 300-acre nature preserve within the Forest Preserve District of Cook County. Daily.

HOTELS
★★Courtyard by Marriott Deerfield
800 Lake Cook Rd., Deerfield,
847-940-8222, 800-321-2211;
www.courtyard.com
131 rooms. High-speed, wireless Internet access. Fitness room. Indoor pool, whirlpool. Airport transportation available. Business center. $

★★★Hyatt Deerfield
1750 Lake Cook Rd., Deerfield,
847-945-3400, 800-633-7313;
www.hyatt.com

Want a hotel that has a cigar humidor on its heated outdoor patio? Or Starbucks coffee and breakfast pastries? Where someone will make a massage appointment for you at a nearby spa? This is the place. High-speed, wireless Internet access, a 24-hour business center and oversized desks will make business travelers happy. The rooms are sleek and contemporary with marble bathrooms.
301 rooms. High-speed, wireless Internet access. Restaurant, bar. Fitness room. Indoor pool, whirlpool. Airport transportation available. Business center. $

★★★Renaissance Chicago North Shore Hotel
933 Skokie Blvd., Northbrook,
847-498-6500, 888-236-2427;
www.renaissancehotels.com
Ten stories of rooms and facilities with a fun chess theme make up the Renaissance Chicago North Shore Hotel. Restaurants include Ruth's Chris Steak House and the American bistro, Rooks Corner.
385 rooms. High-speed, wireless Internet access. Restaurant, bar. Fitness room. Indoor pool, whirlpool. Airport transportation available. Business center. $

RESTAURANTS
★★★Prairie Grass Café
601 Skokie Blvd., Northbrook,

★
★
★
★
★

847-205-4433;
www.prairiegrasscafe.com

Award-winning chef Sarah Stegner, most recently a chef at the Dining Room at the Ritz-Carlton Chicago, has teamed up with former colleague George Bumbaris to open this American cafe, a cross between casual and fine dining. Hardwood floors, exposed brick walls and colorful oil paintings provide a setting for the impeccable American fare. The desserts are prepared by the best pastry chef Stegner could find—her mother.

American menu. Breakfast, lunch, dinner. Closed Monday. Bar. Children's menu. Casual attire. Reservations recommended. **$$$**

★Tonelli's
1038 Waukegan Rd., Northbrook,
847-272-4730
Italian menu. Lunch, dinner. Bar. Children's menu. Casual attire. Outdoor seating. **$$**

OAK BROOK

Known as Fullersburg in the mid-1800s, Oak Brook is the home of Butler National Golf Club. Sports and recreation have long been important in this carefully planned village—it has 12 miles of biking and hiking paths and more than 450 acres of parks and recreation land. Today, Oak Brook is a hub for international polo players and the headquarters of many major corporations.
Information: Village of Oak Brook, 1200 Oak Brook Rd., 630-990-3000

WHAT TO SEE AND DO

Fullersburg Woods Environmental Center
3609 Spring Rd., Oak Brook,
630-850-8110
This center has wildlife in a natural setting, an environmental center and theater, a native marsh ecology exhibit and four nature trails. Daily.

Graue Mill and Museum
York and Spring Roads, Oak Brook,
630-655-2090
A restored mill built in 1852, this was the only operating water-powered gristmill in the state and a former station of the Underground Railroad. Mid-April-mid-November, Tuesday-Sunday 10 a.m.-4:30 p.m.

Oakbrook Center
100 Oakbrook Center, Oak Brook,
630-573-0700,
www.oakbrookcenter.com
This giant center has six major department stores and more than 160 shops and restaurants, all linked by gardens and fountains. Daily, hours vary.

SPECIAL EVENT

Sunday Polo
700 Oak Brook Rd., Oak Brook,
630-990-2394
Mid-June-mid-September.

HOTELS

★Hampton Inn
222 E. 22nd St., Lombard,
630-916-9000, 800-426-7866;
www.hamptoninn.com
128 rooms. Complimentary continental breakfast. High-speed Internet access. Fitness room. **$**

★★★Hilton Suites Oakbrook Terrace
10 Drury Lane, Oakbrook Terrace,
630-941-0100, 800-445-8667;
www.hilton.com
Adjacent to the Drury Lane Theater, this hotel is near the Oak Brook Center Mall. Each two-room suite features a sleeping room with a king or two double beds and a separate living room with a work desk and pull-out couch.
211 rooms, all suites. High-speed wireless Internet access. Restaurant, bar. Fit-

ILLINOIS

ness room. Indoor pool, whirlpool. Airport transportation available. Business center. **$**

★★★Marriott Oak Brook Hills Resort
3500 Midwest Rd., Oak Brook,
630-850-5555; 800-228-9290

This sprawling resort has indoor and outdoor pools, a fitness center and spa, volleyball and basketball courts and seasonal cross-country skiing. The 18-hole Willow Crest Golf Club, considered one of the Midwest's finest courses, is also on the property.

384 rooms. High-speed wireless Internet access. Two restaurants, two bars. Fitness room. Indoor pool, outdoor pool, whirlpool. Golf, 18 holes. Tennis. Airport transportation available. Business center. **$$**

RESTAURANTS
★★Braxton Seafood Grill
3 Oak Brook Center Mall, Oak Brook,
630-574-2155;
www.braxtonseafood.com

Seafood menu. Lunch, dinner, brunch. Bar. Children's menu. Business casual attire. Reservations recommended. **$$**

★★Cafe 36
22 Calendar Court, La Grange,
708-354-5722

French menu. Lunch, dinner. Closed Monday. Bar. Business casual attire. Reservations recommended. Valet parking. **$$**

OAK LAWN

In 1856, Oak Lawn was a settlement known as Black Oaks Grove. When the Wabash Railroad began to lay tracks through the community in 1879, an agreement was made with the railroad builder to create a permanent village. The new town of Oak Lawn was established in 1882. Now, it's a western Chicago suburb.

Information: Chamber of Commerce, 5314 W. 95th St., 708-424-8300

HOTELS
★★★Hilton Oak Lawn
9333 S. Cicero Ave., Oak Lawn,
708-425-7800;
www.oaklawn.hilton.com

This is a hotel designed for business. Located just four miles from Midway airport, the hotel has a courtesy shuttle that picks up travelers curbside. Rooms have high-speed and wireless Internet access and dual-line telephones. The hotel is approximately 15 miles from downtown Chicago.

184 rooms. High-speed, wireless Internet access. Restaurant, bar. Fitness room. Indoor pool, whirlpool. Airport transportation available. Business center. **$**

RESTAURANTS
★Palermo's
4849 W. 95th St., Oak Lawn,
708-425-6262;
www.palermos95th.com

Italian menu. Lunch, dinner. Closed Tuesday. Bar. Children's menu. Casual attire. **$$**

★Whitney's Grille
9333 S. Cicero Ave., Oak Lawn,
708-229-8888;
www.oaklawn.hilton.com

American menu. Breakfast, lunch, dinner, brunch. Bar. Children's menu. Casual attire. Reservations recommended. **$$**

OAK PARK

Oak Park, one of Chicago's oldest suburbs, is a village of well-kept houses and magnificent trees. The town is internationally famous as the birthplace of Ernest Hemingway and for its concentration of Prairie School houses by Frank Lloyd Wright and other modern architects

★
★
★
★
★
★

of the early 20th century. Wright both lived in the town and practiced architecture from his Oak Park studio between 1889 and 1909.

Information: Oak Park-River Forest Chamber of Commerce, Oak Park Village Hall, 123 Madison St., 708-383-6400; www.vil.oak-park.il.us

WHAT TO SEE AND DO

Ernest Hemingway Museum
Arts Center, 200 N. Oak Park Ave., Oak Park, 708-848-2222
A restored 1890s Victorian home, this museum includes rare photos, artifacts and letters from the author. Walking tours of Hemingway sites, including his birthplace. Sunday-Friday 1-5 p.m., Saturday 10 a.m.-5 p.m.

Frank Lloyd Wright Home and Studio
951 Chicago Ave., Oak Park, 708-848-1976; www.wrightplus.org
Wright built this house in 1889, when he was 22 years old. He remodeled the inside on an average of every 18 months, testing his new design ideas while creating the Prairie school of architecture in the process. This is a National Trust for Historic Preservation property. Guided tours daily, inquire for schedule.

Oak Park Visitors Center
158 N. Forest Ave., Oak Park, 708-848-1500; www.oprf.com/opvc
This center offers information guidebooks, an orientation program on the Frank Lloyd Wright Prairie School of Architecture National Historic District, a recorded walking tour (fee), and admission tickets for tours of Wright's home and studio; other walking tours. Daily.

Pleasant Home (John Farson House)
217 S. Home Ave., Oak Park, 708-383-2654; www.oprf.com/phf
An opulent 30-room mansion designed by prominent Prairie school architect George W. Maher in 1897, this house's second floor is home to the Oak Park/River Forest Historical Society and Museum. Thursday-Sunday afternoons, guided tours on the hour.

Unity Temple
875 Lake St., Oak Park, 708-383-8873
Home to a congregation of the Unitarian Universalist Church, this national landmark was designed by Frank Lloyd Wright in 1906. The church was his first Monolithic concrete structure and his first public building. Self-guided tour, Monday-Friday afternoons; weekend tours available.

RESTAURANT

★★Cafe Le Coq
734 Lake St., Oak Park, 708-848-2233
French bistro menu. Dinner, Sunday brunch. Closed Monday. Bar. Business casual attire. Valet parking. $$

★
★
★
★
★
★

OREGON
Generations of artists have found inspiration in the scenic region surrounding Oregon. In 1898, sculptor Lorado Taft and others founded a colony for artists and writers. Located on Rock River, Oregon is the home of the Lorado Taft Field Campus of Northern Illinois University.

Information: Chamber of Commerce, 201 N. 3rd St., 815-732-2100

WHAT TO SEE AND DO

Castle Rock State Park
1365 W. Castle Rd., Oregon.
815-732-7329
This park located on 2,000 acres offers fishing, boating, hiking skiing trails and tobogganing.

Ogle County Historical Society Museum
111 N. 6th St., Oregon,
815-732-6876
The restored frame house located here was the home of Chester Nash, inventor of the cultivator. May-October, Thursday and Sunday, limited hours; also by appointment.

Oregon Public Library Art Gallery
300 Jefferson St., Oregon,
815-732-2724
Displays work of the original Lorado Taft Eagle's Nest art group. Monday-Saturday.

Stronghold Castle
1922 Hwy. 2 N., Oregon,
815-732-6111
This replica of an Old English castle was built in 1929 by newspaper publisher Walter Strong and is now owned by the Presbytery of Blackhawk, Presbyterian Church.

The Eternal Indian
Rising 48 feet above brush-covered bluffs, this monumental work by Lorado Taft was constructed in 1911 of poured Portland cement. The statue is usually referred to as **Black Hawk**.

White Pines Forest State Park
Pines Rd., Morris, 815-946-3717
On 385 acres, the White Pines park contains the northernmost large stand of virgin white pine in Illinois. Fishing, hiking, cross-country skiing, picnicking, concession, lodge, dining facilities, camping.

SPECIALTY LODGING

Pinehill Inn Bed & Breakfast
400 Mix St., Oregon,
815-732-2067, 800-851-0131;
www.pinehillbb.com
This Italianate country estate was built in 1874 and is listed on the National Historic Register. 4 rooms.

OTTAWA

Founded by the commissioners of the Illinois and Michigan Canal, Ottawa took root after the Black Hawk War of 1832. The first of the Lincoln-Douglas debates was held in the town's public square, and a monument in Washington Park marks the site. Located at the confluence of the Fox and Illinois Rivers, many industries are now located in this "Town of Two Rivers."
Information: Ottawa Area Chamber of Commerce and Industry, 100 W. Lafayette St., 815-433-0084; www.ottawa.il.us

WHAT TO SEE AND DO

Buffalo Rock State Park
Buffalo Rock Rd., Ottawa,
815-433-2220
Part of the Illinois and Michigan Canal State Trail on 243 acres. Live buffalo. Hiking, picnicking, playground.

Effigy Tumuli Sculpture
Buffalo Rock State Park, Ottawa,
815-433-2220
The largest earth sculptures since Mount Rushmore were formed as part of a reclamation project on the site of a former strip mine. Fashioned with the use of earthmoving equipment, the five enormous figures— a snake, turtle, catfish, frog and water strider were deliberately designed and formed to recall similar earth sculptures done by pre-Columbian Native Americans as ceremonial or burial mounds called *tumuli*. Daily.

Skydive Chicago
Ottawa Airport, 3215 E. 1969th Rd.,
Ottawa,
815-434-6094
Largest skydiving center in the Midwest.
Daily.

William Reddick Mansion
100 W. Lafayette St., Ottawa,
815-434-2737
This Italianate, antebellum mansion (built
1856-1857) has 22 rooms, ornate walnut
woodwork and ornamental plasterwork.
Period rooms contain many original furnishings. Daily.

HOTELS
★Holiday Inn Express
120 W. Stevenson Rd., Ottawa,
815-433-0029;

www.hiexpress.com
70 rooms. Pets accepted, some restrictions.
Indoor pool, whirlpool. **$**

RESTAURANTS
★Captain's Cove Bar and Grill
Starved Rock Marina, Ottawa,
815-434-0881
Steak, seafood menu. Lunch, dinner. Closed
January-February. Bar. Outdoor seating. **$$**

★Monte's Riverside Inn
903 E. Norris Dr., Ottawa,
815-434-5000
American menu. Lunch, dinner. **$$**

PEORIA
Peoria is the oldest settlement
in the state. Louis Jolliet and
Father Jacques Marquette
discovered the area in 1673.
René Robert Cavelier and
Sieur de La Salle established
Fort Creve Coeur on the eastern shore of Peoria Lake (a
wide stretch in the Illinois
River) in 1680. Between 1691
and 1692, Henri Tonti, Fran-
cois Dauphin and Sieur de
LaForest established Fort St.
Louis II on a site within the
city. The settlement that grew
around the fort has, except
for a brief period during the
Fox Wars, been continuously
occupied. The British flag
flew over Peoria from 1763

to 1778 and, for a short time in 1781, the Spanish held Peoria. The city is named for the
Native Americans who occupied the area when the French arrived.
Information: Peoria Area Convention and Visitors Bureau, 456 Fulton St.,
309-676-0303, 800-747-0302; www.peoria.org

★
★
★
★
☆

WHAT TO SEE AND DO

Spirit of Peoria
100 N.E. Water St., Peoria,
309-636-6166; 800-676-8988
A replica of turn-of-the-century stern-wheeler offers cruises along the Illinois River.

Corn Stock Theatre
1700 N. Park Rd., Peoria
800-220-1185;
www.cornstocktheatre.com
Theater-in-the-round summer stock under a circus-type big top with dramas, comedies and musicals. Call for schedule and pricing. June-August.

Eureka College
300 E. College Ave., Eureka,
309-467-6318, 888-438-7352
One of the first coeducational colleges in the country, this school's most famous graduate is Ronald Reagan. The grounds' Peace Garden honors Reagan's famous 1982 speech regarding the end of the Cold War.

Glen Oak Park and Zoo
2218 N. Prospect Rd., Peoria,
309-686-3365
This park on heavily wooded bluffs includes a zoo with more than 250 species, an amphitheater and tennis courts. Also here is the **George L. Luthy Memorial Botanical Garden,** which is an all-season garden.

Metamora Courthouse State Historic Site
113 E. Partridge, Metamora,
309-367-4470
This site has one of two remaining courthouse structures on the old Eighth Judicial Circuit, in which Abraham Lincoln practiced law for 12 years. On the first floor is a museum containing a collection of pioneer artifacts; on the second floor is the restored courtroom. Tuesday-Saturday.

Pettengill-Morron Museum
1212 W. Moss Ave., Peoria,
309-674-4745
An Italianate/Second Empire mansion, built by Moses Pettengill, this house was purchased by Jean Morron in 1953 to replace her ancestral house, which was being destroyed to make way for a freeway. She moved a two-century accumulation of household furnishings and family heirlooms, as well as such architectural pieces as the old house's cast-iron fence, chandeliers, marble mantles and brass rails from the porch. By appointment.

Wildlife Prairie State Park
3826 N. Taylor Rd., Peoria,
309-676-0998
Wildlife and nature preserve with animals native to Illinois—bears, cougars, bobcats, wolves, red foxes and more—in natural habitats along wood-chipped trails. The pioneer homestead has a working farm from the late 1800s with an authentic log cabin and one-room schoolhouse. March-mid-December: daily.

SPECIAL EVENTS

Spoon River Scenic Drive
Peoria, 309-547-3234
Take an autumn drive through small towns and rolling, wooded countryside noted for fall color (complete drive 140 miles); 19th- and early 20th-century crafts, exhibits, demonstrations; antiques, collectibles; produce, food. Fall festival usually the first two full weekends in October.

HOTELS

★★Best Western Signature Inn
4112 N. Brandywine Dr., Peoria,
309-685-2556;
www.bestwestern.com
123 rooms. Pets accepted, some restrictions; fee. Complimentary continental breakfast. Fitness room. Outdoor pool. Airport transportation available. Business center. **$**

★Comfort Suites
4021 N. War Memorial Dr., Peoria,
309-688-3800
66 rooms. Pets accepted; fee. Complimentary continental breakfast. High-speed Internet access. Indoor pool, whirlpool. **$**

★★Hotel Pere Marquette
501 Main St., Peoria,
309-637-6500, 800-447-1676;
www.hotelperemarquette.com
288 rooms. Pets accepted; fee. High-speed Internet access. Two restaurants, bar. Fitness room. Airport transportation available. **$**

★★Mark Twain Hotel Downtown Peoria
225 N.E. Adams St., Peoria,
309-676-3600, 888-325-6351;
www.marktwainhotels.com
Pets accepted; fee. Complimentary full breakfast. High-speed Internet access. Fitness room. Airport transportation available. **$**

★Stoney Creek Inn
101 Mariners Way, East Peoria,
309-694-1300, 800-659-2220
165 rooms. Complimentary continental breakfast. High-speed Internet access. Bar. Children's activity center. Fitness room. Indoor pool, outdoor pool, whirlpool. Airport transportation available. Business center. **$**

RESTAURANT
★★Carnegie's
501 N. Main, Peoria,
309-637-6500, 800-474-1676;
www.hotelperemarquette.com
American menu. Dinner. Closed Sunday. Bar. Children's menu. Casual attire. Reservations recommended. **$$**

PERU
Once a busy North-Central Illinois river port, Peru is now a commerical center for the area. Information: Illinois Valley Area Chamber of Commerce and Economic Development, 300 Bucklin St., La Salle, 815-223-0227; www.ivaced.org

WHAT TO SEE AND DO
Illinois Waterway Visitor Center
950 N. 27th Rd., Peru,
815-667-4054
Located at the Starved Rock Lock and Dam, this site offers an excellent view across the river to Starved Rock. The history of the Illinois River from the time of the Native Americans, the French explorers, and the construction of canals to the modern Illinois Waterway is portrayed in a series of exhibits. Daily.

Matthiessen State Park
Hwys. 71 and 178, Utica,
815-667-4868
This 1,938-acre park is particularly interesting for its geological formations, which can be explored via seven miles of hiking trails. The upper area and bluff tops are generally dry and easily hiked, but trails into the interiors of the two dells can be difficult, especially in spring and early summer. The dells feature scenic waterfalls. Daily.

SPECIAL EVENTS
Mendota Sweet Corn Festival
Hwy. 34 and Illinois Ave., Mendota,
815-539-6507;
www.sweetcornfestival.com
Each year, the town serves free sweet corn at this festival. There is also a beer garden, a queen pageant and a flea market with more than 200 dealers represented. Second weekend in August.

Winter Wilderness Weekend
Rtes. 71 and 178, Utica,
815-667-4906
This tour departs from Starved Rock visitor center and includes guided hikes to see the spectacular ice falls of Starved Rock. Cross-country skiing rentals and instruction. January.

HOTELS
★Comfort Inn
5240 Trompeter Rd., Peru,
815-223-8585, 800-228-5150;
www.comfortinn.com
50 rooms. Complimentary continental breakfast. Indoor pool. **$**

83

ILLINOIS

RESTAURANTS
★The Maples
1401 Shooting Park Rd., Peru,
815-223-1938
Lunch, dinner. Closed July 4. Bar. Children's menu. **$$**

★★Uptown Grill
601 1st St., La Salle,
815-224-4545;
www.uptowngrill.com
American menu. Lunch, dinner. Bar. Children's menu. Casual attire. Outdoor seating. **$$**

QUINCY
Quincy, the seat of Adams County, was named for President John Quincy Adams. Located on the east bank of the Mississippi River, the town was the site of the sixth Lincoln-Douglas debate on October 13, 1858; a bronze bas-relief in Washington Park marks the spot. Quincy was the second-largest city in Illinois in the mid-19th century. Today, Quincy is known for its historical district and restored Victorian residences.
Information: Quincy Area Chamber of Commerce, 300 Civic Center Plaza, 217-222-7980; www.quincychamber.org

WHAT TO SEE AND DO
John Wood Mansion
425 S. 12th St., Quincy,
217-222-1835
This two-story, Greek Revival mansion was the home of the founder of Quincy and a former governor of Illinois. In about 1864, the house was cut in half and moved across a special bridge to its present location. June-August: daily; April-May, September-October: Saturday-Sunday; also by appointment.

Quincy Museum
1601 Maine St., Quincy,
217-224-7669

Located in the Newcomb-Stillwell mansion, this museum is housed in a Richardson Romanesque-style building. Rotating exhibits and a children's discovery room are featured. Tuesday-Sunday 1 p.m.-5 p.m.

HOTELS
★★Holiday Inn
201 S. Third St., Quincy,
217-222-2666, 800-465-4329;
www.holiday-inn.com
152 rooms. Pets accepted; fee. Complimentary continental breakfast. Restaurant, bar. Indoor pool, whirlpool. Airport transportation available. **$**

ROCKFORD
The state's second-largest city grew up on both sides of the Rock River and took its name from the ford that was used by the Galena-Chicago Stagecoach Line. The early settlers of Rockford were primarily from New England.
Information: Rockford Area Convention and Visitors Bureau, Memorial Hall, 211 N. Main St., 815-963-8111, 800-521-0849; www.gorockford.com

WHAT TO SEE AND DO
Anderson Japanese Gardens
318 Spring Creek Rd., Rockford,
815-229-9390
These formal nine-acre gardens have a waterfall, ponds, bridges, a tea house, guest house and footpaths. May-October: daily.

Burpee Museum of Natural History
737 N. Main St., Rockford,
815-965-3433;
www.burpee.org
This science museum features natural history exhibits including a complete T-Rex-like skeleton called Jane, who is believed to be

ILLINOIS

either a young speciman of the dinosaur or a smaller relative. Daily.

Discovery Center Museum
Riverfront Museum Park, 711 N. Main St., Rockford, 815-963-6769.
This hands-on learning museum has more than 120 exhibits illustrating scientific and perceptual principles. Visitors can leave their shadow hanging on a wall, create a bubble window, see a planetarium show, learn how a house is built, star in a TV show or visit a carboniferous coal forest. Adjacent **Rock River Discovery Park** features a weather station, earth and water exhibits. Daily; closed some Mondays.

Rock Cut State Park
7318 Harlem Rd., Rockford, 815-885-3311
This 3,092-acre park has two artificial lakes with swimming beaches, boating, horseback trails, cross-country skiing and more. Daily

SPECIAL EVENTS

Illinois Snow Sculpting Competition
1401 N. 2nd St., Rockford, 815-987-8800
Teams from throughout Illinois compete to represent the state at national and international competitions. January

New American Theater
118 N. Main St., Rockford, 815-964-6282
A professional theater, the troupe here produces six main-stage shows each season. Late September-late May.

HOTELS
★★Best Western Clock Tower Resort & Conference Center

7801 E. State St., Rockford, 815-398-6000, 800-358-7666; www.clocktowerresort.com
247 rooms. Three restaurants, two bars. Children's activity center. Fitness room, fitness classes available, spa. Indoor pool, two outdoor pools, children's pool, whirlpools. Tennis. Airport transportation available. Business center. $

★★Courtyard by Marriott
7676 E. State St., Rockford, 815-397-6222; www.courtyard.com
147 rooms. High-speed Internet access. Fitness room. Indoor pool, whirlpool. Business center.

★Hampton Inn
615 Clark Dr., Rockford, 815-229-0404
www.hampton-inn.com
122 rooms. Complimentary full breakfast. High-speed Internet access. Fitness room. Indoor pool, whirlpool.

RESTAURANTS
★★Giovanni's
610 N. Bell School Rd., Rockford, 815-398-6411; www.giodine.com

★
★
★
★
★

French, Italian menu. Lunch, dinner. Closed Sunday; holidays. Bar. Children's menu. Business casual attire. Reservations recommended. **$$$**

★★Thunder Bay Grille
7652 Potawatomi Trail, Rockford,
815-397-4800;
www.thunderbaygrille.com
American menu. Lunch, dinner. Bar. Children's menu. Casual attire. Reservations recommended. Outdoor seating. **$$**

SCHAUMBURG

This village has one of suburban Chicago's top shopping centers, and is also the headquarters of Motorola.
Information: Greater Woodfield Convention and Visitors Bureau, 1430 Meacham Rd., 847-490-1010; www.ci.schaumburg.il.us

WHAT TO SEE AND DO

Chicago Athenaeum at Schaumburg
190 S. Roselle Rd., Schaumburg,
815-777-4444;
www.chi-athenaeum.org
This museum honors the history of design in all aspects of civilization, from fashion to urban development. Wednesday-Sunday.

Woodfield Shopping Center
5 Woodfield Dr., Schaumburg,
847-330-1537;
www.shopwoodfield.com
This mall has more than 250 specialty shops and department stores, including Nordstrom and Lord & Taylor. Daily.

HOTELS

★★★Hyatt Regency Woodfield
1800 E. Golf Rd., Schaumburg,
847-605-1234;
www.hyatt.com
This hotel, with Frank Lloyd Wright-inspired public spaces and spacious guest suites, is packed with amenities, including two pools, a health club, Tre Cena Italian restaurant and a sports bar with a nine-foot video wall.

470 rooms. High-speed, wireless Internet access. Two restaurants, two bars. Fitness room. Indoor pool, outdoor pool, whirlpool. Airport transportation available. Business center. **$$**

SKOKIE

In this Chicago suburb's early years, farmers produced food here for the growing city of Chicago and market trails carved by farm wagons later became paved roads. **Information:** Chamber of Commerce, 5002 Oakton St., 847-673-0240; www.skokiechamber.org

WHAT TO SEE AND DO

North Shore Center for the Performing Arts
9501 Skokie Blvd.,
847-679-9501;
www.northshorecenter.org
This center houses two individual theaters that offer many types of performances.

Westfield Old Orchard
34 Old Orchard Center, Skokie,
847-673-6800;
www.westfield.com

Shop at a wide array of stores linked outdoors by landscaped areas. Anchor stores include Bloomingdales, Macy's, Lord & Taylor and Nordstrom. Monday-Saturday 10 a.m.-9 p.m., Sunday 11 a.m.-6 p.m., holiday hours vary.

RESTAURANTS

★★Café La Cave
2777 Mannheim Rd., Des Plaines,
847-827-7818;
www.cafelacaverestaurant.com

Steak menu. Dinner. Bar. Casual attire. Valet parking. **$$**

★★Don's Fishmarket
9335 Skokie Blvd., Skokie,
847-677-3424;
www.donsfishmarket.com
Seafood menu. Lunch, dinner. Bar. Children's menu. Casual attire. **$$**

★Lotawata Creek
311 Salem Place,
Fairview Heights,
618-628-7373;
www.lotawata.com
American menu. Lunch, dinner. Children's menu. Casual attire. **$$**

SPRINGFIELD

Near the geographical center of the state, Springfield, the capital of Illinois, was the home of Abraham Lincoln for a quarter of a century.
Information: Convention and Visitors Bureau, 109 N. 7th, 217-789-2360, 800-545-7300; www.visit-springfieldillinois.com

WHAT TO SEE AND DO

Dana-Thomas House State Historic Site
301 E. Lawrence Ave.,
Springfield,
217-782-6776;
www.dana-thomas.org
Designed by Frank Lloyd Wright for Springfield socialite Susan Lawrence Dana, this house is the best preserved of the architect's Prairie period. The fully restored interior has more than 100 pieces of original furniture. The house was one of the largest and most elaborate of Wright's career. Wednesday-Sunday.

Edwards Place
700 N. 4th St., Springfield,
217-523-2631
Built by Benjamin Edwards (brother of Ninian Edwards, an early Illinois governor married to Mary Todd Lincoln's older sister), this Italianate mansion was Springfield's social and political center in the years before the Civil War; Lincoln addressed the public from the front gallery. By appointment only.

Henson Robinson Zoo
1101 E. Lake Dr., Springfield,
217-753-621.
A 14-acre zoo with exotic and domestic animals, penguin exhibit; contact area; picnic area. Daily.

Lincoln Home National Historic Site
426 S. Seventh St., Springfield,
217-492-4241;
www.nps.gov/liho
This site is the only home Abraham Lincoln ever owned. In 1844, Abraham and Mary Lincoln purchased the house and lived there until their February 1861 departure for Washington, D.C. Daily.

ILLINOIS

LINCOLN'S NEW SALEM STATE HISTORIC SITE

This wooded, 700-acre park incorporates a complete reconstruction, based on original maps and family archives, of New Salem as the village appeared when Abraham Lincoln lived there from 1831-1837. Today, New Salem consists of 12 timber houses, a school, stores and industries, including the Denton Offutt store, where Lincoln first worked. The only original building is the Onstot cooper shop, which was discovered in Petersburg and returned to its original foundation in 1922. Interior furnishings are authentic to the 1830s period of Lincoln's residency. The visitor center offers a 180-minute orientation film and exhibits. Picnicking, concessions and camping are available. Daily; 217-632-4000.

Lincoln Memorial Garden and Nature Center
2301 E. Lake Dr., Springfield,
217-529-1111;
www.lmgnc.com
This park is an 80-acre garden of trees, shrubs and flowers native to Illinois designed in a naturalistic style by landscape architect Jens Jensen. Tuesday-Sunday; closed December 24-January 1.

★
★
★
★

Lincoln Tomb State Historic Site
Oak Ridge Cemetery, 1441 Monument Ave., Springfield,
217-782-2717
Under a 117-foot granite obelisk, a belvedere, accessible via exterior staircases, offers views of a 10-foot statue of Lincoln and four heroic groupings representing Civil War armed forces. In the center of the domed burial chamber is a monumental sarcophagus. Mary Todd Lincoln and three of four Lincoln sons are interred within the wall opposite. Daily; closed holidays.

HOTELS

★Comfort Inn
3442 Freedom Dr., Springfield,
217-787-2250, 800-228-5150;
www.comfortinn.com
67 rooms. Pets accepted; fee. Complimentary continental breakfast. Indoor pool, whirlpool. $

★★Courtyard by Marriott
3462 Freedom Dr., Springfield,
217-793-5300, 800-321-2211;
www.courtyard.com
78 rooms. Bar. Fitness room. Indoor pool, whirlpool. $

★Hampton Inn
3185 S. Dirksen Pkwy., Springfield,
217-529-1100, 800-426-7866;
www.hamptoninn.com
124 rooms. Complimentary continental breakfast. Fitness room. Indoor pool, whirlpool. $

★Hampton Inn and Suites
1400 N. Milwaukee Ave., Lincolnshire,
847-478-1400;
www.hamptoninn.com
117 rooms. Complimentary continental breakfast. High-speed Internet access. Fitness room. Indoor pool, whirlpool. Business center.

★★★Hilton Springfield
700 E. Adams St., Springfield,
217-789-1530;
www.hilton.com
This being the only skyscraper in Springfield, rooms here have great views of the city.
367 rooms. Restaurant, bar. Fitness room. Indoor pool. Airport transportation available. Business center. $

★★★Renaissance Springfield Hotel
701 E. Adams St., Springfield,
217-544-8800, 800-228-9898;
www.renaissancehotels.com
With a concourse leading to the convention center and 13,000 square feet of meeting

space, this hotel is popular with business travelers. Try Lindsay's Gallery Restaurant for Sunday brunch.

316 rooms. Restaurant, bar. Fitness room. Indoor pool, whirlpool. Airport transportation available. Business center. **$**

RESTAURANTS
★★**Chesapeake Seafood House**
3045 Clear Lake Ave., Springfield,
217-522-5220

American, seafood menu. Lunch, dinner. Bar. Children's menu. **$$**

★★**Maldaner's**
222 S. Sixth St., Springfield,
217-522-4313
American menu. Dinner. Closed Sunday-Monday. Bar. **$$**

ST. CHARLES
Located on the Fox River one hour west of Chicago, St. Charles is an affluent suburb with a charming downtown filled with antique and specialty shops housed in historic buildings. Information: Greater St. Charles Convention and Visitors Bureau, 311 N. 2nd St., 630-377-6161, 800-777-4373; www.visitstcharles.com

WHAT TO SEE AND DO
Fox River Valley Trail
St. Charles,
630-897-0516;
www.trailsfromrails.com/fox_river_trail.htm
Located among hills and historic old towns, the Fox River winds a lazy path, making it ideal for recreational canoeing. Several outfitters offer canoe rentals, and there are at least four entry points. If you have a bike, the well-maintained Fox River Trail runs parallel to the river extending as far north as Crystal Lake and as far south as Aurora. Daily.

Pheasant Run Resort and Spa
4051 E. Main St., St. Charles,
800-474-3272;
www.pheasantrun.com
In terms of bang for your buck, Pheasant Run offers great golf for prices lower than most courses in the area. The course also plays only a little more than 6,300 yards, so great scores are definitely within reach. Golfers can play 18 holes for $23, cart included, from 5:30 p.m. until dark.

Pottawatomie Park
North Ave., St. Charles,
630-584-1028

This park has a mile of frontage on the Fox River and is open daily. The *St. Charles Belle II* and *Fox River Queen* paddle-wheel boats offer afternoon sightseeing trips river. Boats depart from the park and follow the river trail of the Pottawatomie. June-August: daily; May and September-mid-October: Saturday-Sunday.

HOTELS
★★★**Hotel Baker**
100 W. Main St., St. Charles,
630-584-2100, 800-284-0110;
www.hotelbaker.com
Built in 1928, this hotel has traditionally decorated rooms with Egyptian cotton linens and wireless internet. The waterfront restaurant hosts everything from wine tastings to a Sunday Champagne brunch.
53 rooms. Restaurant, bar. Airport transportation available. **$$$**

RESTAURANTS
★**Filling Station Pub & Grill**
300 W. Main St., St. Charles,
630-584-4414;
www.filling-station.com
American menu. Lunch, dinner. Bar. Children's menu. Casual attire. Outdoor seating. **$**

★
★
★
★
☆

UTICA/STARVED ROCK STATE PARK

Hwy. 178, Utica, 815-667-4726; www.dnr.state.il.us.

A local favorite for recreation and outdoor sports, Starved Rock State Park, located an hour and a half southwest of Chicago in Utica, has glacial canyons, sandstone bluffs, unusual rock formations and forests. The park offers 13 miles of well-marked hiking trails, fishing and boating along the Illinois River, equestrian trails, picnicking and camping. The park has a refurbished lodge with a hotel wing with 72 luxury rooms, an indoor pool with spa and sauna, and a restaurant; 22 cabins are also available. Though it's open year-round, a prime time to visit is early spring, when waterfalls form at the heads of the more than 18 canyons and create a glittering natural spectacle. Daily.

HOTELS

★★Starved Rock Lodge and Conference Center
Hwy. 178, Utica,
815-667-4211, 800-868-7625
93 rooms. Restaurant, bar. Indoor pool, children's pool, whirlpool. $

WAUKEGAN

On the site of what was once a Native American village and a French trading post, Waukegan was first called Little Fort because of a French stockade there. In April 1860, Abraham Lincoln delivered his "unfinished speech" here—he was interrupted by a fire. Waukegan was the birthplace of comedian Jack Benny and author Ray Bradbury, who used the town as a background in many of his works.

Information: Lake County Chamber of Commerce, 5221 W. Grand Ave., Gurnee, 847-249-3800; www.lakecounty-il.org

HOTELS

★★Courtyard by Marriott
800 Lakehurst Rd., Waukegan,
847-689-8000, 800-321-2211;
www.courtyard.com
149 rooms. High-speed Internet access. Restaurant. Fitness room. Indoor pool, whirlpool. $

★Hampton Inn
5550 Grand Ave., Gurnee,
847-662-1100, 800-426-7866;
www.hamptoninn.com
134 rooms. Complimentary full breakfast. High-speed Internet access. Outdoor pool. $

★★Illinois Beach Resort and Conference Center
1 Lakefront Dr., Zion,
847-625-7300, 866-452-3224;
www.ilresorts.com

RESTAURANT

★★Country Squire
19133 W. Hwy. 120., Waukegan, 847-223-0121; www.csquire.com
American menu. Lunch, dinner, Sunday brunch. Closed Monday. Bar. Children's menu. $$

90

ILLINOIS

WHEATON

Wheaton, the seat of DuPage County, is a residential community with 39 churches and the headquarters of approximately two dozen religious publishers and organizations. The town's most famous citizens are football great Red Grange, Elbert Gary, (who created the Indiana steel city that bears his name); and evangelist Billy Graham.

Information: Wheaton Chamber of Commerce, 108 E. Wesley St., 630-668-6464; www.ewheaton.com

WHAT TO SEE AND DO

Cantigny

1S151 Winfield Rd., Wheaton,
630-668-5161

This is the 500-acre estate of the late Robert R. McCormick, editor and publisher of the *Chicago Tribune.*

Cosley Animal Farm and Museum

1356 N. Gary Ave., Wheaton,
630-665-5534

This farm has a children's petting zoo, antique farm equipment display, railroad caboose, aviary, herb garden and outdoor education center. Daily.

Wheaton College

501 College Ave., Wheaton,
630-752-5000;
www.wheaton.edu

This Christian liberal arts school is home to the **Billy Graham Center Museum,** which features exhibits on the history of evangelism in America.

Marion E. Wade Center

351 E. Lincoln, Wheaton,
630-752-5908

Housed here is a collection of books and papers of seven British authors: Owen Barfield, G. K. Chesterton, C. S. Lewis, George MacDonald, Dorothy L. Sayers, J. R. R. Tolkien and Charles Williams. Monday-Saturday.

RESTAURANTS

★★★Bistro Banlieue

44 Yorktown Convenience Center,
Lombard,
630-629-6560

Don't let the strip mall location fool you. This restaurant is a local favorite for its terrific food and unique touches, such as optional, reduced entree-portions and monthly wine dinners.

French menu. Lunch, dinner. Bar. Business casual attire. Reservations recommended. Outdoor seating. **$$**

★★Greek Islands West

300 E. 22nd St., Lombard,
630-932-4545;
www.greekislands.net

Greek menu. Lunch, dinner. Bar. Casual attire. Outdoor seating. **$$**

WHEELING

The Wheeling area was first occupied by the Potawatomi. Settlers arrived in 1833 and began farming the fertile prairie soil.

Information: Wheeling/Prospect Heights Area Chamber of Commerce and Industry, 395 E. Dundee Rd., 847-541-0170; www.wheeling.com

HOTELS

★Hawthorn Suites

10 Westminster Way Rd., Lincolnshire,
847-945-9300, 800-527-1133;
www.hawthorn.com

125 rooms, all suites. Pets accepted, some restrictions; fee. Complimentary full breakfast. High-speed Internet access. Fitness room. Indoor pool, whirlpool. Business center. **$**

★SpringHill Suites Lincolnshire
300 Marriott Dr., Lincolnshire,
847-793-7500, 888-287-9400;
www.springhillsuites.com
161 rooms. Complimentary continental breakfast. High-speed Internet access. Fitness room. Indoor pool, whirlpool. Business center. **$**

★★★Marriott Lincolnshire Resort
10 Marriott Dr., Lincolnshire,
847-634-0100, 800-228-9290;
www.marriott.com
This hotel has an award-winning theater-in-the-round, seasonal outdoor sports facilities, half a dozen bars and restaurants and an open lobby with wood beams and a roaring fire. Although the hotel hosts many business meetings and conferences, families looking for a little R&R find it a fun getaway.

380 rooms. High-speed wireless Internet access. Two restaurants, three bars. Fitness room. Indoor pool, outdoor pool, whirlpool. Golf, 18 holes. Tennis. Airport transportation available. Business center. **$**

RESTAURANTS
★★94th Aero Squadron
1070 S. Milwaukee Ave., Wheeling,
847-459-3700
American menu. Dinner, Sunday brunch. Closed Monday. Bar. Children's menu. Business casual attire. Reservations recommended. Outdoor seating. **$$**

★★Bob Chinn's Crab House
393 S. Milwaukee Ave., Wheeling,
847-520-3633;
www.bobchinns.com
Seafood menu. Lunch, dinner. Closed holidays. Bar. Children's menu (dinner). Casual attire. Reservations recommended. Valet parking. **$$$**

★★Don Roth's
61 N. Milwaukee Ave., Wheeling,
847-537-5800;
www.donroths.com
Steak menu. Dinner. Bar. Children's menu. Business casual attire. Reservations recommended. Outdoor seating. **$$$**

★★Osteria di Tramanto
601 N. Milwaukee Ave., Wheeling,
847-777-6570;
www.cenitare.com
Italian. Breakfast, lunch, dinner. Bar. Valet parking. **$$**

★★★Tramonto's Steak & Seafood
601 N. Milwaukee Ave., Wheeling,
847-777-6575; 800-837-8461
Chicago chef Rick Tramonto and pastry chef Gale Gand are the culinary duo behind this contemporary steakhouse. Cozy banquettes or white linen-topped tables fill the dining room, while an impressive wine wall displays more than 1,000 bottles from around the world. The menu aptly spotlights grilled steak and seafood from skirt steak frites with carmelized onions to spice-rubbed yellowfin tuna. Steakhouse classics, such as creamy Caesar salad, creamed spinach and garlic whipped potatoes accompany the entrees.

Steak/seafood menu. Dinner. Bar. Valet parking. **$$$**

WILMETTE
This tony North Shore Chicago suburb possesses an idyllic location on Lake Michigan's shoreline. The Wilmette Park District manages 19 public parks, including the popular Gillson Park beach.
Information: Chamber of Commerce, 1150 Wilmette Ave., 847-251-3800; www. wilmettechamber.org

WHAT TO SEE AND DO

Baha'i House of Worship

100 Linden Ave., Wilmette,
847-853-2300

Spiritual center of the Baha'i faith in the
United States, this remarkable nine-sided
structure overlooks Lake Michigan and is
surrounded by nine gardens and fountains.
Exhibits and slide programs in visitor center on lower level. Daily

Gillson Park

Lake and Michigan Avenues, Wilmette,
847-256-9656

This park contains Wilmette Beach, which
has 1,000 feet of sandy shoreline, life-
guards, a beach house, sailing and Sun-
fish and Hobie 16 catamaran rentals. Park.
Daily.

Kohl Children's Museum

165 Green Bay Rd., Wilmette,
847-512-1300;
www.kohlchildrensmuseum.org

This museum offers interactive music,
construction, science and arts participatory
exhibits designed for children up to age 8.
Daily.

RESTAURANTS

★★Betise

1515 N. Sheridan Rd., Wilmette,
847-853-1711

French bistro menu. Lunch, dinner, brunch.
$$

★★Convito Italiano

1515 N. Sheridan Rd., Wilmette,
847-251-3654,
www.convitoitaliano.com

Italian menu. Dinner. **$$**

93

ILLINOIS

★
★
★
★
★

INDIANA

IF SPORTS ARE YOUR THING, INDIANA'S YOUR PLACE. WITH LEGENDARY BALL TEAMS LIKE THE Super Bowl champion Indianapolis Colts, Notre Dame's Fighting Irish and the Indiana University hoosiers, Indiana's fabled sports legacy continues to grow. But if you're out for the ultimate Indiana sporting experience, watch racecar drivers clock 200 laps and 500 miles around the Indianapolis Motor Speedway during the Indianapolis 500.

Prefer shopping to speedways? Experience first-rate stores in Indianapolis' Wholesale District; exotic dining and arts on Mass Ave; and trendy boutiques, clubs and alfresco dining in Broad Ripple Village. Buy the kids a sundae at the old-fashioned soda fountain in the Fountain Square District or stroll along the capital's family-friendly Canal & White River State Park District.

Rather hike on a trail than all over town? With 24 state parks, 22 fish and wildlife areas, nine reservoirs, 13 state forests and 14 nature preserves, Indiana is hardly short on places to scuff the dirt. h ike the marked trails and comb the beaches of the Indiana Duncs National Lakeshore, then rough it on 27 miles of trails on the Adventure hiking Trail in the :arrison-Crawford State Forest.

For an idyllic getaway, the charming resort towns in southern Indiana are your best bet, whether you're taking a family vacation or sneaking off for a romantic weekend. Browse charming craft and antique shops in the historic artist colony of Nashville and sip and swirl your way through the Upland Wine Trail's eight wineries nearby. If you're in need of R&R, the historic resort hotels in French Lick let you rejuvenate amid mineral springs, lush gardens, golf courses, spas and gorgeous surroundings.

Or if you're craving a quirkier adventure, check out wares from more than 1,000 vendors at Shipshewana's outdoor flea market (May-October), sample chocolates at the South Bend Chocolate Museum and see which Big Top biggies made it into Peru, Indiana's Circus Hall of Fame.

95

INDIANA
★
★
★
★
★

ANDERSON

This was once the site of a Delaware village in the hills south of the White River. The city was named for Kikthawenund, also called Captain Anderson, a well-known chief of the Delaware. The discovery of natural gas pockets underneath the city in 1886 sparked a 10-year boom. One hundred Newport-style gaslights have been added to what is now known as historic West 8th Street. Restored Victorian homes reflect the area's fashionable past.

Information: Anderson-Madison County Visitors and Convention Bureau, 6335 S. Scatterfield Rd., 765-643-5633, 800-533-6569; www.madtourism.com

WHAT TO SEE AND DO
Mounds State Park
4306 Mounds Rd., Anderson, 765-642-6627.
Within this 290-acre park of rolling woodlands are several well-preserved earth for-

mations constructed many centuries ago by a prehistoric race of Adena-Hopewell mound builders. On bluffs overlooking the White River are earth structures that were once an important center of an ancient civilization of which very little is known. The largest earth structure is 9 feet high and nearly 1/4 mile in circumference. Smaller structures nearby include conical mounds and a fiddle-shaped earthwork.

SPECIAL EVENTS
Little 500
Anderson Speedway,
1311 Pendleton Ave., Anderson,
765-642-0206

Auto races. Reservations necessary. Weekend of Indianapolis 500.

HOTELS
★Best Inn
5706 S. Scatterfield Rd., Anderson,
765-644-2000, 800-237-8466;
www.bestinn.com
93 rooms. Pets accepted; fee. Complimentary continental breakfast. **$**

★★Holiday Inn
5920 Scatterfield Rd., Anderson,
765-644-2581, 800-465-4329;
www.holiday-inn.com
158 rooms. Restaurant, bar. Indoor pool, outdoor pool, whirlpool. Airport transportation available. **$**

ANGOLA
This tranquil town lies in the northeastern corner of Indiana's resort area. The wooded hills surrounding Angola provide more than 100 lakes for swimming, boating and fishing in the summer and ice skating in the winter.
Information: Steuben County Tourism Bureau, 207 S. Wayne St. 800-525-3101; www.lakes101.org

WHAT TO SEE AND DO
Pokagon State Park
450 Lane 100 Lake James, Angola,
219-833-2012
This is a 1,203-acre park on the shores of Lake James and Snow Lake in northern Indiana lake country. Swimming beach, bathhouse, water-skiing, fishing, boating rentals. h iking trails, saddle barn, skiing, ice skating, tobogganing, ice fishing,

picnicking, concession, camping. Nature center, wildlife exhibit, naturalist service. Daily.

HOTELS
★★Potawatomi Inn
6 Lane 100A Lake James, Angola,
260-833-1077, 877-768-2928
142 rooms. Restaurant. Fitness room. Beach. Indoor pool, whirlpool. **$**

AURORA
A river town located west of Cincinnati, Aurora was settled in the 1800s and has six preserved, historic churches.
Information: www.aurora.in.us

HOTELS
★★Grand Victoria Casino & Resort By Hyatt
600 Grand Victoria Dr., Rising Sun,
812-438-1234, 800-472-6311;
www.hyatt.com

201 rooms. Restaurant. Fitness room. Indoor pool, whirlpool. Business center. **$**

★★★Belterra Casino Resort
777 Belterra Dr., Belterra,
812-427-7777, 888-235-8377;
www.belterracasino.com

There's plenty to do at this resort, from a full-service spa and salon, to an outdoor pool, championship golf and plenty of restaurants. The 38,000-square-foot casino riverboat features 40 table games, a poker room and more than 1,600 slots. Rooms offer views of the Ohio River, the golf course or the hilly Indiana scenery.

308 rooms. High-speed Internet access. Three restaurants, two bars. Fitness room. Outdoor pool, whirlpool. Golf, 18 holes. Airport transportation available. Business center. Casino. **$$**

BATESVILLE

This historic southeastern Indiana town was the first city west of Cincinnati to install streetlights. It has a well-preserved downtown with historic buildings.
Information: Chamber of Commerce, 132 S. Main, Batesville, 812-934-3101; www.batesvilleindiana.us

WHAT TO SEE AND DO
Whitewater Canal State Historic Site
19083 Clayborn St., Metamora,
765-647-6512.
Includes part of a restored 14-mile section of the Whitewater Canal, which provided transportation between Hagerstown and the Ohio River at Lawrenceburg from 1836 to 1860. The Ben Franklin III canal boat offers 25-minute horse-drawn boat cruises through the Duck Creek aqueduct 1848 to the canal's only remaining operating lock May-October, Tuesday Sunday; other times by appointment. Working gristmill in Metamora Wednesday-Sunday.

SPECIALTY LODGINGS
Sherman House
35 S. Main St., Batesville,
812-934-1000, 800-445-4939;
www.sherman-house.com
23 rooms. Restaurant. Fitness room. **$**

RESTAURANTS
★★Sherman House
35 S. Main St., Batesville,
812-934-2407;
www.sherman-house.com
German, American menu. Breakfast, lunch, dinner. Bar. Children's menu. Established in 1852. Lobster tank. **$$$**

BEDFORD

Bedford is the center of Indiana limestone quarrying, one of the state's top industries. Limestone quarried here was used in the construction of the World War II Memorial in Indianapolis, the Empire State Building in New York and the Federal Triangle in Washington, D.C.

The headquarters of the h oosier National Forest and Wayne National Forest are here. Williams Dam, 11 miles southwest on h ighway 450, offers fishing on the White River.
Information: Lawrence County Tourism Commission, 1116 16th St., 812-275-7637, 800-798-0769; www.bedford.in.us

WHAT TO SEE AND DO
Bluespring Caverns
1459 Bluespring Caverns Rd., Bedford
812-279-9471;
www.bluespringcaverns.com
One of the world's largest cavern systems, more than 20 miles of explored passageways and 15 miles of underground streams join to form the large river upon which tour boats travel. Electric lighting reveals many unusual sights, including eyeless blindfish and blind crawfish. April-May: weekends; Memorial Day-late October: daily.

Hoosier National Forest
811 Constitution Ave., Bedford,
812-275-5987,
Approximately 189,000 acres spread through nine counties. Swimming, boating, fishing; picnicking, hiking, horseback

97

INDIANA

★
★
★
★

trails, hunting, nature study; historic sites. Campsites at Hardin Ridge Monroe County, German Ridge, Celina Lake, Tipson Lake, Indian Lake Perry Count and Springs Val-ley Orange County recreation areas. Campsites on first-come, first-served basis. Fees are charged at recreation sites for camping; entrance fee at Hardin Ridge.

BLOOMINGTON

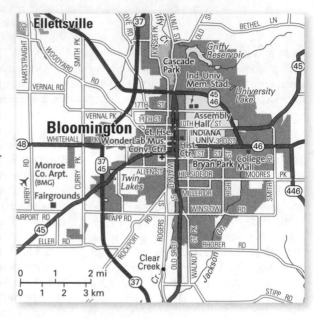

h ome to Indiana University, Bloomington is regarded as one of America's best college towns, thanks to its relaxed atmosphere, eclectic shops and restaurants, vast cultural offerings and scenic setting. Bloomington's official population falls just short of 70,000, a figure that includes few of the 39,000 students at I.U.

Bloomington's downtown, situated a couple of blocks west of the university, is anchored by the Monroe County Courthouse. The town has a vibrant arts scene, including the Indiana University Art Museum, which was designed by I. M. Pei and boasts a collection of more than 35,000 pieces, including paintings by Monet and Picasso. Each fall, Bloomington hosts the Lotus World Music and Arts Festival, a celebration of the world's diverse cultures.

Spring brings the annual Little 500 Bicycle Race, made famous by the 1979 film *Breaking Away.* Many avid cyclists live in Bloomington, and they can be seen pedaling on the streets and numerous riding trails in and around town. Basketball is popular throughout Indiana, and locals take pride in the fact that I.U.'s men's program has won five national championships.
Information: Bloomington-Monroe County Convention and Visitors Bureau,
2855 N. Walnut St., 812-334-8900, 800-800-0037;
www.visitbloomington.com

WHAT TO SEE AND DO
Little 500 Bicycle Race
Indiana University campus,
1606 N. Fee Lane, Bloomington,
812-855-9152
Bicycle and tricycle races, golf jamboree, entertainment. Late April.

HOTELS
★★Courtyard by Marriott
310 S. College Ave., Bloomington,
812-335-8000, 800-321-2211;

www.courtyard.com
117 rooms. Fitness room. Indoor pool, whirlpool. **$**

★★Fourwinds Resort
9301 Fairfax Rd., Bloomington,
812-824-2628;
www.fourwindsresort.com
126 rooms. Restaurant, bar. Children's activity center. Beach. Indoor pool, outdoor pool, whirlpool. Airport transportation available. Overlooks Lake Monroe Reservoir. **$**

98

INDIANA

★
★
★
★
★

★Hampton Inn
2100 N. Walnut, Bloomington,
812-334-2100, 800-426-7866;
www.hamptoninn.com
131 rooms. Pets accepted. Outdoor pool. **$**

★★Holiday Inn
1710 N. Kinser Pike, Bloomington,
812-334-3252;
www.holiday-inn.com
189 rooms. Restaurant, bar. Indoor pool, whirlpool. Airport transportation available. **$**

RESTAURANTS
★★Colorado Steakhouse
1635 N. College Ave., Bloomington,
812-339-9979;
www.colorado-steakhouse.com
Steak menu. Lunch, dinner. Bar. Children's menu. Atrium dining area. **$$**

★Le Petit Cafe
308 W. 6th St., Bloomington,
812-334-9747.
American menu. Lunch, dinner. Closed Monday. **$$**

CENTERVILLE
Founded in 1814, this town was a stopoff for those making their way to the Gold Rush. It is now *the* place for antiquing.
Information: www.centervillein.com

SPECIALTY LODGINGS
Lantz House Inn B&B
214 W. Main St., Centerville,
765-855-2936, 800-495-2689
This inn is located in a historical commercial building in old Centerville, within walking distance to shops and restaurants. All rooms have private baths.
5 rooms. **$**

RESTAURANTS
★★Palais Royal Cafe
822 E. Main St., Centerville,
765-391-1990;
www.palaisroyalcafe.com
American menu. Dinner. Closed Sunday-Wednesday. **$$**

CHESTERTON
This small town is nestled between the Indiana Dunes State Park and Chicago, and takes advantage of its Lake Michigan access with plenty of boating, fishing and recreation.
Information: www.chesterton.net

RESTAURANTS
★★Lucrezia
428 S. Calumet Rd., Chesterton,
219-926-5829;
www.lucreziacafe.com
Italian menu. Lunch, dinner. Bar. Casual attire. Outdoor seating. **$$**

COLUMBUS
The architectural designs of many modern buildings in Columbus have attracted international attention. In the heart of the prairie, the project was launched in the late 1930s with the commissioning of Eliel Saarinen to design a church. Since then, more than 50 public and private buildings have been designed by architects such as John Carl Warnecke, Harry Weese, I. M. Pei, Kevin Roche, Eliot Noyes and J. M. Johansen.
Information: Visitors Center, 506 5th St.,
812-378-2622, 800-468-6564; www.columbus.in.us

HOTELS

★★Holiday Inn
2480 Jonathan Moore Pike, Columbus,
812-372-1541, 800-465-4329;
www.holiday-inn.com

253 rooms. Pets accepted, some restrictions; fee. Restaurant, bar. Fitness room. Indoor pool, whirlpool. Turn-of-the-century atmosphere. **$**

CORYDON

Corydon was the scene of the only Civil War battle fought on Indiana soil. A Confederate raiding party under General John Hunt Morgan occupied the town briefly on July 9, 1863, holding the home guard captive.

Information: Chamber of Commerce of Harrison County, 310 N. Elm St., 812-738-2137, 888-738-2137

WHAT TO SEE AND DO
Squire Boone Caverns and Village
100 Squire Boone Rd. S.W., Mauckport,
812-732-4381
These caverns, discovered in 1790 by Daniel Boone's brother, Squire, contain travertine formations, stalactites, stalagmites, underground streams and waterfalls. Aboveground village includes restored working gristmill, craft shops, demonstrations. hayrides; 110 acres of forest with nature trails and picnic areas. One-hour cavern tours. Admission includes all activities and facilities. Memorial Day Labor Day: daily.

RESTAURANTS
★Magdalena's
103 E. Chestnut St., Corydon,
812-738-8075
Lunch, dinner. Casual attire. **$$**

CRAWFORDSVILLE

Crawfordsville has been the home of nearly a dozen authors and playwrights, including General Lew Wallace, who wrote Ben Hur, Maurice Thompson, author of Alice of Old Vincennes and Meredith Nicholson, author of h ouse of a Thousand Candles. The all-male Wabash College is located here.

Information: Montgomery County Visitors & Convention Bureau, 218 E. Pike St., 765-362-5200, 800-866-3973; www.crawfordsville.org

HOTELS
★★Holiday Inn
2500 N. Lafayette Rd., Crawfordsville,
765-362-8700, 800-465-4329;
www.holiday-inn.com
150 rooms. Pets accepted, some restrictions; fee. Restaurant, bar. Fitness room. Outdoor pool. **$**

RESTAURANTS
★Bungalow
210 E. Pike St., Crawfordsville,
765-362-2596
Italian, American menu. Lunch, dinner. Closed Sunday. Bar. **$$**

★

★

★

★

★

EVANSVILLE

Separated from Kentucky by the Ohio River, Evansville has retained some of the atmosphere of the busy river town it once was when steamboats cruised the Ohio and Mississippi Rivers. Evansville is the principal transportation, trade and industrial center of southwestern Indiana.

Information: Evansville Convention & Visitors Bureau, 401 S.E. Riverside Dr., 800-433-3025; www.evansvillecvb.org

WHAT TO SEE AND DO

Angel Mounds State Historic Site

8215 Pollack Ave., Evansville, 812-853-3956

Largest and best-preserved group of prehistoric mounds (1100-1450) in Indiana. Approximately 100 acres. Interpretive center has film, exhibits and artifacts; reconstructed dwellings on grounds. Mid-March-December: Tuesday-Sunday.

Evansville Museum of Arts, History and Science

411 S.E. Riverside Dr., Evansville, 812-425-2406; www.emuseum.org

Permanent art, history and science exhibits; sculpture garden; Koch Planetarium; re-creation of turn-of-the-century village. Tours. Tuesday-Sunday.

HOTELS

★Hampton Inn

8000 Eagle Crest Blvd., Evansville, 812-473-5000, 800-426-7866; www.hamptoninn.com

143 rooms. Complimentary continental breakfast. Fitness room. Indoor pool. $

★★Holiday Inn

4101 Hwy. 41 N., Evansville, 812-424-6400, 800-465-4329; www.holiday-inn.com

198 rooms. Restaurant, bar. Fitness room. Indoor pool, children's pool, whirlpool. Airport transportation available. Business center. $

★Signature Inn

1101 N. Green River Rd., Evansville, 812-476-9626, 800-822-5252; www.signatureinn.com

125 rooms. Complimentary continental breakfast. Outdoor pool. $

★★★Marriott Evansville Airport

7101 Hwy. 41 N., Evansville, 812-867-7999, 800-228-9290; www.marriott.com

A glass-enclosed atrium encloses the lobby of this airport hotel. Rooms have wireless Internet and spacious work areas. 199 rooms. Restaurant, bar. Fitness room. Indoor pool, whirlpool. Airport transportation available. $

RESTAURANTS

★The Old Mill Restaurant

5031 New Harmony Rd., Evansville, 812-963-6000.

American menu. Lunch, dinner. $

101

INDIANA

★
★
★
★
★

FORT WAYNE

The Fort Wayne area is one of the most historically significant in Indiana. The point where the St. Joseph and St. Mary's Rivers meet to form the Maumee was, for many years before and after the first European explorers came to Indiana, the headquarters of the Miami Native Americans. A French fort was established here about 1690 by fur traders. The settlement became known as Miami Town and Frenchtown. In 1760, English troops occupied the French fort, but were driven out three years later by warriors led by Chief Pontiac. During the next

30 years, Miami Town became one of the most important trading centers in the West. President Washington sent out two armies in 1790 to establish a fort for the United States at the river junction, but both armies were defeated. A third American army, under General "Mad Anthony" Wayne, succeeded and set up a post called Fort Wayne across the river from Miami Town. Today, Fort Wayne is the second-largest city in Indiana.

Information: Fort Wayne-Allen County Convention and Visitors Bureau, 1021 S. Calhoun St., 260-424-3700, 800-767-7752; www.fwcvb.org

102

INDIANA

WHAT TO SEE AND DO

Allen County Fort Wayne Historical Society Museum

302 E. Berry St., Fort Wayne,
260-426-2882

Exhibits on six themes: earliest times to the Civil War; 19th-century industrialization 1860s-1894; culture and society 1894-1920; 20th-century technology and industry 1920-present; old city jail and law enforcement 1820-1970; ethnic heritage. Special temporary exhibits. Tuesday-Sunday.

Foellinger-Freimann Botanical Conservatory

1100 S. Calhoun St., Fort Wayne,
260-427-6440

Showcase h ouse with seasonally changing displays of colorful flowers; Tropical h ouse with exotic plants; Arid house with cacti

and other desert flora native to Sonoran Desert. Cascading waterfall. Daily.

Fort Wayne Children's Zoo

3411 Sherman Blvd., Fort Wayne,
260-427-6800;
www.kidszoo.com

Especially designed for children, this zoo has exotic animals, pony rides, a train and contact area. The 22-acre African Veld area allows animals to roam free while visitors travel by miniature safari cars; tropical rain forest; five-acre Australian Outback area with dugout canoe ride, kangaroos, Tasmanian devils. Late April-mid-October: daily.

HOTELS

★★Courtyard by Marriott

1619 W. Washington Center Rd., Fort Wayne,
260-489-1500, 800-321-2211;
www.courtyard.com

142 rooms. Fitness room. Indoor pool, outdoor pool, whirlpool. **$**

★★Holiday Inn
300 E. Washington Blvd., Fort Wayne,
260-422-5511, 800-465-4329;
www.holiday-inn.com
208 rooms. Restaurant, bar. Fitness room. Indoor pool, whirlpool. Airport transportation available. **$**

★Signature Inn
1734 W. Washington Center, Fort Wayne,
260-489-5554, 800-822-5252,
102 rooms. Complimentary continental breakfast. Outdoor pool. **$**

★★★Hilton Fort Wayne Convention Center
1020 S. Calhoun St., Fort Wayne,
219-420-1100, 800-445-8667,
www.hilton.com
Located in downtown Fort Wayne, this hotel and convention center has rooms decorated with contemporary furnishings. The hotel also has an onsite fitness center and indoor pool.
250 rooms. Three restaurants, three bars. Fitness room. Indoor pool, whirlpool. Airport transportation available. **$**

★★★Marriott Fort Wayne
305 E. Washington Center Rd.,
Fort Wayne,
260-484-0411, 800-228-9290;
www.marriott.com
Rooms at this Fort Wayne hotel have been updated with luxury linens and beds. Try Red River Steaks and BBQ Restaurant for a pleasurable dining experience.
222 rooms. Pets accepted; fee. Restaurant, bar. Fitness room. Indoor pool, outdoor pool, whirlpool. Airport transportation available. **$$**

RESTAURANTS
★Don Hall's Factory
5811 Coldwater Rd., Fort Wayne,
260-484-8693;
www.donhalls.com
Lunch, dinner. Bar. Children's menu. **$$**

★★Flanagan's
6525 Covington Rd., Fort Wayne,
260-432-6666
Lunch, dinner. Bar. Children's menu. Victorian decor; garden gazebo, carousel. **$$**

103

INDIANA

FRENCH LICK
In the early 18th century, this was the site of a French trading post. The post, and the existence of a nearby salt lick, influenced the pioneer founders of the later settlement to name it French Lick.

Today, this small community is a well-known health and vacation resort centered around the French Lick springs and surrounding woodlands. The water contains a high concentration of minerals.

Information: French Lick-West Baden Chamber of Commerce, 812-936-2405

HOTELS
★★★West Baden Springs Hotel
8538 West Baden Ave., French Lick,
812-936-1902;
www.French Lick.com
This more than 100-year-old property recently underwent a massive restoration. When it was built in 1902, this grand structure with its massive domed roof (deemed architecturally impossible to build at the time) was considered one of the finest hotels in the country. The number of rooms has been reduced by half to create new, spacious retreats with plush beds topped by luxury bedding. The spa offers cutting edge treatments as well as the original Pluto mineral water baths, drawn from local springs. 246 rooms. Restaurant, Bar. Pool. Tennis. Golf. Casino. Fitness room. Spa. WiFi. Pets accepted, fee. **$$**

★
★

★

★

★

★

★★★French Lick Springs Resort & Spa
8670 W. Hwy. 56, French Lick,
812-936-9300;
www.French Lick.com
This historic resort is set among gardens, mineral springs and blooming flowers and features comfortable suites, golf, tennis, a spa, and 500 rooms. Restaurants, bar. Children's activity center. Fitness room, spa. Indoor pool, outdoor pool, whirlpool. Golf. Tennis. **$**

GARY

An industrial center located on Lake Michigan just outside Chicago, Gary is probably best known for its most famous residents, Michael Jackson and the Jackson family.
www.gary.in.us

RESTAURANTS
★★★Miller Bakery Cafe
555 S. Lake St., Gary,
219-938-2229
Located in the Miller Beach area, this charming restaurant's name comes from its setting in a renovated bakery building. The kitchen serves up mostly modern American fare, with specialties including pasta and seafood dishes.
International menu. Lunch, dinner. Closed Monday. Casual attire. Reservations recommended. **$$**

GOSHEN

This historic town is located in the heart of Amish country and surrounded by farmland.
Information: Chamber of Commerce, 232 S. Main St. 574-533-2102, 800-307-4204;
www.goshen.org

HOTELS
★★Courtyard by Marriott
1930 Lincolnway E., Goshen,
574-534-3133, 800-321-2211
www.courtyard.com
98 rooms. High-speed Internet access. Restaurant. Fitness room. Indoor pool, outdoor pool, whirlpool. **$**

★★★Essenhaus Inn and Conference Center
240 Hwy. 20, Middlebury,
574-825-9471; 800-455-9471;
www.essenhaus.com
Essenhaus Inn and Conference Center is surrounded by Amish countryside in northern Indiana. Comfortable guest rooms have refrigerators and some feature balconies. Within walking distance is the Village Shops, carriage rides, a covered bridge and miniature golf.
40 rooms. Restaurant. **$$**

GREENCASTLE

Greencastle is located within 15 miles of two man-made lakes—Raccoon Lake Reservoir and Cataract Lake. It is also the home of DePauw University, a small liberal arts school.
Information: Chamber of Commerce, 2 S. Jackson St., 765-653-4517;
www.greencastle.com

HOTELS

★★Walden Inn
2 W. Seminary St., Greencastle,
765-653-2761, 800-225-8655;
www.waldeninn.com
Located within minutes of DePauw University and the area's covered bridges, this country inn has warmth and charm. 55 rooms. Restaurant. **$**

RESTAURANTS

★★Different Drummer
2 W. Seminary St., Greencastle,
765-653-2761;
www.waldeninn.com
Located inside the Walden Inn, this restaurant serves classic fare such as chicken cordon bleu, roasted eggplant with spinach, lamb chops, and veal medallions. Appetizers include warm duck breast pâté. Breakfast, lunch, dinner. Closed holidays. Bar. **$$**

GREENFIELD

This town, located east of Indianapolis, is the birthplace of poet James Whitcomb Riley.
Information: Greater Greenfield Chamber of Commerce, 1 Courthouse Plaza, 317-477-4188; www.greenfieldcc.org

HOTELS

★Lees Inn
2270 N. State St., Greenfield,
317-462-7112
100 rooms. Pets accepted, some restrictions; fee. Complimentary continental breakfast. **$**

RESTAURANTS

★Carnegie's
100 W. North St., Greenfield,
317-462-8480
American menu. Lunch, dinner. Closed Sunday-Monday. **$**

HAMMOND

Hammond is one of the Calumet area industrial cities on the southwest shore of Lake Michigan. The Indiana-Illinois state line is two blocks from h ammond's business district and separates it from its neighbor community, Calumet City, Illinois. Hammond is also adjacent to Chicago.
Information: Chamber of Commerce, 7034 Indianapolis Blvd., 219-931-1000; www.hammondchamber.org

HOTELS

★★Best Western Northwest Indiana Inn
3830 179th St., Hammond,
219-844-2140, 800-937-8376;
www.bestwestern.com
101 rooms. Complimentary continental breakfast. Restaurant, bar. Fitness room. Outdoor pool. **$**

RESTAURANTS

★★Cafe Elise
435 Ridge Rd., Munster,
219-836-2233
American menu. Lunch, dinner. Closed Monday. Bar. Children's menu. Casual attire. **$$**

★★Phil Smidt's
1205 N. Calumet Ave., Hammond,
219-659-0025, 800-376-4534;
www.froglegs.com
Seafood menu. Lunch, dinner. Closed Monday. Bar. Children's menu. Casual attire. **$$**

INDIANAPOLIS

The present site of Indianapolis was an area of rolling woodland when it was selected by a group of 10 commissioners as the location of the new Indiana state capital on June 7, 1820. Only scattered Native American villages and two white settler families were located in the region at the time. The city was laid out in the wheel pattern of Washington, D.C.

The annual 500-mile Formula One automobile race at the Indianapolis Motor Speedway has brought international fame to the city. Indianapolis is also called the nation's amateur sports capital, and has hosted more than 400 national and international amateur sporting events.

In the middle of Indianapolis is Circle Centre Mall, which is home not only to the largest mall in the area, but also to the Indianapolis Artsgarden, which has concerts, botanical displays and other cultural events. Also downtown are the RCA Dome, home to the Indianapolis Colts, Conseco Fieldhouse, home of the Indiana Pacers, and Victory Field, where the Indianapolis Indians play. Victory Field is consistently voted one of the top ballparks in minor league baseball.

Information: Convention and Visitors Association, 1 RCA Dome, 317-639-4282, 800-323-4639; www.indy.org

SPOT★ LIGHT

★ 1980S TV SITCOM ONE DAY AT A TIME WAS SET IN INDIANAPOLIS.

★ DRIVERS WHO WIN THE INDY 500 IMMEDIATELY DRINK A BOTTLE OF MILK, A 72-YEAR-OLD TRADITION.

WHAT TO SEE AND DO

Children's Museum of Indianapolis
3000 N. Meridian St., Indianapolis,
317-334-3322;
www.childrensmuseum.org
The largest of its kind, this outstanding children's museum has exhibits covering science, culture, space, history and exploration. The largest gallery, the Center for Exploration, is designed for ages 12 and up. March-Labor Day: daily 10 a.m.-5 p.m.; Labor Day-February: Tuesday-Sunday 10 a.m.-5 p.m.

City Market
222 E. Market St., Indianapolis.
317-634-9266,
www.indianapoliscitymarket.com
This renovated marketplace was constructed in 1886. Shops in the building and two adjacent areas sell smoked meats, dairy products, specialty baked goods and fruits and ethnic foods. Live music is featured on Wednesdays and Fridays in the summer. Monday-Friday 6 a.m.-6 p.m.

Colonel Eli Lilly Civil War Museum
1 Monument Circle, Indianapolis,
317-232-7615

At this museum underneath the Soldiers and Sailors Monument on downtown's Monument Circle, exhibits describe h oosier involvement in the Civil War. Exhibits include photos, letters and diaries of Indiana soldiers. Wednesday-Sunday 10 a.m.-6 p.m.

Easley Winery
205 N. College Ave., Indianapolis,
317-636-4516;
www.easleywine.com
Wine tastings; outdoor garden; sales room and gift shop. Tours: Monday-Saturday, 9 a.m.-6 p.m., Sunday noon-4 p.m.

Indianapolis Motor Speedway and Hall of Fame Museum
4790 W. 16th St., Indianapolis,
317-484-6747;
www.indianapolismotorspeedway.com
Site of the famous 500-mile automobile classic held each year the Sunday before Memorial Day. Many innovations in modern cars have been tested at races here. The oval track is 2 1-2 miles long, lined by grandstands, paddocks and bleachers. Designated a National historic Landmark, the h all of Fame Museum displays approximately 75 cars, including a 1957 SSI Corvette and the Marmon "Wasp," which, with Ray h arroun behind the wheel, won the first-ever Indy 500 in 1911. Daily.

Indianapolis Museum of Art
4000 Michigan Rd., Indianapolis,
317-920-2659;
www.ima-art.org
Extensive collections with many special exhibits fee. Tours. Tuesday-Sunday.

Madame Walker Theatre Center
617 Indiana Ave., Indianapolis,
317-236-2099
The Walker Theatre, erected and embellished in an African and Egyptian motif, was built in 1927 as a tribute to Madame C. J. Walker, America's first self-made female millionaire. The renovated theater now features theatrical productions, con-

INDIANA DUNES NATIONAL LAKESHORE
In 1966, 8,000 acres surrounding Indiana Dunes State Park were established as Indiana Dunes National Lakeshore. Another 7,139 acres have since been acquired and development continues. The lakeshore contains a number of distinct environments—clean, sandy beaches; huge sand dunes, many covered witHtrees and shrubs; and several bogs and marshes. To preserve these environments, dune buggies and off-road vehicles are prohibited.

The visitor center is located at the junction of Kemil Road and Highway 12, three miles east of Highway 49. On Highway 12 near Michigan City is Mount Baldy, the largest dune in the lakeshore, witHhiking trails and a beach.
Information: 1100 N. Mineral Springs Rd., Porter. 219-926-7561.

INDIANA

certs and other cultural events. The center serves as an educational and cultural center for the city's African-American community. Tours by appointment.

President Benjamin Harrison Home
1230 N. Delaware St., Indianapolis,
317-631-1888;
www.presidentbenjaminharrison.org
This is the former residence of the 23rd president of the United States. Guided tours depart every 30 minutes and take visitors through 16 rooms with original furniture, paintings and the family's personal effects. Monday-Saturday 10 a.m.-3:30 p.m.; closed first three weeks in January, 500 Race Day.

Indianapolis Zoo
1200 W. Washington St., Indianapolis,
317-630-2001;

★
★
★

www.indyzoo.com

This zoo includes the state's largest aquarium, an enclosed whale and dolphin pavilion and more than 3,000 animals from around the world. h orse-drawn streetcar, elephant, camel, carousel and miniature train rides. Stroller and locker rentals. Daily.

NCAA Hall of Champions
700 W. Washington St., Indianapolis, 800-735-6222

This center celebrates intercollegiate athletics through photographs, video presentations and displays covering 22 men's and women's sports and all NCAA championships. The 25,000-square-foot area contains two levels of interactive displays and multimedia presentations. Monday-Saturday 10 a.m.-5 p.m.; Sunday noon-5 p.m.; closed Monday, Labor Day-Memorial Day.

Indianapolis 500
Indianapolis Motor Speedway, 4790 W. 16th St., Indianapolis, 317-484-6780;
www.indianapolismotorspeedway.com

This 500-mile auto race is the nation's premiere event for racing. Watching and partying from the track's inner circle is a popular annual event. Sunday before Memorial Day.

HOTELS

★★Courtyard By Marriott Downtown
501 W. Washington St., Indianapolis, 317-635-4443, 800-321-2211;
www.courtyard.com

235 rooms. Restaurant, bar. Outdoor pool. Business center. $

★Courtyard Indianapolis at The Capitol
320 N. Senate Ave., Indianapolis, 317-684-7733, 800-321-2211;
www.courtyard.com

124 rooms. Indoor pool, whirlpool. Business center. $

★Hampton Inn
105 S. Meridian St., Indianapolis, 317-261-1200, 800-426-7866;
www.hamptoninn.com

180 rooms. Complimentary continental breakfast. Fitness room. $

★★Hilton Garden Inn Indianapolis Downtown
10 E. Market St., Indianapolis, 317-955-9700

180 rooms. Restaurant, bar. Fitness room. Indoor pool. $

★★★Canterbury Hotel
123 S. Illinois St., Indianapolis, 317-634-3000, 800-538-8186;
www.canterburyhotel.com

Since the 1850s, this hotel has been Indianapolis' leading hotel. Mahogany furniture and traditional artwork decorate the guest rooms. The restaurant dishes up American and continental favorites for breakfast, lunch and dinner, while the traditional afternoon tea is a local institution.
99 rooms. Wireless Internet access. Restaurant. Fitness room. $$$

★★★Crowne Plaza Hotel Union Station
123 W. Louisiana St., Indianapolis, 317-631-2221, 888-303-1746;
www.crowneplaza.com-ind-downtown

Located in historic Union Station, this hotel offers 26 authentic Pullman sleeper train cars for overnight stays, with each one named for a famous personality from the early 1900s. Full of old-world charm and modern convenience, this hotel is within walking distance of downtown restaurants and sports and cultural hot spots.
273 rooms. High-speed Internet access. Restaurant, bar. Fitness room. Indoor pool, whirlpool. Airport transportation available. Business center. $

★★Doubletree Guest Suites
11355 N. Meridian St., Carmel, 317-844-7994, 800-222-8733;
www.doubletree.com

137 rooms. Restaurant, bar. Fitness room. Indoor pool, outdoor pool, whirlpool. $

★★★Hyatt Regency Indianapolis
1 S. Capitol Ave., Indianapolis,

317-632-1234;
www.hyatt.com
This hotel is located eight miles from the Indianapolis International Airport, and connected to the Indiana Convention Center, RCA Dome and Circle Centre Mall by a skywalk.
497 rooms. Restaurant, bar. Fitness room. Indoor pool, whirlpool. Business center. **$$**

★★★Marriott Indianapolis Downtown
350 W. Maryland St., Indianapolis,
317-822-3500, 877-640-7666;
www.marriott.com
Superior customer service is the hallmark of this downtown hotel. Guest rooms are tastefully decorated with modern furnishings. The on-site Champions Sports Bar features more than 30 TVs, making it the perfect spot to watch a big race or game.
615 rooms. Restaurant, bar. Fitness room. Indoor pool, whirlpool. Business center. **$**

★★★Omni Severin Hotel
40 W. Jackson Place, Indianapolis,
317-634-6664;
www.omnihotels.com
This historic hotel is connected to the Circle Centre Mall and located opposite Union Station. Rooms feature luxury linens and full stocked refreshment centers.
424 rooms. Pets accepted, some restrictions; fee. Restaurant, bar. Fitness room. Indoor pool. Business center. **$$**

★★★Sheraton Hotel and Suites
8787 Keystone Crossing, Indianapolis,
317-846-2700;
www.sheraton.com
Connected to the city's most upscale mall, Keystone Crossing, this hotel is close to several restaurants and a nearby Bally's h ealth Club. The hotel has rooms and suites that feature refrigerators, wet bars and spacious seating areas.
506 rooms. Pets accepted, some restrictions. Restaurant, bar. Indoor pool, whirlpool. Business center. **$**

★★★The Westin Indianapolis
50 S. Capitol Ave., Indianapolis,
317-262-8100;
www.westin.com
Located near the IMAX theater and connected to the RCA Dome and a shopping center, this hotel is convenient for business and leisure travelers. Rooms have plush, duvet-topped beds and views of the city.
573 rooms. Pets accepted, some restrictions. Restaurant, bar. Fitness room. Indoor pool, whirlpool. Business center. **$**

SPECIALTY LODGINGS
Nestle Inn
637 N. East St., Indianapolis,
317-610-5200;
www.nestleindy.com
This restored Victorian has individually decorated rooms with private baths and wireless Interent access.
5 rooms. Complimentary full breakfast. **$**

Old Northside Inn
1340 N. Alabama St., Indianapolis,
317-635-9123, 800-635-9127;
www.oldnorthsideinn.com
This historic inn has hardwood floors, flowers and antiques throughout. A piano room, fully stocked snack bar, and books and movies are all offered here.
7 rooms. Complimentary full breakfast. **$$**

Stone Soup Inn
1304 N. Central Ave., Indianapolis,
317-639-9550, 866-639-9550;
www.stonesoupinn.com
This 1901 Colonial Revival style mansion is located north of downtown Indianapolis. The living room features comfortable large chairs and a fireplace.
9 rooms. Complimentary full breakfast. Check-in by appointment, check-out by 11a.m. **$**

The Looking Glass Inn
1319 N. New Jersey, Indianapolis,
317-639-9550

109

INDIANA

★
★
★
★
★

The Looking Glass Inn is a historic 1905 Free Classic style mansion located north of downtown. Each room is unique and decorated with antiques. A butler's pantry offers snacks and beverages, games, videos, magazines and books.
6 rooms. Complimentary full breakfast. Check-in by appointment, check-out 11 a.m. $

Yellow Rose Inn
1441 N. Delaware St., Indianapolis, 317-636-7673;
www.yellowroseinn.com
This inn is located north of town in an area with many historic mansions. The restored yellow building, once a family home, has guest rooms decorated in styles ranging from 17th century to 21st century.
4 rooms, all suites. Complimentary full breakfast. $$

RESTAURANTS

★Aristocrat Pub
5212 N. College Ave., Indianapolis, 317-283-7388
American menu. Lunch, dinner, Sunday brunch. Bar. Children's menu. Casual attire. Outdoor seating. $$

★Cafe Patachou
4911 N. Pennsylvania St., Indianapolis, 317-925-2823;
www.cafepatachou.com
American menu. Breakfast, lunch, brunch. Children's menu. Casual attire. Outdoor seating. $

★★★Chanteclair
2501 S. HigHSchool Rd., Indianapolis, 317-243-1040;
www.genhotels.com-chanteclair.html
This eatery, located on the top floor of the Holiday Inn Select, is not a typical hotel restaurant. Classic French dishes like steak Diane and Dover sole make up the menu, while candlelight and violinists set the mood. Jackets for men are suggested, but not required.
French menu. Dinner. Closed Sunday; holidays. Bar. Business casual attire. Reservations recommended. $$$

★★Daddy Jack's
9419 N. Meridian St., Indianapolis, 317-843-1609;
www.konajacksindy.com
American menu. Lunch, dinner. Closed Sunday. Bar. Casual attire. Reservations recommended. Outdoor seating. $$

★★Glass Chimney
12901 Old Meridian St., Carmel, 317-844-0921
French, American menu. Dinner. Closed Sunday. Bar. Outdoor seating. $$$

★★Hollyhock Hill
8110 N. College Ave., Indianapolis, 317-251-2294;
www.hollyhockhill.com
American menu. Dinner, lunch Sunday only. Closed Monday. Bar. Children's menu. Casual attire. $$

★Loon Lake Lodge
6880 E. 82nd St., Indianapolis, 317-845-9011
American menu. Lunch, dinner, Sunday brunch. Bar. Children's menu. Casual attire. $$

★★Palomino
49 W. Maryland St., Indianapolis, 317-974-0400;
www.palomino.com
Mediterranean menu. Lunch, dinner. Bar. Children's menu. Business casual attire. Reservations recommended. Outdoor seating. $$

★★★Restaurant at the Canterbury
123 S. Illinois St., Indianapolis, 317-634-3000, 800-538-8186;
www.canterburyhotel.com
Located downtown in the Canterbury hotel, this eatery is decorated more like an English club than a restaurant. American Continental cuisine is the focus here, with classics like Steak Diane and surf and turf served at dinner.
American, Continental menu. Breakfast, lunch, dinner, brunch bar. Business casual attire. Reservations recommended. Valet parking. $$$

★★Rick's Cafe Boatyard
4050 Dandy Trail, Indianapolis,
317-290-9300
International menu. Lunch, dinner, Sunday brunch. Bar. Children's menu. Business casual attire. Outdoor seating. $$

★❋ St. Elmo Steak House
127 S. Illinois St., Indianapolis.
317-635-0636
www.stelmos.com
Steak menu. Dinner. Bar. Casual attire. Reservations recommended. $$$

★★★The Oceanaire Seafood Room
30 S. Meridian St., Indianapolis,
317-955-2277;
www.theoceanaire.com

This modern seafood house is located in downtown Indianapolis and is a popular choice for power lunches. The menu changes daily and features fresh seafood from ahi tuna to black bass. The oyster bar features mollusks from both the Atlantic and Pacific Oceans.
Seafood menu. Lunch, dinner. Bar. Casual attire. Reservations recommended. Valet parking. $$$

★Yats
5463 College Ave., Indianapolis,
317-253-8817;
www.yatscajuncreole.com
Cajun-creole menu. Lunch, dinner. Casual attire. Outdoor seating. $

JASPER
This small southern Indiana town was settled in 1866 and populated by German settlers, whose influence can still be felt in the area.
Information: Dubois County Tourism Commission, 610 Main St., 812-482-9115, 800-968-4578; www.jasperindiana.gov

HOTELS
★★Holiday Inn
951 Wernsing Rd., Jasper,
812-482-5555, 800-872-3176;
www.holiday-inn.com
200 rooms. Restaurant, bar. Fitness room. Indoor pool, children's pool, whirlpool. $

RESTAURANTS
★★Schnitzelbank
393 Third Ave., Jasper,
812-482-2640
German, American menu. Breakfast, lunch, dinner. Closed Sunday. Bar. $$

JEFFERSONVILLE
Jeffersonville, perched on the north bank of the Ohio River and opposite Louisville, Kentucky, has a history as a shipbuilding center. One of the oldest towns in Indiana, it was built according to plans drawn up by Thomas Jefferson.
Information: Southern Indiana Convention and Tourism Bureau, 315 Southern Indiana Ave., 812-282-6654, 800-552-3842; www.sunnysideoflouisville.org

WHAT TO SEE AND DO
Howard Steamboat Museum
1101 E. Market St., Jeffersonville,
812-283-3728, 888-472-0606;
www.steamboatmuseum.org
This museum is housed in a 22-room mansion featuring stained- and leaded-glass windows, hand-carved panels, brass chandeliers and Victorian furniture; steam-boat models, shipyard artifacts and tools, and other memorabilia. Tours. Tuesday-Saturday 10 a.m.-4 p.m., Sunday 1-4 p.m.

HOTELS
★Best Western Green Tree Inn
1425 Broadway, Clarksville,
812-288-9281, 800-950-9281;

www.bestwestern.com
107 rooms. Pets accepted, some restrictions. Outdoor pool. **$**

★★Ramada Inn
700 W. Riverside Dr., Jeffersonville,

812-284-6711, 800-537-3612;
www.ramada.com
187 rooms. Pets accepted; fee. Restaurant, bar. Outdoor pool. Airport transportation available. **$**

KOKOMO

This lively manufacturing center is where Elwood Haynes invented the first clutch-driven automobile with an electric ignition. Since then, Kokomo manufacturers have invented several more useful items, from the first pneumatic rubber tire to canned tomato juice. Chrysler and Delphi-Delco Electronics have plants here, which manufacture automotive entertainment systems, semiconductor devices, transmissions and aluminum die castings. Indiana University has a branch here, and Grissom Air Reserve Base is located 14 miles north of town.
Information: Kokomo Indiana Visitors Bureau, 1504 N. Reed Rd.,
765-457-6802, 800-837-0971; www.kokomo-in.org

WHAT TO SEE AND DO
Elwood Haynes Museum
1915 S. Webster St., Kokomo,
765-456-7500
This museum was the home of Elwood Haynes, creator of one of the earliest American automobiles. Includes memorabilia, 1905 and 1924 Haynes cars and the Haynes Stellite alloy used in spaceships. Daily; closed holidays.

Seiberling Mansion
1200 W. Sycamore St., Kokomo.
765-452-4314
This late Victorian mansion houses exhibits of historical and educational interest, county history, manufacturing artifacts. Tuesday-Sunday afternoons; closed January.

HOTELS
★Best Western Signature Inn
4021 S. LaFountain St., Kokomo,
765-455-1000, 800-822-5252;
www.bestwestern.com
101 rooms. Complimentary continental breakfast. Fitness room. Indoor pool, whirlpool. **$**

★★Clarion Hotel
1709 E. Lincoln Rd., Kokomo.
765-459-8001
132 rooms. Restaurant, bar. Fitness room. Indoor pool. Airport transportation available. **$**

★Hampton Inn
2920 S. Reed Rd., Kokomo,
765-455-2900, 800-426-7866;
www.hamptoninnkokomo.com
105 rooms. Pets accepted, some restrictions. Complimentary continental breakfast. Fitness room. Indoor pool. **$**

RESTAURANTS
★★Sycamore Grille
115 W. Sycamore, Kokomo,
765-457-2220
Lunch, dinner. Closed Sunday. Bar. Children's menu. **$$**

112

INDIANA

LA PORTE

This busy manufacturing center is a popular resort area in both winter and summer. City lakes offer fishing, ice fishing, snowmobiling and other recreational activities. Seven lakes with fishing and boating facilities border the town on the north and west. The area's chief industrial products are industrial fans, coil coating, corrugated and plastic containers, rubber products and iron and metal castings.

Information: Greater La Porte Chamber of Commerce, 414 Lincolnway, 219-362-3178; www.lpchamber.com

HOTELS

★Best Value

444 Pine Lake Ave., La Porte,
219-362-4585, 888-298-2054;
www.bestvalueinn.com

146 rooms. Pets accepted, some restrictions; fee. Complimentary continental breakfast. Restaurant, bar. Fitness room. Indoor pool, outdoor pool, whirlpool

★★★Arbor Hill

263 W. Johnson Rd., La Porte,
219-362-9200;
www.arborhillinn.com

Built in 1910, this historic Greek Revival inn welcomes guests with its fusion of old-world, turn-of-the-century charm and luxurious modern amenities. Nearby attractions include the Prime Outlet Mall, Notre Dame and Lake Michigan.

12 rooms. Complimentary full breakfast. $

RESTAURANTS

★Reed's State Street Pub

502 State St., La Porte,
219-326-8339

Lunch, dinner. Closed Sunday. Bar. Children's menu. $$

LAFAYETTE

Lafayette, a farming community on the east bank of the Wabash River, was named for the Marquis de Lafayette, who served as a general under George Washington in the Revolutionary War. On the west bank of the river in West Lafayette is Purdue University. Established as an agricultural college in 1869, Purdue is known for its engineering school.

Information: Convention and Visitors Bureau,
301 Frontage Rd.,
765-447-9999, 800-872-6648;
www.lafayette-in.com

WHAT TO SEE AND DO

Purdue University

504 Northwestern Ave., West Lafayette,
765-494-4636;

www.purdue.edu

This Big Ten conference member has 38,208 students and more than 140 major buildings on 1,579 acres.

Tippecanoe Battlefield Museum and Park
200 Battleground Ave., Battle Ground,
I-65 at Hwy. 43 exit,
765-567-2147
This is the site of the 1811 battle in which soldiers and local militia led by General William h . h arrison, territorial governor of Indiana, defeated a confederation of Native Americans. Wabash h eritage Trail begins here. Daily.

Wolf Park
4012 E. 800 N., Battle Ground,
765-567-2265
Education-research facility; home to several packs of wolves, a small herd of bison, some coyotes and foxes. See wolves close at hand as they eat and socialize. May-November: Tuesday-Sunday afternoons.

HOTELS
★★Best Western
4343 Hwy. 26 E., Lafayette,
765-447-0575
124 rooms. Pets accepted, some restrictions; fee. Restaurant, bar. Indoor pool, whirlpool. $

★Fairfield Inn
4000 Hwy. 26 E., Lafayette,
765-449-0083, 888-236-2427;
www.fairfieldinn.com

79 rooms. Complimentary continental breakfast. High-speed Internet access. Indoor pool, whirlpool. $

★Signature Inn
4320 Hwy. 26 E., Lafayette,
765-447-4142, 800-526-3766;
www.signatureinn.com
121 rooms. Pets accepted; fee. Complimentary continental breakfast. Wireless Internet access. Outdoor pool. Business center, business center. $

★★University Inn Conference Center and Suites
3001 Northwestern Ave., West Lafayette
765-463-5511; 800-777-9808;
www.uiccwl.com
171 rooms. Restaurant, bar. Fitness room. Indoor pool, outdoor pool, whirlpool. Airport transportation available. $

SPECIALTY LODGINGS
Loeb House Inn B & B
708 Cincinnati St., Lafayette,
765-420-7737;
www.loebhouseinn.com
This charming inn was built in 1882 and features period antiques.
5 rooms. Children over 12 years only. Complimentary full breakfast.

LOGANSPORT
Located where the Wabash and Eel Rivers meet, Logansport is situated in the agricultural heartland. The town was named in honor of James Logan, nephew of the famous Shawnee chief, Tecumseh. Logan was fatally wounded by British-led Native Americans after serving with distinction as leader of a company of scouts fighting for the United States in the War of 1812.
Information: Logansport-Cass County Chamber of Commerce, 300 E. Broadway, 574-753-6388; www.logan-casschamber.com

HOTELS
★★Holiday Inn
3550 E. Market St., Logansport,
574-753-6351, 800-465-4329;
www.holiday-inn.com
95 rooms. Pets accepted. Restaurant, bar. Outdoor pool. Airport transportation available. $

LINCOLN LOGS

Lincoln spent his boyhood years (1816–1830) in this area, reading books, clerking at James Gentry's store and helping his father withHfarmwork. When Lincoln was 21, his family moved to Illinois, where the future president launched his political career.

This 200-acre wooded and landscaped park includes the grave of Lincoln's mother, Nancy Hanks Lincoln, who died at 35 years old in 1818. The memorial visitor center has information available on the park, including the cabin site memorial, two miles of walking trails and the gravesite. A film is shown at the visitor center every hour depicting Lincoln's Indiana years. Nearby, on the original Thomas Lincoln tract, is the Lincoln Living Historical Farm, witHa furnished log cabin similar to the one in whicHthe Lincolns lived. Costumed pioneers carry out activities typical of an early 19th-century farm. Farm May-September: Daily.

The Lincoln Amphitheatre has an outdoor musical-theatrical production about Lincoln's life in Indiana. Mid-June-mid-August, Tuesday-Sunday. Information: Santa Claus, four miles west on Hwy. 162, 812-937-4541; 800-264-4223. www.nps.gov/libo

MARION

A farm town, Marion is located on the banks of the Mississinewa River. Indiana Wesleyan University, established in 1920, is located here. Film legend James Dean is from Marion. Information: Marion-Grant County Convention and Visitors Bureau, 217 S. Adams St., 765-668-5435, 800-662-9474; www.jamesdeancountry.com

INDIANA

WHAT TO SEE AND DO

James Dean Memorial Gallery
6508 E. Museum Blvd., Fairmount, 765-998-2080
This gallery has an extensive collection of memorabilia and archives on James Dean. Exhibit includes clothing from his films, high school yearbooks, original movie posters from around the world. Daily 9 a.m.-6 p.m.

Matthews Covered Bridge
Third and Front Streets, Matthews, 765-998-2928
This 175 feet long bridge spans the Mississinewa River.

HOTELS

★★Clarion Hotel
501 E. 4th St., Marion, 765-668-8801, 800-228-5151; www.choicehotels.com
121 rooms. Restaurant, bar. Outdoor pool. $

★Comfort Inn
1345 N. Baldwin Ave., Marion, 765-651-1006.
62 rooms. Pets accepted, some restrictions; fee. Complimentary continental breakfast. Fitness room. Indoor pool, outdoor pool, whirlpool. $

MERRILLVILLE

Once a thriving stop-off point for the many wagon trains headed west, Merrillville has abandoned its rural beginnings to become a leader in commercial and industrial development.
Information: Chamber of Commerce, 255 W. 80thPlace, 219-769-8180; www.merrillvillecoc.org

HOTELS
★Fairfield Inn
8275 Georgia St., Merrillville,
219-736-0500, 800-228-2800;
www.fairfieldinn.com
132 rooms. Complimentary continental breakfast. Outdoor pool. **$**

★★Radisson Hotel at Star Plaza
800 E. 81st Ave., Merrillville,
219-769-6311, 800-333-3333;
www.radisson.com

347 rooms. High-speed Internet access. Two restaurants, two bars. Children's activity center. Fitness room. Indoor pool, outdoor pool, whirlpool. Business center. **$$**

RESTAURANTS
★★Cafe Venezia
405 W. 81st Ave., Merrillville,
219-736-2203
Italian menu. Lunch, dinner. Closed Sunday. Casual attire. **$$**

MICHIGAN CITY
This is Indiana's summer playground on the southeast shore of Lake Michigan. Located in the famous Indiana sand dunes region, Michigan City offers miles of fine beaches. For fishermen, the lake has coho salmon from late March to November, as well as chinook salmon, lake trout and perch.
Information: La Porte County Convention and Visitors Bureau, 1503 S. Meer Rd., 800-634-2650; www.harborcountry-in.org

WHAT TO SEE AND DO
Barker Mansion
631 Washington St., Michigan City,
219-873-1520
This circa 1900 38-room mansion was modeled after an English manor house. Tours June-October: daily; rest of year: Monday-Friday.

John G. Blank Center for the Arts
101 Avenue of the Arts, Michigan City,
219-874-4900
Paintings, sculptures and graphic art exhibits of regional, national and international origin can be viewed here. Tuesday-Sunday; closed holidays.

Lighthouse Place Outlet Center
601 Wabash St., Michigan City,
219-879-6506;
www.premiumoutlets.com/lighthouseplace
This center has more than 135 outlet stores, including J. Crew and Polo Ralph Lauren. Daily.

Washington Park Zoo
115 Lakeshore Dr., Michigan City,
219-873-1510.

Swimming beach, yacht basin, marina, fishing; picnic facilities, concession; tennis courts; observation tower. Zoo daily. Recreational facilities daily. Amphitheater summer, Thursday evenings, weekend band concerts. Senior citizens center Monday-Friday. Some fees March-December.

Old Lighthouse Museum
Heisman Dr., Michigan City,
219-872-6133
This is the site of the launching of the first submarine on the Great Lakes in 1845. March-December, Tuesday-Sunday.

HOTELS
★★Blue Chip Hotel and Casino
2 Easy St., Michigan City,
219-879-7711, 888-879-7711;
www.bluechip-casino.com
188 rooms. Restaurant, bar. Fitness room. Indoor pool, whirlpool. Business center. Casino. **$**

SPECIALTY LODGINGS
Creekwood Inn
5727 N. 600 W., Michigan City,
219-872-8357, 800-400-1981;
www.creekwoodinn.com

★

★

★

★

★

This English cottage-style inn has rooms with charming fireplaces and patios. Relax in an overstuffed chair in the conservatory, or hit the fitness room.
13 rooms. Closed early January. Complimentary continental breakfast. Fitness room. Whirlpool. **$$**

Dune Land BeacHInn
3311 Pottawattamie Trail, Michigan City, 219-874-7729, 800-423-7729;
www.dunelandbeachinn.com
This turn-of-the-century country inn was built in 1892.
9 rooms. Pets accepted, some restrictions; fee. Complimentary continental breakfast. Restaurant. Beach. **$**

MUNCIE

This area was once the home of the Munsee tribe of the Delaware. The town became a farming center during the first half of the 19th century, but with the construction of railroads and the discovery of natural gas, it became an industrial city.

Ball Corporation, which for years produced the classic Ball jars, has its international headquarters in Muncie. The five Ball brothers took an active part in the city's life and contributed substantially to Ball State University.

Muncie became famous in the 1930s as the subject of Robert and Helen Lynd's sociological studies of a "typical" small city: Middletown and Middletown in Transition.
Information: Muncie-Delaware County Convention and Visitors Bureau,
425 N. High St., 765-284-2700, 800-568-6862; www.muncievisitorsbureau.org

HOTELS

★★Best Value Inn
3400 S. Madison St., Muncie,
765-288-1911, 888-315-2378;
www.bestvalueinn.com
148 rooms. Pets accepted, some restrictions; fee. Complimentary continental breakfast. Restaurant, bar. Outdoor pool, whirlpool. **$**

★★Clubhouse Inn
420 S. High St., Muncie,
765-741-7777

130 rooms. Pets accepted, some restrictions; fee. Restaurant, bar. Indoor pool, whirlpool. **$**

★Signature Inn
3400 N. Chadam Lane, Muncie,
765-284-4200, 800-822-5252;
www.signatureinn.com
101 rooms. Pets accepted, some restrictions; fee. Complimentary continental breakfast. Indoor pool. **$**

★
★
★
★
★

NAPPANEE

Many Amish-owned farms dot the countryside surrounding Nappanee. Rich soil makes agriculture a major part of the town's economy.
Information: Amish Acres Visitor Center, 1600 W. Market St., 574-773-4188,
800-800-4942; www.amishacres.com

HOTELS

★★The Inn at Amish Acres
1234 W. Market St., Nappanee,
574-773-2011, 800-800-4942;
www.amishacres.com
64 rooms. Complimentary continental breakfast. Outdoor pool. Airport transportation available. **$**

★★The Nappanee Inn
2004 W. Market St., Nappanee,
574-773-5999, 800-800-4942;
www.amishacres.com
66 rooms. Complimentary continental breakfast. Outdoor pool. **$**

NASHVILLE

Driving south from Indianapolis on State Road 135, the scenery quickly evolves from bland to beautiful as the pavement, at first level and unbending, begins to rise and fall and gently curve. On either side of the road, fields give way to dense forests. Within an hour, travelers arrive at the charming village of Nashville in Brown County. This area is also known as the art colony of the Midwest, a moniker earned in the early 1900s when the area was one of six art colonies established in the United States. The impressionist painter T. C. Steele moved here in 1907, and his homestead, the h ouse of the Singing Winds, is now a state historic site. Many artists followed Steele's lead and moved to Brown County, and today Nashville is filled with shops and galleries featuring the works of local artists. Like the larger city of the same name, Nashville has a vibrant country music scene. Two popular venues include the Little Nashville Opry and the Country Time Music h all. Information: Brown County Convention and Visitors Bureau, Main and Van Buren Streets, 812-988-7303, 800-753-3255; www.nashville-indiana.com

HOTELS

★★Brown County Inn
Hwy. 46, Nashville,
812-988-2291, 800-772-5249;
www.browncountyinn.com
99 rooms. Restaurant, bar. Indoor pool, outdoor pool. Tennis. $

★★The Seasons Lodge
560 Hwy. 46 E., Nashville,
812-988-2284, 800-365-7327;
www.seasonslodge.com
80 rooms. Restaurant, bar. Indoor pool, outdoor pool. $

SPECIALTY LODGINGS

Cornerstone Inn
54 E. Franklin St., Nashville,
812-988-0300, 888-383-0300;
www.cornerstoneinn.com
20 rooms. Complimentary full breakfast. $

RESTAURANTS

★★Harvest Dining Room
Hwys. 135 and 46, Nashville,
812-988-2267, 800-772-5249;
www.browncountyinn.com
Breakfast, lunch, dinner, Sunday brunch. Bar. Children's menu. Outdoor seating. $$

★Nashville House
Main St., Nashville,
812-988-4554
Bake shop. Lunch, dinner. Closed Tuesday, except in October; also late December-early January. Children's menu. $$

★The Ordinary
Van Buren St., Nashville,
812-988-6166;
www.seasonslodge.com-the-ordinaryhtm
Lunch, dinner. Closed Monday, except in October. Bar. Children's menu. $$

INDIANA

★

★

★

★

★

NEW HARMONY

During the first half of the 19th century, this was the site of two social experiments in communal living. A town was founded here by religious leader George Rapp and members of the Harmony Society, who came from Germany and settled in Harmony, Pennsylvania. In 1814, the society moved to Indiana. The deeply religious members believed in equality, mutual protection and common ownership of property. They practiced celibacy and believed in the imminent return of Christ. In a 10-year period, they transformed 30,000 acres of dense forest and swampland into farms and a town that was the envy of the surrounding region. In 1825, the group returned to Pennsylvania and sold Harmony to Robert Owen, a Welsh social reformer and communal idealist. Owen, with his four sons and geologist William Maclure, attempted to organize a new social order, eliminating financial exploitation, poverty and competition. h e tried to establish a model society in New Harmony, with equal opportunities for all, full cooperative effort and advanced educational facilities to develop the highest type of human beings. Within a short time, many of the world's most distinguished scientists, educators, scholars and writers came to New Harmony, which became a scientific center for America. Though Owen's original experiment failed, mainly because of his absence from the community and rivalry among his followers, the scientists and educators stayed on. The first U.S. Geological Survey was done here, and the Smithsonian Institution has its origins in this community.

The town is in a rural area surrounded by rich farmland. historic New Harmony and the New Harmony State historic Sites are dedicated to thc founders of this community. Many of the buildings and old homes still dominate New Harmony today.
Information: www.newharmony.biz or www.usi.edu/hnh

WHAT TO SEE AND DO

Atheneum Visitors Center
NortHand Arthur Streets, New Harmony,
812-682-4474, 800-231-2168;
www.newharmony.org
Documentary film. Orientation area in building designed by Richard Meier. All tours begin here. April-October: daily; March, November-December: call for hours; closed January-February.

1830 Owen House
Tavern and Brewery Streets,
New Harmony,
800-231-2168
Example of English architectural style.

Harmonist Cemetery
Church, West, Arthur and North Streets,
New Harmony,
800-231-2168
Buried here in unmarked graves dating from 1814 to 1824 are 230 members of the Harmony Society. Site includes several prehistoric Woodland mounds and an apple orchard.

Labyrinth
Main St., New Harmony,
800-231-2168
Circular maze of shrubbery created to symbolize the twists and choices along life's pathway.

Robert Henry Fauntleroy House
West and Church Streets, New Harmony,
800-231-2168
1822–1840 h armonist family residence. Enlarged and restyled by Robert and Jane Owen Fauntleroy. h ouse museum contains period furniture.

Thrall's Opera House
Church St., New Harmony,
800-231-2168
Originally the h armonist Dormitory Number 4, this building was later converted to a concert hall by Owen descendants.

Roofless Church
NortHand Main Streets, New Harmony,
800-231-2168
This interdenominational church, designed by Philip Johnson in 1959, commemorates New Harmony's religious heritage. Jacques

119

★
★
★
★
★
★

Lipchitz's sculpture, Descent of the h oly Spirit, is in its center.

HOTELS

★★New Harmony Inn
504 North St., New Harmony,
812-682-4491, 800-782-8605;
www.newharmonyinn.com

90 rooms. Restaurant, bar. Fitness room. Indoor pool, whirlpool. Tennis. $

RESTAURANTS

★★Red Geranium
504 North St., New Harmony,
812-682-4431, 800-782-8605;
Lunch, dinner. Closed Monday. Bar. $$

PLYMOUTH

Plymouth is a farming and industrial center. Southwest of the town was the site of the last Potawatomi village in this area. The chief, Menominee, refused to surrender his village to white settlers. The surviving men, women and children were removed by the government and sent to Kansas in 1838. So many members of the tribe died of malaria that fresh graves were left at every campsite during their journey.

Information: Marshall County Convention and Visitors Bureau, 220 N. Center St. 574-936-9000, 800-626-5353; www.blueberrycountry.org

HOTELS

★★Ramada Inn
2550 N. Michigan St., Plymouth,
574-936-4013, 800-272-6232;

www.ramada.com
108 rooms. Pets accepted; fee. Restaurant, bar. Outdoor pool. $

RICHMOND

Established by Quakers, this city on the Whitewater River is one of Indiana's leading industrial communities.

Information: Richmond-Wayne County Tourism Bureau, 5701 National Rd. E. 765-935-8687, 800-828-8414; www.visitrichmond.org

WHAT TO SEE AND DO

Hayes Regional Arboretum
801 Elks Rd., Richmond,
2 miles W. of Hwy. 40 and I-70.,
765-962-3745
A 355-acre site with trees, shrubs and vines native to this region; 40-acre beech-maple forest; auto tour 3 1-2 miles of site. Fern garden; spring house. h iking trails; bird sanctuary; nature center with exhibits; gift shop. Tuesday-Sunday.

Indiana Football Hall of Fame
815 N. A St., Richmond,
765-966-2235
h istory of football in Indiana; photos, plaques, memorabilia of more than 300 inductees. high schools, colleges and universities are represented. Monday-Friday, also by appointment.

HOTELS

★Knights Inn Richmond
3020 E. Main St., Richmond,
765-966-1505
44 rooms. Complimentary continental breakfast. Outdoor pool. $

RESTAURANTS

★★Olde Richmond Inn
138 S. 5th St., Richmond,
765-962-2247
American menu. Lunch, dinner. Bar. Children's menu. Outdoor seating. $$

★Taste of the Town
1616 E. Main St., Richmond,
765-935-5464
Italian menu. Lunch, dinner. Closed Monday. Bar. Children's menu. Casual attire. $$

SOUTHBEND

South Bend is probably most famous, at least in the eyes of football fans, for being the home of the Fighting Irish of the University of Notre Dame. A visit to the campus, distinguished by the massive golden dome of the Administration Building, is worth the trip. Indiana University also has a branch here.

Two Frenchmen, Peré Jacques Marquette and Louis Jolliet, were the first Europeans to explore the South Bend area. In 1679, the famous French explorer Rene-Robert Cavelier proceeded from here with 32 men to the Mississippi River. During a second trip in 1681, Cavelier negotiated a peace treaty between the Miami and Illinois Confederations under an oak tree known as the Council Oak. The first permanent settlers arrived in 1820, when Pierre Freischuetz Navarre set up a trading post for the American Fur Company.

South Bend was founded in 1823 by Alexis Coquillard who, with his partner Francis Comparet, bought a fur trading agency from John Jacob Astor. Joined by Lathrop Taylor, another trading post agent, Coquillard was instrumental in promoting the European settlement of the area and in the construction of ferries, dams and mills, which began the industrial development of the town.

Information: SouthBend-Mishawaka Convention and Visitors Bureau, 401 E. Colfax Ave., Suite 310, 574-234-0051, 800-519-0577; www.livethelegends.com

WHAT TO SEE AND DO

Notre Dame Stadium
Juniper and Edison Streets, South Bend, 574-631-5267

Few sports arenas have as much history and tradition as Notre Dame Stadium. The stadium has hosted several national championship teams and some of the greatest players and coaches in collegiate history. It was expanded in 1997 to hold more than 80,000 fans and is well attended—if not sold out—for almost every regular-season game.

HOTELS

★★Holiday Inn City Center
213 W. Washington St., South Bend, 574-232-3941, 800-465-4329; www.holiday-inn.com

176 rooms. Two restaurants, two bars. Fitness room. Indoor pool. Airport transportation available. Business center. $

★★Inn At Saint Mary's
53993 State Rd. 933, South Bend, 574-232-4000, 800-947-8627; www.innatsaintmarys.com

150 rooms. Complimentary full breakfast. High-speed Internet access. Bar. Fitness room. Whirlpool. Airport transportation available. Business center. $

★★Morris Inn
Notre Dame Ave., South Bend, 574-631-2000; www.morrisinn.com

★
★
★
★
★

92 rooms. Closed 10 days during Christmas break. Complimentary full breakfast. High-speed Internet access. Restaurant, bar. Fitness room. Business center. **$**

★Signature Inn
215 Dixie Way S., South Bend,
574-277-3211;
www.signatureinn.com
123 rooms. Pets accepted, some restrictions; fee. Complimentary continental breakfast. Fitness room. Indoor pool, whirlpool. Business center. **$**

★★★Marriott SoutHBend
123 N. St. Joseph St., South Bend,
574-234-2000, 800-328-7349;
www.marriott.com
This downtown South Bend hotel has a nine-story atrium and lobby decorated in an Art Deco style. A skywalk connects the hotel to the Century Center Convention and Civic Complex, and the downtown location makes it accessible to local businesses, attractions and schools, including, the University of Notre Dame.
298 rooms. Pets accepted; fee. High-speed Internet access. Restaurant, bar. Fitness room. Indoor pool, whirlpool. Airport transportation available. Business center. **$**

SPECIALTY LODGINGS
Oliver Inn Bed & Breakfast
630 W. Washington St., South Bend,
574-232-4545, 888-697-4466;
www.oliverinn.com
This Victorian inn was built in 1886.
9 rooms. Pets accepted, some restrictions; fee. Complimentary continental breakfast. **$**

Queen Anne Inn
420 W. Washington St., South Bend,
574-234-5959, 800-582-2379;
www.queenanneinn.net
This charming bed-and-breakfast has rooms furnished with antiques.
6 rooms. Complimentary full breakfast. **$**

RESTAURANTS
★★Damon's Grill

52885 Hwy. 31 Business, South Bend,
574-272-5478; www.damons.com
Barbecue menu. Lunch, dinner. Bar. Children's menu. Casual attire. **$$**

★★★La Salle Grill
115 W. Colfax, South Bend,
574-288-1155;
www.lasallegrill.com
This acclaimed restaurant in downtown South Bend offers such creative American dishes as grilled Amish chicken with honey and raisin barbecue sauce and black pepper mashed potatoes The dining room has high ceilings and tables topped with white linens and imported crystal. Its wine list includes nearly 350 selections.
American menu. Dinner. Closed Sunday. Bar. **$$$**

★★Sorin's
Notre Dame Ave., South Bend,
574-631-2000
American, French menu. Breakfast, lunch, dinner. Closed mid-December-early January. Bar. Children's menu. Business casual attire. Reservations recommended. **$$**

★★★The Carriage House Dining Room
24460 Adams Rd., South Bend,
574-272-9220
A historic church is the setting for this South Bend gem, where an inventive American menu is complemented by professional, friendly service. All dishes, including signatures like hickory-smoked salmon, beef Wellington with Burgundian sauce, and steak Diane with dauphinoise potatoes, are prepared using classic French techniques as well as fresh, seasonal produce. American menu. Dinner. Closed Sunday-Monday; also early January. Bar. Outdoor seating. **$$$**

★★★Tippecanoe Place
620 W. Washington St., South Bend,
574-234-9077; www.tippe.com
This 1880s stone mansion once owned by the Studebaker family is now an elegant restaurant. The menu features classics

like filet mignon or roasted salmon with mustard-basil glaze. The extensive wine list features bottles from around the world, but spotlights winemakers from California.

American menu. Lunch, dinner, Sunday brunch. Bar. Children's menu. Business casual attire. Reservations recommended. **$$**

TERRE HAUTE

Terre Haute was founded as a river town on the lower Wabash River and has become an important industrial, educational and cultural center.

The plateau on which the city is built was named Terre Haute or high land by the French, who governed this area until 1763. The dividing line that separated the French provinces of Canada and Louisiana runs through this section. American settlers arrived with the establishment of Fort h arrison in 1811. Many wagon trains with westbound settlers passed through here.

Novelist Theodore Dreiser, author of *Sister Carrie* and *An American Tragedy,* and his brother, Paul Dresser, composer of Indiana's state song, "On the Banks of the Wabash," lived here. Eugene V. Debs founded the American Railway Union, the first industrial union in America, in Terre h aute. The city is the home of Rose-h ulman Institute of Technology, established in 1874.

Information: Terre Haute Convention and Visitors Bureau, 643 Wabash Ave., 812-234-5555, 800-366-3043; www.terrehaute.com

HOTELS

★**Drury Inn**
3050 Hwy. 41 S., Terre Haute, 812-234-4268, 800-282-8733; www.druryhotels.com
64 rooms. Pets accepted, some restrictions.

★**Fairfield Inn**
475 E. Margaret Ave., Terre Haute, 812-235-2444; www.fairfieldinn.com
62 rooms. Complimentary continental breakfast. Check-in 3 p.m., check-out noon. Indoor pool, whirlpool. **$**

★★**Holiday Inn**
3300 Dixie Bee Hwy., Terre Haute, 812-232-6081, 800-465-4329; www.holiday-inn.com
230 rooms. Pets accepted. Restaurant, bar. Fitness room. Indoor pool, whirlpool. **$**

SPECIALTY LODGINGS

The Farrington Bed & Breakfast
931 S. 7th St., Terre Haute; 812-238-0524
Located in the historical district of Terre h aute and built in 1898.
5 rooms. Complimentary full breakfast. **$**

VALPARAISO

This northern Indiana town, located two hours from Chicago, has a quaint and historic town center.

Information: Chamber of Commerce, 150 Lincolnway, 219-462-1105; www.ci.valparaiso.in.us

HOTELS

★Best Western Expressway Inn
760 Morthland Dr., Valparaiso,
219-464-8555, 800-321-2211;
www.bestwestern.com
54 rooms. $

★★Courtyard by Marriott
2301 E. Morthland Dr., Valparaiso,
219-465-1700;
www.courtyard.com
111 rooms. Restaurant. Fitness room. Indoor pool, outdoor pool, whirlpool. $

★★Indian Oak Resort & Spa
558 Indian Boundary Rd., Chesterton,
219-926-2200, 800-552-4232;
www.indianoak.com
93 rooms. Complimentary continental breakfast. Restaurant. Fitness room. Indoor pool, whirlpool. Business center. $

RESTAURANTS

★Billy Jack's Cafe & Grill
2904 N. Calumet Ave., Valparaiso,
219-477-3797
Italian, Southwestern menu. Lunch, dinner. Bar. Children's menu. Casual attire. $$

★Bistro 157
157 Lincolnway, Valparaiso,
219-462-0992
International menu. Lunch, dinner. Closed Monday. Casual attire. Outdoor seating. $$

★★Dish Restaurant
3907 Calumet Ave., Valparaiso,
219-465-9221
American menu. Lunch, dinner. Closed Sunday. Bar. Casual attire. $$

★Don Quijote
119 E. Lincolnway, Valparaiso,
219-462-7976;
www.donquijoterestaurant-in.com
Spanish menu. Lunch, dinner. Closed Sunday. Children's menu. Casual attire. Reservations recommended. Outdoor seating. $$

★★Strongbow Inn
2405 E. Route 30, Valparaiso,
219-462-5121;
www.strongbowinn.com
American menu. Lunch, dinner. Bar. Children's menu. Casual attire. $$

WARSAW

Warsaw is located in the Indiana lake region and is a popular vacation spot. Many lakes in surrounding Kosciusko County have excellent swimming and boating facilities. Kosciusko County is also home to the world's largest duck producer, Maple Leaf Farms.

Information: Kosciusko County Convention and Visitors Bureau, 313 S. Buffalo St., 574-269-6090, 800-800-6090; www.wkchamber.com

HOTELS

★★Ramada Plaza
2519 E. Center St., Warsaw,
574-269-2323, 800-272-6232;
www.ramada.com
156 rooms. Pets accepted. Restaurant, bar. Fitness room. Indoor pool, outdoor pool, whirlpool. $

OHIO

NOT EVERY VACATION LEAVES YOU FEELING AS SPRIGHTLY AS A YOUTH. BUT WITH ITS renowned art museums and orchestras, quaint Lake Erie resorts and famous amusement parks, Ohio can bring out the kid in you, no matter what your age.

Between fishing on Lake Erie and the area's miles of hiking trails, Northeast Ohio is an ideal stop for nature lovers. For the ultimate outdoor adventure, visit Cuyahoga Valley National Park, covering 33,000 acres along the banks of the Cuyahoga River. Whether you like sweating it out on steep backcountry slopes, cycling or taking a stroll on the groomed Ohio and Erie Canal Towpath Trail, the park offers something for all outdoor enthusiasts.

Since you're already in the neighborhood, and in a sporting mood, make a stop at the Pro Football Hall of Fame in nearby Canton and learn about the game's heroes.

Or continue on to Cleveland, where a rich arts scene, stellar sports teams and diverse neighborhoods make it one of the Midwest's most unique cities. Enjoy a night at the theater at Playhouse Square or experience University Circle, where you can see famed paintings at the Cleveland Museum of Art, explore 10 acres of landscaped gardens at the Cleveland Botanical Garden and hear the Cleveland Orchestra's symphonic sounds at Severance Hall.

Prefer rock to Ravel? No problem. Head to the Rock and Roll Hall of Fame. Perched on Cleveland's lakefront, the museum houses some of the world's most legendary rock-and-roll memorabilia, including Janis Joplin's car and Jimi Hendrix' guitars.

If you'd rather feel the beat of feet stomping in a deafening stadium, don scarlet and gray and hasten to Ohio State University in Columbus. The state's capital and largest city is home not only to the Columbus Museum of Art and a popular ethnic dining scene, but also to the Ohio State Buckeyes—and their storied football and basketball history.

For a fun family getaway, a trip to southern Ohio is a must. Take a whitewater rafting trip down the Ohio River, learn about Ohio's integral role in the anti-slavery movement at Cincinnati's National Underground Railroad Freedom Center and get a thrill on one of 80 rollercoasters, water rides and other attractions at nearby Paramount's Kings Island.

Want even more amusement? Make your way to Cedar Point in Sandusky. The second oldest amusement park in North America boasts the most rides and some of the highest and fastest coasters in the world.

★
★
★
☆
☆

 SPOTLIGHT

★ Seven U.S. presidents were born in Ohio, making it the home state to the most presidents in history after Virginia.

★ Aviation pioneers Wilbur and Orville Wright, Neil Armstrong and John Glenn are all Ohioans.

★ Cleveland disc jockey Alan Freed coined the term "rock and roll" in 1951.

★ Ohio State University, with 60,000 students, is the largest university in the country.

★ A unique Ohio treat is the buckeye—a candy version of the nut of the state tree made of peanut butter fudge dipped in chocolate.

AKRON

Once called the "rubber capital of the world," Akron is the headquarters for four major rubber companies, including Goodyear and Firestone.

Akron owes its start to the Ohio and Erie Canal, which was opened in 1827. The town was already thriving when Dr. Benjamin Franklin Goodrich launched the first rubber plant here in 1870. When automobiles were invented, Akron became a boomtown. ThougHindustry isn't quite what it once was, the signs of the city's past affluence can still be seen.

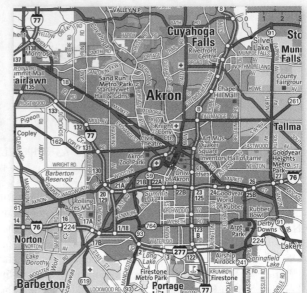

Information: Akron-Summit Convention and Visitors Bureau, 77 E. Mill St., 330-374-7560, 800-245-4254; www.visitakron-summit.org

WHAT TO SEE AND DO

Hale Farm and Village
2686 Oak Hill Rd., Bath, 330-666-3711, 800-589-9703; www.wrhs.org-halefarm

Authentic Western Reserve house circa 1825; other authentic buildings in a village setting depict northeastern Ohio's rural life in the mid-1800s. Memorial Day-October: Wednesday-Saturday 11 a.m.-5 p.m., Sunday noon-5 p.m.

Quaker Square
135 S. Broadway, Akron, 330-253-5970; www.quakersquare.com

Shopping, restaurants and an entertainment center can be found in the original mills and silos of the Quaker Oats Company. historical displays include famous Quaker Oats advertising memorabilia. Monday-Thursday 10 a.m.-8 p.m., Saturday 10-a.m.-9 p.m., Sunday 10 a.m.-6 p.m.

Stan Hywet Hall and Gardens
714 N. Portage Path, Akron,

330-836-5533; www.stanhywet.org

This Tudor Revival manor house built by F. A. Seiberling, co-founder of Goodyear Tire & Rubber, contains 65 rooms with antiques and art, with some pieces dating from the 14th century. More than 70 acres of grounds and gardens. Daily 9 a.m.-6 p.m.; also January.

HOTELS

★Best Western Executive Inn
2677 Gilchrist Rd., Akron, 330-794-1050, 800-528-1234; www.bestwestern.com

112 rooms. Complimentary continental breakfast. Fitness room. Outdoor pool. $

★★Holiday Inn
4073 Medina Rd., Akron, 330-666-4131, 800-465-4329; www.holiday-inn.com

166 rooms. Restaurant. Fitness room. Outdoor pool. $

★★Radisson Inn Akron-Fairlawn
200 Montrose West Ave., Akron,

330-666-9300, 800-333-3333;
www.radisson.com
128 rooms. Restaurant, bar. Fitness room. Indoor pool, whirlpool. Airport transportation available. **$**

★★★Crowne Plaza Quaker Square
135 S. Broadway St., Akron,
330-253-5970, 866-668-6689;
www.crowneplaza.com
Constructed from 19th-century silos and mills that once produced or stored oats for Quaker Oats Company, this historic hotel (which has round guest rooms) is a landmark for Akron. There's also a large entertainment complex with restaurants and shops connected to the hotel.
190 rooms. High-speed Internet access. Four restaurants, two bars. Fitness room. Indoor pool. Airport transportation available. Business center. **$**

★★★Hilton Akron-Fairlawn
3180 W. Market St., Akron,
330-867-5000, 800-445-8667;
www.akronfairlawn.hilton.com
This locally owned hotel is located in the Akron suburb of Fairlawn. Rooms are large and feature marble bathrooms and high-speed Internet access.
203 rooms. Restaurant, bar. Fitness room. Indoor pool, outdoor pool, whirlpool. Airport transportation available. Business center. **$**

RESTAURANTS
★★★Lanning's
826 N. Cleveland-Massillon Rd., Akron,
330-666-1159;
www.lannings-restaurant.com
On the banks of Yellow Creek, this fine dining room offers fresh fish and hand-cut steaks and has been in business since 1967. Everything is made in-house, including salad dressings, sauces, soups, breads and desserts.
American menu. Dinner. Closed Sunday. Bar. Business casual attire. Reservations recommended. Valet parking. **$$$**

★★★Tangier
532 W. Market St., Akron,
330-376-717, 800-826-4437;
www.thetangier.com
This local gem is considered one of Ohio's top spots for live music, from jazz to light rock. Listen to the entertainment while sampling the eclectic Middle Eastern cuisine.
American, Middle Eastern menu. Lunch, dinner. Closed Sunday. Bar. Children's menu. Business casual attire. Reservations recommended. Outdoor seating. **$$$**

★★The Triple Crown
335 S. Main, Munroe Falls,
330-633-5325
American menu. Lunch, dinner. Closed Monday. Bar. Children's menu. Casual attire. Reservations recommended. Outdoor seating. **$$**

★
★
★
★
★

ASHTABULA
This modern harbor at the mouth of the Ashtabula River is an important shipping center for coal and iron ore. The location on Lake Erie makes swimming and fishing popular pastimes here.
Information: Ashtabula Area Chamber of Commerce, 4536 Main Ave., 440-998-6998

HOTELS
★Comfort Inn
1860 Austinburg Rd., Austinburg,
440-275-2711, 800-516-3268;
www.comfortinn.com
119 rooms. Pets accepted; fee. Restaurant, bar. Outdoor pool. **$**

RESTAURANTS
★★El Grande
2145 W. Prospect St., Ashtabula,
440-998-2228
American, Italian menu. Lunch, dinner. Closed Sunday-Monday. **$$**

ATHENS

The founding in 1804 of Ohio University, the oldest college in what was the Northwest Territory, created the town of Athens. Life in this small town revolves around the almost 30,000 students who attend the school.

Information: Athens County Convention and Visitors Bureau, 667 E. State St., 740-592-1819, 800-878-9767; www.athensohio.com

HOTELS

★AmeriHost Inn
20 Home St., Athens,
740-594-3000, 800-434-5800;
www.amerihostinn.com
102 rooms. Complimentary continental breakfast. Fitness room. Indoor pool, whirlpool. $

★★Ohio University Inn and Conference Center
331 Richland Ave., Athens,

740-593-6661; www.ouinn.com
139 rooms. Pets accepted, some restrictions; fee. Restaurant, bar. Outdoor pool. $

RESTAURANTS

★★Seven Sauces
66 N. Court, Athens,
740-592-5555;
www.sevensauces.com
International menu. Dinner. Bar. $$

AURORA

This small city, situated between Cleveland and Akron, attracts visitors for its Geauga Lake theme park (which has everything from roller coasters to waterslides) and the premium outlets located here.

Information: Aurora Chamber of Commerce, 12 W. Garfield, 330-562-3355; www.auroraohiochamber.com

★
★
★
★
★

HOTELS

★★★The Bertram Inn and Conference Center
600 N. Aurora Rd., Aurora,
330-995-0200, 877-995-0200;
www.thebertraminn.com
This sprawling resort attracts large conferences. Rooms are decorated with traditional furnishings. The onsite Leopard Restaurant is acclaimed for its creative cooking—the menu includes everything from lacquered duck with black Thai sticky rice to classic Dover sole.
162 rooms. High-speed Internet access. Restaurant, bar. Outdoor pool, whirlpool. Airport transportation available. Business center. $$

BEACHWOOD

This eastern Cleveland suburb has some of the area's best shopping, thanks to the Beachwood Place Mall and many stores surrounding it.

Information: Beachwood Chamber of Commerce, 24500 Chagrin Blvd., 216-831-0003

HOTELS

★★Courtyard by Marriott
3695 Orange Place, Beachwood,
216-765-1900, 800-321-2211;
www.beachwoodcourtyard.com

113 rooms. High-speed Internet access. Restaurant, bar. Fitness room. Indoor pool, whirlpool. Business center. $

★★Embassy Suites
3775 Park East Dr., Beachwood,
216-765-8066, 800-362-2779;

www.embassysuites.com
216 rooms, all suites. Complimentary full breakfast. High-speed Internet access. Restaurant, bar. Fitness room. Indoor pool, whirlpool. Business center. **$$**

★★**Holiday Inn**
3750 Orange Place, Beachwood,
216-831-3300, 800-465-4329;
www.holiday-inn.com
170 rooms. Pets accepted, some restrictions; fee. Restaurant, bar. Fitness room. Indoor pool, outdoor pool. Airport transportation available. **$**

RESTAURANTS
★★★**Ristorante Giovanni**
25550 Chagrin Blvd., Beachwood,
216-831-8625;
www.giovanniscleveland.com
Dine in a romantic setting at this restaurant, which serves fine classic Italian dishes and pastas. Enjoy a good cigar with dessert. Italian menu. Lunch, dinner. Closed Sunday. Bar. Jacket required. Reservations recommended. Valet parking. **$$$**

BURTON
This historic town in Geauga County has several well-preserved buildings as well as a working maple syrup farm.
Information: www.burtonchamberofcommerce.org

RESTAURANTS
★★**Welshfield Inn**
14001 Main Market, Burton,
440-834-4164
American, Italian menu. Lunch, dinner. Closed Tuesday. Children's menu. **$$**

CAMBRIDGE
Cambridge, an important center for the glassmaking industry, was named by settlers who came from England's Isle of Guernsey. At one time a center of mining and oil, it is located at the crossroads of three major federal highways.
Information: Visitors and Convention Bureau, 627 Wheeling Ave., 740-432-2022, 800-933-5480; www.visitguernseycounty.com

HOTELS
★**Best Western Cambridge**
1945 Southgate Pkwy., Cambridge,
740-439-3581, 800-528-1234;
www.bestwestern.com
95 rooms. Pets accepted. Bar. Outdoor pool. **$**

★★**Holiday Inn**
2248 Southgate Pkwy., Cambridge,
740-432-7313, 800-465-4329;
www.holiday-inn.com
108 rooms. Pets accepted. Restaurant, bar. Outdoor pool. **$**

RESTAURANTS
★**Bears Den**
13320 E. Pike, Cambridge,
740-432-5285
American menu. Dinner. Closed Sunday. **$**

★**Theo's**
632 Wheeling Ave., Cambridge,
740-432-3878
Eclectic menu. Lunch, dinner. Closed Sunday. Bar. Casual attire. **$$**

CANTON

In 1867, president-to-be William McKinley opened a law office in Canton and later conducted his "front porch campaign" for the presidency here. After his assassination, his body was brought back to Canton for burial. Because of his love for the red carnation, it was made the state flower.

This large steel-processing city, important a century ago for farm machinery, is in the middle of rich farmland, on the edge of "steel valley" where the three branches of Nimishillen Creek come together. It's also home to the Pro Football Hall of Fame.

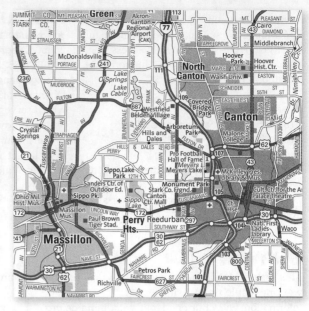

Information: Canton-Stark County Convention and Visitors Bureau, The Millennium Centre, 222 Market Ave. N., 330-454-1439, 800-533-4302; www.visitcantonohio.com

WHAT TO SEE AND DO

Pro Football Hall of Fame
2121 George Halas Dr. N.W., Canton, 330-456-8207; www.profootballhof.com
This museum, a five-building complex, is dedicated to the game of football and its players. It houses memorabilia, a research library, a movie theater and a museum store. Memorial Day-Labor Day: daily 9 a.m.-8 p.m.; rest of year: daily 9 a.m.-5 p.m.

HOTELS

★★Four Points by Sheraton
4375 Metro Circle N.W., Canton, 330-494-6494, 877-867-7666; www.fourpoints.com
152 rooms. Pets accepted. Restaurant, bar. Fitness room. Indoor pool, outdoor pool. Airport transportation available. Business center. $

★Hampton Inn
5335 Broadmoor Circle N.W., Canton, 330-492-0151, 800-426-7866; www.hamptoninn.com
107 rooms. Pets accepted, some restrictions; fee. Complimentary continental breakfast. $

★★Holiday Inn
4520 Everhard Rd. N.W., Canton, 330-494-2770, 800-465-4329; www.holiday-inn.com
194 rooms. Restaurant, bar. Fitness room. Outdoor pool. Airport transportation available. $

RESTAURANTS

★John's
2749 Cleveland Ave., Canton, 330-454-1259; www.johnsgrille.com
American menu. Breakfast, lunch, dinner. Closed Sunday. Bar. Casual attire. $

★★★Lolli's
4801 N.W. Dressler Rd., Canton, 330-492-6846
This restaurant and banquet center in the Belden Village Mall hosts many of the area's special events and has space for up to 375 people. Try reserving a table at the weekly murder mystery dinner theater. Italian, seafood menu. Dinner. Closed Sunday-Wednesday. Bar. $$

★
★
★
★
★
★

CHARDON

This northeastern Ohio town is a Cleveland exurb, and was founded in the late 1700s by pioneers from New England. The charming downtown reflects that heritage in the look of the buildings and the names of the streets.

Information: Chardon Area Chamber of Commerce, 112 E. Park St. 440-285-9050; www.chardon.cc

RESTAURANTS

★★Bass Lake Taverne
426 South St., Chardon,
440-285-3100;
www.basslaketaverne.com
American menu. Lunch, dinner. Bar. Casual attire. Outdoor seating. **$$**

★★The Inn at Fowler's Mill
10700 Mayfield Rd., Chardon,
440-286-3111
American menu. Dinner, Sunday brunch. Closed Monday. Bar. Children's menu. Outdoor seating. **$$$**

CHILLICOTHE

Chillicothe, first capital of the Northwest Territory, became the first capital of Ohio in 1803. Among the early settlers from Virginia who helped Ohio achieve statehood were Edward Tiffin, first state governor, and Thomas Worthington, governor and U.S. senator. Greek Revival mansions built for these statesmen can be seen on Chillicothe's Paint Street.

Information: Ross-Chillicothe Convention and Visitors Bureau, 25 E. Main St., 740-702-7677, 800-413-4118; www.chillicotheohio.com-rccvb

HOTELS

★Comfort Inn
20 N. Plaza Blvd., Chillicothe,
740-775-3500, 800-542-7919;
www.comfortinn.com
106 rooms. Pets accepted. Complimentary continental breakfast. Bar. Outdoor pool. **$**

★Hampton Inn
100 N. Plaza Blvd., Chillicothe,
740-773-1616, 800-426-7866;
www.hamptoninn.com

71 rooms. Complimentary continental breakfast. Fitness room. Indoor pool, whirlpool. Business center. **$**

RESTAURANTS

★Damon's
10 N. Plaza Blvd., Chillicothe,
740-775-8383;
www.damons.com
American menu. Lunch, dinner. Bar. Children's menu. Casual attire. **$$**

CINCINNATI

Cincinnati was a busy frontier riverboat town and one of the largest cities in the nation when poet Henry Wadsworth Longfellow called it the "queen city of the West." Although other cities farther west have since outstripped it in size, Cincinnati is still the Queen City to its inhabitants and to the many visitors who are rediscovering it. With a wealth of fine restaurants, a redeveloped downtown with a Skywalk, its own Montmartre in Mount Adams and the beautiful Ohio River, Cincinnati has a cosmopolitan flavor uniquely its own.

Early settlers chose the site because it was an important river crossroads used by Native Americans. In 1790, Arthur St. Clair, governor of the Northwest Territory, changed the name of Losantiville to Cincinnati in honor of the revolutionary officers' Society of Cincinnati. Despite smallpox, insects, floods and crop failures, approximately 15,000 settlers came in the next five years. They had the protection of General Anthony Wayne, who broke the resistance of the Ohio Native Americans. In the early 1800s, a large influx of immigrants, mostly German, settled in the area.

During the Civil War, the city was generally loyal to the Union, althougHits location on the Mason-Dixon line and the interruption of its trade with the SoutHcaused mixed emotions. After the Civil War, prosperity brought art, music, a new library and a professional baseball team. A period of municipal corruption in the late 19tHcentury was ended by a victory for reform elements and the establishment of a city manager form of government, which has earned Cincinnati the title of America's best-governed city.

Today, the city is the home of two universities and several other institutions of higher education and has its own symphony orchestra, opera and ballet. Major hotels, stores, office complexes, restaurants, entertainment centers and the Cincinnati Convention Center are now connected by a skywalk system, making the city easy to walk, even in winter. Information: Greater Cincinnati Convention and Visitors Bureau, 300 W. 6th St., 800-246-2987; www.cincyusa.com

132

OHIO

SPOT★ LIGHT

★TV HOST JERRY SPRINGER WAS MAYOR OF CINNCINNATI IN THE 1970S.

★CINNCINNATI CHILI IS MADE WITH CINNAMON AND CHOCOLATE AND SERVED OVER SPAGHETTI.

WHAT TO SEE AND DO

Cincinnati Zoo and Botanical Garden
3400 Vine St., Cincinnati,
513-281-4700;
www.cincyzoo.org
More than 700 species can be seen in a variety of naturalistic habitats, including the world-famous gorillas and white Bengal tigers. The Cat house features 16 species of cats; the Jungle Trails exhibit is an indoor-outdoor rain forest. Rare okapi, walrus, Komodo dragons and giant eland also are on display. Participatory children's zoo. Animal shows summer. Elephant and camel rides. Picnic areas, restaurant. Daily, hours vary.

Eden Park
Gilbert Ave., Cincinnati
More than 185 acres initially called "the Garden of Eden." Ice skating on Mirror Lake. The Murray Seasongood Pavilion features spring and summer band concerts and other events. Four overlooks with scenic views of the Ohio River, the city and Kentucky hillsides.

Harriet Beecher Stowe House
2950 Gilbert Ave., Cincinnati,

513-632-5120
The author of Uncle Tom's Cabin lived here from 1832 to 1836. Completely restored with some original furnishings. Tuesday-Thursday, by appointment only.

Museum of Natural History & Science
1301 Western Ave., Cincinnati,
513-287-7000
This museum depicts the natural history of the Ohio Valley. Wilderness Trail with Ohio flora and fauna and full-scale walk-through replica of a cavern with 32-foot waterfall; Children's Discovery Center. Monday-Saturday 10 a.m.-5 p.m., Sunday 11 a.m.-6 p.m.

William Howard Taft National Historic Site
2038 Auburn Ave., Cincinnati,
513-684-3262;
www.nps.gov-wiho
This is the birthplace and boyhood home of the 27th president and chief justice of the United States. Four rooms with period furnishings; other rooms contain exhibits on Taft's life and careers. Daily 8 a.m.-4 p.m.

Cincinnati Ballet
Aronoff Center, 1555 Central Pkwy., Cincinnati, 513-621-5219;
www.cincinnatiballet.com
Performs a five-series program at the Aronoff Center of both contemporary and classical works. October-May; the Nutcracker is staged at Cincinnati Music h all during December.

Cincinnati Opera
Cincinnati Music Hall, 1241 Elm St., Cincinnati,
513-241-2742;
www.cincinnatiopera.com
The nation's second-oldest opera company offers a summer season; capsulized English translations projected above the stage complement all productions. Mid-June-mid-July.

Cincinnati Symphony Orchestra
Cincinnati Music Hall, 1241 Elm St., Cincinnati, 513-381-3300;

www.cincinnatisymphony.org
The fifth-oldest orchestra presents symphony and pops programs. September-May.

HOTELS
★Comfort Inn Northeast
9011 Fields Ertel Rd., Cincinnati,
513-683-9700, 800-424-6423;
www.comfortinn.com
112 rooms. Complimentary continental breakfast. High-speed Internet access, wireless Internet access. Outdoor pool. **$**

★★Courtyard by Marriott Cincinnati Blue Ash
4625 Lake Forest Dr., Cincinnati,
513-733-4334, 800-321-2211;
www.courtyard.com
Designed for business travelers but also family-friendly, this stylish, affordable hotel is conveniently located near major highways and about 15 minutes from downtown. The casual lobby features plenty of overstuffed seating and a large flat-screen TV. The well-appointed guest rooms are spacious and wired for work needs. 149 rooms. High-speed Internet access. Fitness room. Indoor pool, whirlpool. Business center. **$**

★★Embassy Suites
4554 Lake Forest Dr., Blue Ash,
513-733-8900, 800-362-2779;
www.embassysuites.com
235 rooms, all suites. Complimentary full breakfast. Restaurant, bar. Fitness room. Indoor pool, whirlpool. **$$**

★Hampton Inn
10900 Crowne Point Dr., Cincinnati,
513-771-6888
130 rooms. Complimentary continental breakfast. Outdoor pool. **$**

★★Holiday Inn Cincinnati Eastgate
4501 Eastgate Blvd., Cincinnati,
513-752-4400, 800-465-4329;
www.holiday-inn.com
247 rooms. Check-in 3 p.m., check-out 1 p.m. Wireless Internet access. Restaurant,

133

OHIO

bar. Fitness room. Indoor pool, whirlpool. Business center. **$**

★★Vernon Manor Hotel
400 Oak St., Cincinnati,
513-281-3300, 800-543-3999;
www.vernon-manor.com
177 rooms. Pets accepted, some restrictions; fee. Wireless Internet access. Restaurant, bar. Fitness room. Business center. **$**

★★★★Cincinnatian Hotel
601 Vine St., Cincinnati,
513-381-3000, 800-942-9000;
www.cincinnatianhotel.com
Open since 1882, the Cincinnatian hotel was one of the first hotels in the world to have elevators and incandescent lighting and now is listed on the National Register of historic Places. The accommodations are lovingly maintained and incorporate modern technology, like high-speed Internet access and multiline telephones. Furnishings lean toward the contemporary, while some rooms feature balconies and fireplaces. The eight-story atrium of the Cricket Lounge serves afternoon tea and evening cocktails. The fine dining and impeccable service at the Palace Restaurant make it one of the top tables in town.
146 rooms. Pets accepted. High-speed Internet access, wireless Internet access. Restaurant, bar. Fitness room. **$$**

★★★Hilton Cincinnati Netherland Plaza
35 W. Fifth St., Cincinnati,
513-421-9100, 800-445-8667;
www.hilton.com
The h ilton Cincinnati Netherland Plaza is a showpiece of Art Deco design in the heart of the city. Listed on the National Register of historic Places, this elegant hotel marries historic character with modern amenities. The hotel's restaurant, the Palm Court Restaurant, is one of the city's most fashionable dining rooms.
561 rooms. High-speed Internet access. Three restaurants, bar. Fitness room, fitness classes available. Indoor pool. Business center. **$$**

★★★Hyatt Regency Cincinnati
151 W. 5th St., Cincinnati,
513-579-1234, 800-233-1234;
www.cincinnati.hyatt.com
This well-appointed, moderately priced hotel is located across from the convention center and connected to the business district and a shopping mall by an enclosed skywalk. The bright and airy atrium lobby, with its huge skylight and fountain complements the cheery guest rooms with traditional furnishings. One restaurant serves breakfast and lunch buffets, while a sports bar offers televisions, pool tables and traditional bar food.
488 rooms. Wireless Internet access. Two restaurants, two bars. Fitness room. Indoor pool, whirlpool. Business center. **$$**

★★★Marriott Cincinnati Airport
2395 Progress Dr., Hebron, Kentucky,
859-586-0166;
www.marriott.com
This airport has a fitness center, indoor pool and rooms updated with plush beds and linens. Complimentary shuttle service to the airport is available 24 hours a day.
295 rooms. Restaurant. Fitness room. Indoor pool. Business center. **$$**

★★★Marriott Cincinnati North
6189 Muhlhauser Rd., West Chester,
513-874-7335, 800-228-9290;
www.marriott.com
Located near Interstate 75 between Cincinnati and Dayton, this hotel is ideal for business travelers. Guest rooms and suites have traditional furniture, luxury bedding and 24-hour room service.
295 rooms. Wireless Internet access. Restaurant, bar. Fitness room. Indoor pool. Business center. **$$**

★★★Millennium Hotel Cincinnati
141 W. Sixth St., Cincinnati,
513-352-2100, 866-866-8086;
www.millenniumhotels.com
Business travelers choose this downtown hotel for amenities like an on-site car rental desk and the enclosed skywalk leading to the convention center. Rooms are decorated

134

OHIO

★
★
★
★
★

with natural wood and glass furnishings and have ergonomic desk chairs. A poolside bar and grill livens up warmer months.
872 rooms. Pets accepted, some restrictions; fee. High-speed Internet access. Restaurant, bar. Fitness room. Outdoor pool. Business center. **$**

★★★The Westin Cincinnati
Fountain Square, Cincinnati,
513-621-7700, 800-937-8461;
www.westin.com
Overlooking the city's Fountain Square and within steps of restaurants, museums and other cultural attractions, this stylish 450-room hotel is connected to a shopping center and the convention center by an enclosed skywalk. Guest rooms feature subdued contemporary furnishings. The on-site restaurant serves American fare while the lounge offers pub food in a sports bar setting.
450 rooms. Pets accepted, some restrictions. High-speed Internet access. Two restaurants, two bars. Fitness room. Indoor pool, whirlpool. Business center. **$$**

RESTAURANTS
★Aglamesis Bros
3046 Madison Rd., Cincinnati,
513-531-5196;
www.aglamesis.com
Deli menu. Lunch. Children's menu. Casual attire. **$**

★★★Celestial
1071 Celestial St., Cincinnati,
513-241-4455;
www.thecelestial.com
This restaurant's name could just as easily refer to its stunning view of the Ohio River and city as to its street address. Dining takes place in a clubby atmosphere of carved wood. Stop at the Incline Lounge to sip a cocktail and watch the sunset.
Steak menu. Dinner. Bar. Business casual attire. Reservations recommended. Valet parking. Outdoor seating. **$$**

★★Ferrari's Little Italy
7677 Goff Terrace, Madeira,

513-272-2220;
www.ferrarilittleitaly.com
Italian menu. Lunch, dinner. Bar. Children's menu. Casual attire. Reservations recommended. Outdoor seating. **$$$**

★★Germano's
9415 Montgomery Rd., Cincinnati,
513-794-1155;
www.germanosrestaurant.com
Italian menu. Lunch, dinner. Closed Sunday-Monday. Business casual attire. Reservations recommended. **$$$**

★★Grand Finale
3 E. Sharon Rd., Glendale,
513-771-5925;
www.grandfinale.info
American menu. Lunch, dinner. Closed Monday. Bar. Children's menu. Business casual attire. Reservations recommended. Outdoor seating. **$$$**

★House of Tam
889 W. GalbraitHRd., Cincinnati,
513-729-5566
Chinese menu. Lunch, dinner. Closed Sunday. Business casual attire. **$$**

★★Iron Horse Restaurant
40 Village Square, Glendale.
513-771-4787
www.ironhorseinn.com
American menu. Lunch, dinner. Bar. Children's menu. Casual attire. Outdoor seating. **$$**

★★★★Jean-Robert at Pigall's
127 W. Fourth St., Cincinnati,
513-721-1345;
www.pigalls.com
Jean-Robert at Pigall's serves the sort of inventive, high-quality food that has fans, who pay $75 for three courses, feel as though they've had a bargain. Chef Jean-Robert de Cavel reinvigorated the hoary Pigall's with fresh, sophisticated decor and a lively new menu. Although changed to reflect the season, Pigall's French cuisine is typified by cauliflower vichyssoise with truffles, crab and melon salad with caviar,

and bacon-wrapped guinea fowl. The chef engenders goodwill by frequently issuing surprise plates on the house.
French menu. Lunch, dinner. Closed Sunday-Monday. Bar. Business casual attire. Reservations recommended. Valet parking. $$

★★Jeanro
413 Vine St., Cincinnati,
513-621-1465;
www.bistrojeanro.com
Country French menu. Lunch, dinner. Bar. Casual attire. Reservations recommended. $$$

★Le Boxx Cafe
819 Vine St., Cincinnati,
513-721-5638
www.leboxxcafe.com
American menu. Lunch. Closed Saturday-Sunday. Bar. Casual attire. $

★Christy's and Lenhardt's
151 W. McMillan St., Cincinnati,
513-281-3600;
www.christysandlenhardts.com
German, h ungarian menu. Lunch, dinner, late-night. Closed Sunday-Monday. Bar. Casual attire. Reservations recommended. Outdoor seating. $$

★Mecklenburg Gardens
302 E. University, Cincinnati,
513-221-5353;
www.mecklenburgs.net
German menu. Lunch, dinner. Closed Sunday. Bar. Children's menu. Casual attire. Reservations recommended. Outdoor seating. $$

★★Montgomery Inn
9440 Montgomery Rd., Montgomery,
513-791-3482;
www.montgomeryinn.com
American menu. Lunch, dinner. Bar. Children's menu. Casual attire. Valet parking. $$

★★Montgomery Inn at the Boathouse
925 Eastern Ave., Cincinnati,
513-721-7427;

www.montgomeryinn.com
American menu. Lunch, dinner. Bar. Children's menu. Casual attire. Valet parking. Outdoor seating. $$

★★National Exemplar
6880 Wooster Pike, Mariemont,
513-271-2103;
www.nationalexemplar.com
American menu. Breakfast, lunch, dinner. Bar. Children's menu. Casual attire. Reservations recommended. $$

★★Nicola's
1420 Sycamore St., Cincinnati,
513-721-6200;
www.nicolasrestaurant.com
Italian menu. Dinner. Closed Sunday. Bar. Business casual attire. Reservations recommended. Valet parking. Outdoor seating. $$$

★★★Orchids at Palm Court
35 W. 5th St., Cincinnati,
513-421-9100;
www.hilton.com
The Orchids at Palm Court, located in the h ilton Cincinnati Netherland Plaza, has an elegant dining room with friendly, accommodating service. Menu standouts include the phyllo venison wrapped in bacon. On Fridays and Saturdays, a jazz trio and pianist perform.
American menu. Breakfast, lunch, dinner, Sunday brunch. Bar. Children's menu. Business casual attire. Reservations recommended. Valet parking. $$

★★★Precinct
311 Delta Ave., Cincinnati,
513-321-5454, 877-321-5454;
www.jeffruby.com
This restaurant, housed in a former police precinct that was used from the 1900s to the 1940s, offers steakhouse classics—from aged Angus beef to the perfect ribeye broiled to perfection and seasoned with a secret spice mix. At night, the exterior of this historic building is bathed in neon light. Dishes such as steak Diane, fettuccine and bananas Foster are prepared tableside.

Steak menu. Dinner. Bar. Business casual attire. Reservations recommended. Valet parking. $$$$

★★★Primavista
810 Matson Place, Cincinnati,
513-251-6467;
www.pvista.com
The view of Cincinnati from its floor-to-ceiling windows is one reason to dine at Primavista, but it's not the only one. A menu of creative but classic Italian fare including fresh seafood, meat and veal specialties as well as pizzas and pasta dishes are featured. Dishes include pine nut crusted salmon over fettuccine with pesto cream sauce and roasted tomatoes, filet mignon broiled and served with calamari, and linguine tossed in fresh cream, pancetta, egg and green peas.
Italian menu. Dinner. Bar. Business casual attire. Reservations recommended. $$$

★★★The Palace
601 Vine St., Cincinnati,
513-381-3000, 800-942-9000;
www.palacecincinnati.com
This elegant restaurant inside the Cincinnatian hotel is now under the direction of Alsatian chef Romuald Jung. The menu features traditional, French-influenced dishes such as rack of lamb with fava beans and fingerling potatoes, or prime ribeye with potato puree.
American menu. Breakfast, lunch, dinner. Closed Sunday. Bar. Children's menu. Business casual attire. Reservations recommended. Valet parking. $$$

★★★The Phoenix Restaurant
812 Race St., Cincinnati,
513-721-8901;
www.thephx.com
Built in 1893, this traditional restaurant serves dinner in the wood-paneled President's Room, while the rest of the historic building, whichis adorned with two elegant chandeliers, is used for weddings or special events. The menu features steaks and other classics like the grilled pork chop with walnut stuffing and sage buerre blanc.
Continental menu. Dinner. Closed Sunday-Tuesday. Bar. Business casual attire. Reservations recommended. Valet parking. $$$

137

CLEVELAND
Ohio's second-largest city extends 50 miles east and north along the shore of Lake Erie and 25 miles south inland. It is a combination of industrial flats, spacious suburbs, wide principal streets and an informal spirit, due partially to its diverse population. Many nationalities have contributed to the city's growth—Poles, Italians, Croats, Slovaks, Serbs, Lithuanians, Germans, Irish, Romanians, Russians and Greeks. In the past, the various national groups divided regionally, but this is less true today.

Cleveland's history is peppered with industrial giants—John D. Rockefeller, the Mathers of iron and shipping, Mark Hanna of steel and political fame, the Van Sweringens, and others. The village, founded by Moses Cleaveland, profited from the combination of Great Lakes transportation and fertile farm land. At the time, northern Ohio was still almost entirely unoccupied, and growtHwas slow. Not until 1827, when the Ohio Canal was opened to join Lake Erie with the Ohio River, did the town start to expand. Incoming supplies of coal and iron ore jump-started a manufacturing industry. The boom era after World War I brought bedroom communities like Shaker Heights, one of the more affluent suburbs; the Terminal Tower Group of buildings downtown; and the Group Plan, with civic buildings surrounding a central mall.

The layout of the city is systematic. All the main avenues lead to the Public Square Tower City Center, where the Terminal Tower is located. The east-west dividing line is Ontario Street, which runs nortHand soutHthrougHthe square. Euclid Avenue is the main business street running througHCleveland and many of its suburbs. Many of the early buildings have been razed and replaced by planned urban architecture, including "Millionaire's Row" and the magnificent mansions on Euclid Avenue.

Sports are a favorite pastime here, whether it's Cleveland Browns football (so beloved the city sued to stop the team from leaving for Baltimore in the 1990s; the team went, but the city kept the name and launched an expansion franchise in 1999), Indians baseball or Cavaliers basketball. In 1995, the Rock and Roll Hall of Fame opened on the city's lakefront in an I. M. Pei–designed building. This and new stadiums for all three sports teams continue to draw visitors to the city's downtown.

Information: Convention and Visitors Bureau of Greater Cleveland, 3100 Terminal Tower, 216-621-4110, 800-321-1001, www.travelcleveland.com

138

OHIO

★

★

★

★

★

SPOT★ LIGHT

★THE CLEVELAND BROWNS ARE THE ONLY TEAM IN THE NFL TO HAVE A LOGO-FREE HELMET.

★THE MOONDOG CORONATION BALL, HELD IN CLEVELAND IN 1952, WAS THE FIRST ROCK AND ROLL CONCERT.

WHAT TO SEE AND DO

Cleveland Metroparks Zoo
3900 Wildlife Way, Cleveland,
216-661-6500;
www.clemetzoo.com
The seventh-oldest zoo in the country, this zoo has more than 3,300 animals. Includes mammals, land and water birds; animals displayed in naturalized settings. More than 600 animals and 7,000 plants are featured in the two-acre Rain Forest exhibit. Daily 10 a.m.-5 p.m.

Cleveland Metroparks
4101 Fulton Pkwy., Cleveland,
216-635-2300;
www.clemetparks.com

Established in 1917, this park system circles the city with more than 20,000 acres of land in 14 reservations, their connecting parkways and the Cleveland Metroparks Zoo. Bike paths lace throughout the park, and driving through the heavily wooded areas is a favorite fall pastime. Also available are swimming, boating and fishing, picnic areas and play fields; wildlife management areas and waterfowl sanctuaries; hiking and bridle trails, stables; golf courses; tobogganing, sledding, skating and cross-country skiing areas; eight outdoor education facilities offer nature exhibits and programs.

Cleveland Museum of Art
11150 East Blvd., Cleveland,

216-421-7340;
www.clemusart.com
Extensive collections of approximately 30,000 works of art represent a wide range of history and culture. Included are arts of the Islamic Near East, the pre-Columbian Americas and European and Asian art; also African, Indian, American, ancient Roman and Egyptian art. Concerts, lectures, special exhibitions, films; cafe. Parking fee. Tuesday-Sunday.

Cleveland Museum of Natural History
1 Wade Oval, Cleveland,
216-231-4600, 800-317-9155;
www.cmnh.org
Dinosaurs, mammals, birds, geological specimens, gems; exhibits on prehistoric Ohio, North American native cultures, ecology; Woods Garden, live animals; library. Monday-Saturday 10 a.m.-5 p.m., Wednesday to 10 p.m., Sunday from noon.

Cleveland Orchestra
Severance Hall, 11001 Euclid Ave.,
Cleveland, 216-231-1111;
www.clevelandorchestra.com
One of the world's finest orchestras. International soloists and guest conductors are featured each season. During summer months, the orchestra performs at Blossom Music Center, approximately 28 miles south via Interstate 71. Mid-September-mid-May, Tuesday and Thursday-Sunday.

Great Lakes Science Center
601 Erieside Ave., Cleveland,
216-694-2000; www.greatscience.com
More than 350 hands-on exhibits explain scientific principles and topics specifically relating to the Great Lakes region. Also features an Omnimax domed theater. Daily.

Playhouse Square Center
1501 Euclid Ave., Cleveland,
216-241-6000, 800-766-6048;
www.playhousesquare.org
Five restored theaters form the nation's second-largest performing arts and entertainment center. Performances include theater, Broadway productions, popular and classical music, ballet, opera, children's theater and concerts.

Rock and Roll Hall of Fame and Museum
1 Key Plaza, Cleveland,
216-781-7625, 888-764-7625;
www.rockhall.com
A striking composition of geometric shapes, this I. M. Pei–designed building is the permanent home of the rock 'n' roll hall of fame. More than 50,000 square feet of exhibition areas explore rock's ongoing evolution and its impact on culture. Interactive database of rock and roll songs; videos; working studio with DJs conducting live broadcasts; exhibits on rhythm and blues, soul, country, folk and blues music. Thursday-Tuesday 10 a.m.-5:30 p.m., Wednesday to 9 p.m.

Cleveland Botanical Garden
11030 East Blvd., Cleveland,
216-721-1600
h erb, rose, perennial, wildflower, Japanese, and reading gardens. Grounds April-October: Monday-Saturday 10 a.m.-5 p.m., Sunday from noon; November-March: Tuesday-Saturday 10 a.m.-5 p.m., Sunday from noon.

Frederick C. Crawford Auto-Aviation Museum
Magnolia Dr. and E. 108th, Cleveland,
216-721-5722
This museum has an extensive collection of antique cars, planes, and 20th-century motorcycles and bicycles. Monday-Saturday 10 a.m.-5 p.m., Sunday from noon.

HOTELS
★Comfort Inn
17550 RosboughDr., Middleburg Heights,
440-234-3131, 800-424-6423;
www.comfortinn.com
136 rooms. Pets accepted, some restrictions; fee. Complimentary continental breakfast. Outdoor pool. Airport transportation available. Business center. $

★Hampton Inn
1460 E. Ninth St., Cleveland,

★
★
★
★
★

216-241-6600;
www.hamptoninn.com
192 rooms. Fitness room. **$**

★★Hilton Garden Inn
1100 Carnegie Ave., Cleveland,
216-658-6400, 877-782-9444;
www.hiltongardeninn.com
240 rooms. Restaurant, bar. Fitness room.
Indoor pool, whirlpool. Business center. **$**

★Howard Johnson Cleveland Airport
16644 Snow Rd., Brook Park,
216-676-5200; 800-446-4656;
www.howardjohnson.com
135 rooms. Pets accepted; fee. Complimentary continental breakfast. Outdoor pool. **$**

★★Radisson Hotel Cleveland Airport
25070 Country Club Blvd., North Olmsted,
440-734-5060, 800-333-3333;
www.radisson.com
Though this hotel is actually located about a 10-minute drive from the airport, it still caters to business travelers with its high-speed Internet access, spacious work areas and upgraded plush beds. The Great Northern Mall and its many shops and restaurants are nearby.
140 rooms. Pets accepted, some restrictions; fee. Restaurant, bar. Fitness room. Indoor pool, whirlpool. Airport transportation available. **$**

★★★Cleveland Airport Marriott
4277 W. 150th St., Cleveland,
216-252-5333, 800-228-9290;
www.marriott.com
This hotel is located near Cleveland h opkins Airport and 10 miles from downtown. It is near tennis courts, golf courses and attractions.
375 rooms. Pets accepted; fee. Restaurant, bar. Fitness room. Indoor pool, whirlpool. Airport transportation available. **$$**

★★★Embassy Suites
1701 E. 12th St., Cleveland,
216-523-8000, 800-362-2779;
www.embassysuites.com

Located in downtown Cleveland, this all-suite hotel is two blocks away from the Galleria and Playhouse Square, and just seven blocks away from the Rock and Roll h all of Fame.
268 rooms, all suites. Complimentary full breakfast. High-speed Internet access. Restaurant, bar. Fitness room. Indoor pool. Business center. **$$**

★★★Hyatt Regency Cleveland at The Arcade
420 Superior, Cleveland,
216-575-1234, 800-233-1234;
www.cleveland.hyatt.com
Attached to the 1890 Cleveland Arcade, one of America's first indoor shopping malls, this hotel has updated rooms featuring Portico bath products and luxury linens. The onsite-spa offers a complete menu of services.
293 rooms. High-speed Internet access. Two restaurants, bar. Fitness room. Business center. **$**

★★★InterContinental Hotel & Conference Center
9801 Carnegie Ave., Cleveland,
216-707-4100, 888-424-6835;
www.intercontinental.com
This hotel has rooms with flat-screen TVs, minibars, easy chairs and Audley bath amenities. There's a state-of-the-art fitness facility and well-equipped business center, and the friendly staff will arrange everything from laundry and dry cleaning to babysitting. The Rock and Roll h all of Fame, Cleveland Art Museum, and Cleveland Clinic are all nearby.
299 rooms. High-speed Internet access. Three restaurants, two bars. Fitness room. Airport transportation available. Business center. **$$$**

★★★★The Ritz-Carlton, Cleveland
1515 W. Third St., Cleveland,
216-623-1300, 866-372-7868;
www.ritzcarlton.com
Adjacent to Cleveland's Tower City Center and close to the Cleveland Indians' Jacobs Field, this elegant hotel offers downtown

visitors a place to stay in style. The guest rooms, with city and water views, are luxuriously appointed, from the marble-clad bathrooms to the plush terry robes. Even pets are pampered here, with cookies upon check-in, a personalized water bowl and pet room-service menu; walking service is available for a fee. All-day dining at Muse features a seafood-heavy menu dotted with updated comfort-food like truffled macaroni and cheese. By day, the Lobby Lounge serves afternoon tea, while in the evening live entertainment attracts hotel guests and locals alike.

208 rooms. Pets accepted; fee. High-speed Internet access. Restaurant, two bars. Fitness room, spa. Indoor pool, whirlpool. Airport transportation available. Business center.

★★★Wyndham Cleveland at Playhouse Square
1260 Euclid Ave., Cleveland,
216-615-7500, 800-996-3426;
www.wyndhamcleveland.com
The city's historic theaters are located just around the corner from this downtown hotel. Rooms are spacious with plenty of work space and feature h erman Miller Aeron desk chairs.
205 rooms. Restaurant, bar. Fitness room. Indoor pool, whirlpool. Airport transportation available. $

★★★Baricelli Inn
2203 Cornell Rd., Cleveland,
216-791-6500; www.baricelli.com
This charming 1896 brownstone with individually decorated rooms is known for its superb restaurant. The chef combines American cuisine with European flare.
7 rooms. Complimentary continental breakfast. Restaurant. $$

★★★Glidden House Inn
1901 Ford Dr., Cleveland,
216-231-8900, 800-759-8358;
www.gliddenhouse.com
With its location on the campus of Case Western Reserve University, this charming inn is close to the medical centers—

including the Cleveland Clinic—and attractions of the school. The contemporary guest rooms have plasma TVs and luxury bedding.
52 rooms. High-speed Internet access Restaurant, bar. Fitness room. Airport transportation available. Business center. $

★★Clarion Hotel
5300 Rockside Rd., Independence,
216-524-0700, 800-424-6423;
www.clarionhotel.com
179 rooms. Pets accepted; fee. High-speed Internet access, wireless Internet access. Restaurant, bar. Children's activity center. Fitness room. Indoor pool, outdoor pool, whirlpool. Tennis. Airport transportation available. Business center. $

★★★Doubletree Hotel Cleveland South
6200 Quarry Lane, Independence,
216-447-1300.
A contemporary stay in a country setting, this hotel located just south of Cleveland includes an amphitheater, an indoor-outdoor pool, a fitness facility and Shula's Steak 2 Restaurant. Local attractions such as Jacob's Field are just a short drive away.
193 rooms. High-speed Internet access, wireless Internet access. Restaurant, bar. Fitness room. Indoor pool, outdoor pool, whirlpool. Airport transportation available. Business center. $

RESTAURANTS
★★★Baricelli Inn
2203 Cornell Rd., Cleveland,
216-791-6500; www.baricelli.com
Located in University Circle's Little Italy neighborhood, this inn and Italian restaurant are perched on a bluff in a large, turn-of-the-century brownstone mansion. The Little Italy location delivers romantic, old-world charm, and the seasonal menu features thoughtful preparations of local ingredients.
Continental menu. Dinner. Closed Sunday. Outdoor seating. $$

★Cafe Sausalito
1301 E. Ninth St., Cleveland,

141

OHIO

216-696-2233
Seafood menu. Lunch, dinner. Closed
Saturday-Sunday. Valet parking. **$$**

★★Don's Lighthouse Grille
8905 Lake Ave., Cleveland,
216-961-6700;
www.donslighthouse.com
American, seafood menu. Lunch, dinner.
Bar. Valet parking. **$$**

★Great Lakes Brewing Co.
2516 Market Ave., Cleveland,
216-771-4404;
www.greatlakesbrewing.com
American menu. Lunch, dinner. Bar. Chil-
dren's menu. Outdoor seating. **$$**

★Guarino's
12309 Mayfield Rd., Cleveland,
216-231-3100
Italian, American menu. Lunch, dinner.
Bar. Children's menu. Reservations recom-
mended. Valet parking. Outdoor seating.
$$

★John Q's Steakhouse
55 Public Square, Cleveland,
216-861-0900;
www.johnqssteakhouse.com
Steak menu. Lunch, dinner. Bar. Children's
menu. Valet parking Sat. Outdoor seating.
$$$

★★★Johnny's Bar
3164 Fulton Rd., Cleveland,
216-281-0055
This Ohio city restaurant serves huge por-
tions of traditional Italian dishes in a classic
setting. Favorites such as veal picatta and
handmade pastas make an appearance on
the menu.
Italian menu. Lunch, dinner. Closed Sunday.
Bar. Reservations recommended. **$$$**

★★★Morton's, The Steakhouse
1600 W. 2nd, Cleveland,
216-621-6200;
www.mortons.com

This branch of the national steakhouse
chain offers more than 10 different cuts
of perfectly prepared steaks, and plenty
of classics from Caesar salad to creamed
spinach to go with them. Traditional
desserts such as thick, creamy cheese-
cake and warm apple pie complete the
experience.
Steak menu. Dinner. Bar. **$$$**

★Players on Madison
14523 Madison Ave., Lakewood,
216-226-5200;
www.playersonmadison.com
Italian menu. Dinner, Sunday brunch. Bar.
$$

★★★Sans Souci
24 Public Square, Cleveland,
216-696-5600
Fine cuisine is served in this comfortable
dining room which has exposed beams and
a stone hearth. This Renaissance hotel space
is sectioned into intimate rooms where classic cooking is served.
Mediterranean menu. Lunch, dinner. Bar.
$$$

★★Black Forest
8675 Cincinnati-Columbus Rd.,
West Chester,
513-777-7600
German menu. Lunch, dinner. Closed
Sunday. Bar. Children's menu. **$$**

★Cabin Club
30651 Detroit Rd., Westlake,
440-899-7111;
www.hrcleveland.com
Seafood, steak menu. Lunch, dinner. Bar.
Children's menu. **$$$**

★Lemon Grass
2179 Lee Rd., Cleveland Heights,
216-321-0210
Thai menu. Lunch, dinner. Bar. Outdoor
seating. **$$**

142

OHIO

★

★

★

★

★

COLUMBUS

Columbus was created to be the capital of Ohio. The streets here are attractive, broad, and tree-lined, and are the perfect setting for the nation's largest public university, Ohio State University.

With its more than 50,000 students, Ohio State influences much of what happens in Columbus, as does the state government. The people of Columbus are civic-minded, sports-minded and cultured. The city has more than 1,130 churches and congregations and 12 colleges and universities.
Information: Greater Columbus Convention and Visitors Bureau, 90 N. HigHSt., 614-221-6623, 800-345-4386; www.columbuscvb.org

143

OHIO

WHAT TO SEE AND DO

Columbus Museum of Art
480 E. Broad St., Columbus, 614-221-6801;
www.columbusmuseum.org
Collections focus on 19th- and 20th-century European and American paintings, sculptures, works on paper and decorative arts; contemporary sculpture; 16th- and 17th-century Dutch and Flemish Masters. Galleries arranged chronologically. Museum shop; indoor atrium; sculpture garden; cafe. Tuesday-Sunday.

Ohio State Capitol
HigHand Broad Streets, Columbus, 614-728-2695
This capitol building has a group of bronze statues by Levi T. Scofield at its northwest corner that depict Ohio soldiers and statesmen under Roman matron Cornelia. h er words, "These are my jewels," refer to Grant, Sherman, Sheridan, Stanton,

Garfield, Hayes and Chase, who stand below her. Rotunda; observation window on 40th floor of State Office Tower Building, across from rotunda. Daily.

Opera Columbus
Palace Theatre, 117 Naghten, Columbus, 614-469-0939;
www.operacolumbus.org
English translation projected onto screen above stage. October-May.

HOTELS

★Best Western Franklin Park Suites-Polaris
2045 Polaris Pkwy., Columbus, 614-396-5100, 800-528-1234;
www.bestwestern.com
64 rooms, all suites. Complimentary continental breakfast. High-speed Internet access. Bar. Fitness room. Indoor pool, whirlpool. Business center. $

★Best Western Suites
1133 Evans Way Ct., Columbus,
614-870-2378, 888-870-2378;
www.bestwestern.com
66 rooms. Complimentary continental breakfast. Fitness room. Indoor pool, whirlpool. $

★★Clarion Hotel Dublin
600 Metro Place N., Dublin,
614-764-2200.

217 rooms. Pets accepted; fee. Restaurant, bar. Fitness room. Indoor pool. $

★Comfort Inn
4270 Sawyer Rd., Columbus,
614-237-5847, 800-424-6423;
www.comfortsuites.com
67 rooms. Pets accepted, some restrictions. Complimentary continental breakfast. Outdoor pool. Airport transportation available. $

TOURING GERMAN VILLAGE

German Village is a neighborhood of uneven brick streets hand-laid in a herringbone pattern and lined with trees and the plain, simple brick cottages of German brewery workers. The village offers a huge Oktoberfest, a clutcHof German restaurants and genuine old-world charm. There is a noticeable absence of neon. In fact, the entire historic district is listed on the National Register of Historic Places. Start at the German Village Meeting Haus (588 S. Third St.), where an 11-minute video tells the story of the settlement. Head soutHto the Golden Hobby Shop (630 S. Third St.). This 125-year-old former schoolhouse is full of handmade quilts, ceramics, jewelry, stained glass, woodcrafts and holiday decorations. The Book Loft (631 S. Third St.) has 32 rooms of bargain paperbacks and hardcovers, many 50 to 90 percent off original prices. Next door is Cup O Joe (627 S. Third St.), where comfy couches and chairs make for a favorite hangout for locals and visitors. Grab a cup of house blend and one of the fresHpastries, cheesecakes, scones or muffins. Hausfrau Haven (769 S. Third St.) is a general store with an eclectic stock of wine, beer, political T-shirts and a local confection known as buckeyes: rich peanut butter-filled chocolates resembling the horse chestnuts that give Ohio its nickname. Turn left to KossutHStreet and Helen Winnemore's Contemporary Craft Gallery (150 E. KossutHSt.), one of the nation's oldest, continuously operating fine crafts shops, with jewelry and works of clay, metal and wood.

Mohawk dead-ends into Schiller Park, a 23-acre urban park named after German poet-philosopher Friederich von Schiller. Actors Summer Theatre stages Shakespeare productions and musicals in the amphitheater. The park, containing a large statue of the eponymous Schiller, is ringed by large homes built by German brewery owners in the early and mid-19tHcentury. Stroll nortHdown City Park Avenue, arguably the prettiest street in the village. Quilts & Stuff (911 City Park Ave.) has sold quilted items at this location for many years. Continue north, make a left on Beck, a right on Third Street and end your tour at Katzingers Delicatessen (475 S. Third St.) SandwicH#59, hot corned beef and Swiss on pumpernickel, was renamed "Bill's Day at the Deli" after former President Clinton sampled one. Other eateries include Schmidt's Sausage Haus (240 E. KossutHSt.), a historic landmark specializing in German-American foods. At Juergen's Backerei & Konditorei (525 S. FourtHSt.), proprietor Rosemarie Keidel serves up German pastries and foods in a former boardinghouse where waitresses wear traditional dirndls.

★★Courtyard by Marriott
35 W. Spring St., Columbus,
614-228-3200, 800-321-2211;
www.courtyard.com-cmhcy
149 rooms. High-speed Internet access. Restaurant, bar. Fitness room. Indoor pool, whirlpool. **$**

★★Embassy Suites
2700 Corporate Exchange Dr., Columbus,
614-890-8600, 800-362-2779;
www.embassysuites.com
This hotel, with a beautiful atrium setting, is perfect for guests who want extra space and comfort. With its two-room suites, guests can also enjoy a complimentary breakfast, an evening reception to unwind and much more.
221 rooms, all suites. Complimentary full breakfast. Restaurant, bar. Fitness room. Indoor pool, outdoor pool, whirlpool. Airport transportation available. Business center. **$**

★Fairfield Inn & Suites
3031 Olentangy River Rd., Columbus,
614-267-1111, 800-228-2800;
www.fairfieldinn.com
200 rooms. Complimentary continental breakfast. Restaurant, bar. **$**

★Signature Inn Columbus
6767 Schrock Hill Ct., Columbus,
614-890-8111, 800-822-5252;
www.signatureinn.com
125 rooms. Pets accepted, some restrictions; fee. Complimentary continental breakfast. Outdoor pool. Business center. **$**

★★★Columbus Marriott North
6500 Doubletree Ave., Columbus,
614-885-1885, 800-228-9290;
www.marriott.com
This hotel is situated close to such attractions as the Polaris Amphitheater, Columbus Zoo and Center of Science and Industry.
300 rooms. Restaurant, bar. Fitness room. Indoor pool, outdoor pool, whirlpool. Airport transportation available. Business center. **$**

★★★Crowne Plaza
33 E. Nationwide Blvd., Columbus,
614-461-4100, 800-227-6963;
www.crowneplaza.com
Connected to the Columbus Convention Center, this hotel is perfectly located near the city's top attractions. With a convenient shuttle service, guests are just minutes away from downtown.
377 rooms. High-speed Internet access. Restaurant, two bars. Fitness room. Indoor pool. Business center. **$**

★★★Hyatt on Capitol Square
75 E. State St., Columbus,
614-228-1234, 800-233-1234;
www.hyatt.com
This hotel is in the downtown area across from Capitol Park and connected to the Columbus City Center shopping and historic Ohio Theater. The health club overlooks the State Capitol.
400 rooms. Restaurant, bar. Fitness room. Business center. **$$**

★★★Hyatt Regency Columbus
350 N. HigHSt., Columbus,
614-463-1234, 800-233-1234;
www.hyatt.com
Connected to the Columbus Convention Center, this hotel is conveniently located for both business and leisure travel. The luxurious guest suites are spacious. The hotel also houses a deli, cafe and 63,000 square feet of meeting space.
631 rooms. Restaurant, bar. Fitness room. Indoor pool. Business center. **$$**

★★★Marriott Columbus Northwest
5605 Paul G, Blazer Memorial Pkwy., Dublin,
614-791-1000, 800-228-9290;
www.marriott.com
This hotel is located in one of Columbus' fastest-growing entertainment and business districts. Nearby attractions include the Columbus Zoo, Murfield Village and Golf Club and Anheuser Busch Brewery.
303 rooms. Pets accepted, some restrictions. Restaurant, bar. Fitness room. Indoor pool. Business center. **$**

★★★The Blackwell
2110 Tuttle Park Place, Columbus,
614-247-4000, 866-247-4003;
www.theblackwell.com
151 rooms. High-speed Internet access. Restaurant, bar. Airport transportation available. Business center. **$$**

★★★The Lofts
55 E. Nationwide Blvd., Columbus,
614-461-2663, 800-735-6387;
www.55lofts.com
Located in downtown Columbus, the 100-year-old warehouse that houses this hotel has been energized with contemporary design. Clean, simple lines and furnishings create an uncluttered look in the guest rooms, while Frette linens and Aveda bath products make things more comfortable.
44 rooms. Complimentary continental breakfast. High-speed Internet access. Restaurant, bar. Fitness room. Indoor pool. **$$**

SPECIALTY LODGINGS
Short North Bed and Breakfast
50 E. Lincoln St., Columbus,
614-299-5050, 888-299-5051;
www.columbus-bed-breakfast.com
8 rooms. Complimentary full breakfast. **$$**

Harrison House B&B
313 W. 5thAve., Columbus.
614-421-2202; 800-827-4203.
4 rooms. Complimentary full breakfast. **$**

RESTAURANTS
★★Alex's Bistro
4681 Reed Rd., Columbus,
614-457-8887
French bistro menu. Lunch, dinner. Closed Sunday. Bar. Business casual attire. Reservations recommended. **$$**

★★Bexley's Monk
2232 E. Main St., Bexley,
614-239-6665;
www.bexleysmonk.com
Continental menu. Lunch, dinner. Bar. **$$$**

★Cap City Diner-Grandview
1299 Olentangy River Rd., Columbus,
614-291-3663;
www.cameronmitchell.com
American menu. Lunch, dinner, Sunday brunch. Bar. Children's menu. Casual attire. Outdoor seating. **$$**

★★★Handke's Cuisine
520 S. Front St., Columbus,
614-621-2500;
www.chefhandke.com
Located in the brewery district, this restaurant is set in a former 19th-century brewery, with three dining rooms and vaulted ceilings. The menu includes such dishes as grilled tenderloin with morels, potatoes and French green beans.
International menu. Dinner. Closed Sunday. Business casual attire. Reservations recommended. Valet parking. **$$$**

★★Hunan House
2350 E. Dublin-Granville Rd., Columbus,
614-895-3330
Chinese menu. Lunch, dinner. Bar. **$$**

★★Hunan Lion
2038 Bethel Rd., Columbus,
614-459-3933
Chinese, Thai menu. Lunch, dinner. Bar. Business casual attire. **$$**

★Katzinger's Delicatessen
475 S. 3rd St., Columbus,
614-228-3354;
www.katzingers.com
Deli menu. Breakfast, lunch, dinner. Children's menu. Casual attire. Outdoor seating. **$**

★★★L'Antibes
772 N. HigHSt., Columbus,
614-291-1666;
www.lantibes.com
Sophisticated French fare served in an unpretentious atmosphere defines dining at this small restaurant. The sweetbreads are the talk of the town.
French menu. Dinner. Closed Sunday-Monday; also last week in January and one week

in July. Business casual attire. Reservations recommended. Valet parking. **$$$**

★★Lindey's
169 E. Beck St., Columbus,
614-228-4343;
www.lindeys.com
American bistro menu. Lunch, dinner, brunch. Bar. Children's menu. Business casual attire. Reservations recommended. Valet parking. Outdoor seating. **$$**

★★★Morton's, The Steakhouse
280 N. HigHSt., Columbus,
614-464-4442;
www.mortons.com
For the freshest lobster and steaks, this branch of the national chain is a sure bet. Professional service and a club-like setting make for a seamless dining experience. Steak menu. Dinner. Bar. Business casual attire. Reservations recommended. Valet parking. **$$$**

★Old Mohawk
819 Mohawk St., Columbus,
614-444-7204
American menu. Lunch, dinner. Bar. Casual attire. **$$**

★★★Refectory
1092 Bethel Rd., Columbus,
614-451-9774;
www.therefectoryrestaurant.com
Housed in a historic church, this fine French restaurant is known as one of the area's most romantic. For a great deal, try

chef Richard Blondin's three-course bistro menu served Monday through Thursday in the lounge or on the outdoor patio. French menu. Dinner. Closed Sunday. Bar. Business casual attire. Reservations recommended. Outdoor seating. **$$$**

★★Rigsby's Cuisine Volatile
698 N. HigHSt., Columbus,
614-461-7888
Italian menu. Lunch, dinner. Closed Sunday. Bar. Business casual attire. Reservations recommended. Valet parking. **$$**

★★RJ Snappers
700 N. HigHSt., Columbus,
614-280-1070;
www.rjsnappers.com
Seafood menu. Dinner. Bar. Children's menu. Business casual attire. Reservations recommended. Valet parking. **$$**

★★Schmidt's Sausage Haus
240 E. Kossuth St., Columbus,
614-444-6808;
www.schmidthaus.com
German menu. Lunch, dinner. Bar. Children's menu. Casual attire. **$$**

★★Tony's Italian Ristorante
16 W. Beck St., Columbus,
614-224-8669;
www.tonysitalian.net
Italian menu. Lunch, dinner. Closed Sunday. Bar. Business casual attire. Reservations recommended. Outdoor seating. **$$**

147

OHIO

DAYTON

Dayton is located on a fork of the Miami River, which curves through the city from the northeast, uniting with the Stillwater River half a mile above the Main Street Bridge. The Mad River flows from the east and Wolf Creek from the west to join the others four blocks away. Dayton has 28 bridges crossing these rivers.

The first flood, in 1805, started a progression of higher levees. In 1913, the most disastrous flood took 361 lives and property wortH$100 million and inspired a flood-control plan effective to date.

ThougHthe city itself can seem like something of a ghost town these days, with most of the action happening in the suburbs, plenty of famous residents have put the city on the map, including Orville and Wilbur Wright, inventors of the airplane.

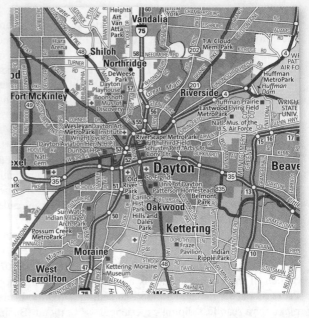

Information: Dayton-Montgomery County Convention and Visitors Bureau, 937-226-8211, 800-221-8235; www.daytoncvb.com

HOTELS

★Comfort Inn
7907 Brandt Pike, Huber Heights, 937-237-7477, 800-228-5150; www.comfortinn.com
53 rooms. Complimentary continental breakfast. Fitness room. **$**

★Days Inn
100 Parkview Dr., Brookville, 937-833-4003, 800-329-7466; www.daysinn.com
62 rooms. Pets accepted; fee. Complimentary continental breakfast. Outdoor pool. **$**

★★Doubletree Guest Suites
300 Prestige Place, Dayton, 937-436-2400, 800-222-8733; www.doubletree.com
137 rooms, all suites. Pets accepted, some restrictions; fee.
Restaurant, bar. Fitness room. Indoor pool, outdoor pool, whirlpool. **$**

★Fairfield Inn
6960 Miller Lane, Dayton, 937-898-1120, 800-228-2800; www.fairfieldinn.com
135 rooms. Pets accepted; fee. Complimentary continental breakfast. Outdoor pool. **$**

★Hampton Inn
2550 Paramount Place, Fairborn, 937-429-5505, 800-426-7866; www.hamptoninn.com
63 rooms. Complimentary continental breakfast. Indoor pool, whirlpool. **$**

★★★Crowne Plaza
33 E. 5th St., Dayton, 937-224-0800, 800-227-6963; www.crowneplaza.com
Located in the business district, this hotel is adjacent to the convention center and near many local attractions. The rooftop restaurant, with views of the city, serves dinner nightly.

283 rooms. Restaurant, bar. Fitness room. Outdoor pool. **$**

★★★Marriott Dayton
1414 S. Patterson Blvd., Dayton,
937-223-1000, 800-450-8625;
www.marriott.com
Rooms at this hotel, located just outside downtown, have been updated with plush new beds and luxury bedding. Fitness and business centers are just a few of the amenities.
399 rooms. Pets accepted, some restrictions; fee. Restaurant, bar. Fitness room. Indoor pool, outdoor pool, whirlpool. Business center. **$**

RESTAURANTS
★Amber Rose
1400 Valley St., Dayton,
937-228-2511; www.theamberrose.com
American, European menu. Lunch, dinner. Closed Sunday. Bar. **$$**

★Barnsider
5202 N. Main St., Dayton,
937-277-1332.
Steak menu. Dinner. Bar. Children's menu. **$$**

★★B. R. Scotese's
1375 N. Fairfield Rd., Beavercreek,
937-431-1350
Italian menu. Dinner. Closed Sunday. Bar. Children's menu. **$$**

★China Cottage
6290 Far Hills Ave., Dayton,
937-434-2622
Chinese menu. Lunch, dinner. Bar. **$$**

★★El Meson
903 E. Dixie Dr., West Carrolltown,
937-859-8229;
www.elmeson.net
Latin American, Spanish menu. Lunch, dinner. Closed Sunday; also first three weeks in January. Bar. Reservations recommended. Outdoor seating. **$$**

★★Jay's
225 E. 6th St., Dayton,
937-222-2892; www.jays.com
Seafood menu. Dinner. Bar. Children's menu. **$$$**

★★★L 'Auberge
4120 Far Hills Ave., Kettering,
937-299-5536; www.laubergedayton.com
For more than 20 years, serious lovers of classic French fare have dined at L'Auberge. Owner Josef Reif has succeeded in creating an elegant restaurant filled with flowers. The food spotlights seasonal ingredients of the region, prepared with a light, classic French hand.
French, seafood menu. Lunch, dinner. Closed Sunday. Bar. Jacket required. Outdoor seating. **$$$**

★★Lincoln Park Grille
580 Lincoln Park Blvd., Dayton,
937-293-6293
American menu. Lunch, dinner. Closed Sunday. Bar. Outdoor seating. **$$**

★★Oakwood Club
2414 Far Hills Ave., Oakwood,
937-293-6973
Seafood, steak menu. Dinner. Closed Sunday. Bar. **$$**

★★Pine Club
1926 Brown St., Dayton,
937-228-7463; www.thepineclub.com
Steak menu. Dinner. Closed Sunday. Bar. Children's menu. **$$**

★★Bravo! Italian Kitchen
2148 Miamisburg Centerville Rd., Centerville,
937-439-1294;
www.bestitalianusa.com
Upscale family dining. Italian menu. Lunch, dinner. Bar. Children's menu. **$$**

★★J. Alexander's
7970 Washington Village Dr., Centerville,
937-435-4441; www.jalexanders.com
American menu. Lunch, dinner. Bar. Children's menu. Casual attire. **$$**

149

OHIO

★
★
★
★
★

DELAWARE

Delaware, on the Olentangy River, is a college town, trading center for farmers, and site of diversified industry. The area was chosen by Native Americans as a campsite because of its mineral springs. The Mansion house—a famous sulphur-spring resort built in 1833—is now Elliot h all, the first building of Ohio Wesleyan University. There is a legend that President Rutherford B. Hayes (a native of Delaware) proposed to his bride-to-be, Lucy Webb, one of the school's first coeds, at the sulphur spring.

Information: Delaware County Convention and Visitors Bureau, 44 E. Winter St., 740-368-4748, 888-335-6446; www.visitdelohio.com

SPECIALTY LODGINGS

Welcome Home Inn
6640 Home Rd., Delaware,
740-881-6588, 800-381-0364;
www.welcomehomeinn.com
5 rooms. Complimentary full breakfast. $

RESTAURANTS

★Branding Iron
1400 Stratford Rd., Delaware,
740-363-1846
American, steak menu. Dinner, Sunday brunch. Closed Monday; also first two weeks in August. Bar. Children's menu. $$

★Bun's of Delaware
14 W. Winter St., Delaware,
740-363-3731
American menu. Lunch, dinner. Bar. Children's menu. $$

EAST LIVERPOOL

Located where Ohio, Pennsylvania and West Virginia meet on the Ohio River, East Liverpool was called Fawcett's Town after its first settler arrived until 1860. Its clay deposits determined its destiny as a pottery center; everything from dinnerware to brick is produced here.

Information: East Liverpool Chamber of Commerce, 529 Market St., 330-385-0845; www.elchamber.com

SPECIALTY LODGINGS

The Sturgis House
122 W. 5th St., East Liverpool,
330-382-0194;
www.sturgishouse.com
Located in a restored Victorian mansion. 6 rooms. Complimentary continental breakfast. $

ELYRIA

This retailing and industrial city, at the junction of the east and west branches of the Black River, is the seat of Lorain County. The novelist Sherwood Anderson managed a paint factory here before launching his literary career.

Information: Lorain County Visitors Bureau, 611 Broadway, Lorain, 440-245-5282, 800-334-1673; www.lcvb.org

HOTELS

★Comfort Inn
739 Leona St., Elyria,
440-324-7676, 800-424-6423;
www.comfortinn.com
66 rooms. Pets accepted; fee. Complimentary continental breakfast. $

★★Holiday Inn
1825 Lorain Blvd., Elyria,
440-324-5411, 800-465-4329;
www.holiday-inn.com
250 rooms. Pets accepted. Restaurant, bar. Outdoor pool. Airport transportation available. $

FINDLAY

Named for Fort Findlay, one of the outposts of the War of 1812, this town is located 45 miles south of Toledo in the state's rich farm area.

Tell Taylor, educated in Findlay, was inspired to write the song "Down by the Old Mill Stream" while fishing along the Blanchard River. Marilyn Miller, Russell Crouse, Dr. Howard T. Ricketts and Dr. Norman Vincent Peale also came from Findlay.

Information: Findlay- Hancock County Convention and Visitors Bureau, 123 E. Main Cross St., 419-422-3315, 800-424-3315; www.findlayhancockchamber.com

WHAT TO SEE AND DO

Fort Ancient State Memorial

Seven miles southeast of Lebanon on Hwy. 350.
513-932-4421;
www.ohiohistory.org

Fort Ancient is one of the largest and most impressive prehistoric earthworks of its kind in the United States. The Fort Ancient earthworks were built by the h opewell people between 100 b.c.-a.d. 500. This site occupies an elevated plateau overlooking the Little Miami River Valley. Its massive earthen walls, more than 23 feet high in places, enclose an area of 100 acres. Within this area are earth mounds once used as calendar markers and other archaeological features. Relics from the site and the nearby prehistoric Native American village are displayed in Fort Ancient Museum. h iking trails, picnic facilities. March-November, daily.

HOTELS

★Fairfield Inn

2000 Tiffin Ave., Findlay,
419-424-9940, 800-228-2800;
www.fairfieldinn.com

57 rooms. Complimentary continental breakfast. Indoor pool, whirlpool. $

★★Findlay Inn & Conference Center

200 E. Main Cross St., Findlay,
419-422-5682, 800-825-1455;
www.findlayinn.com

80 rooms. Complimentary continental breakfast. Restaurant, bar. Fitness room. Indoor pool, whirlpool. $

151

OHIO

★
★
★
★
★

GALLIPOLIS

Gallipolis, "the old French city" along the Ohio River, was the second permanent settlement in Ohio. The columnist O. O. McIntyre lived in Gallipolis, often wrote about it and is buried here. The district library has an extensive collection of his work.

Information: www.gallipolisohio.com

HOTELS

★★Holiday Inn

577 State Route 7 N., Gallipolis,
740-446-0090, 800-465-4329;
www.holiday-inn.com

100 rooms. Pets accepted, some restrictions. Restaurant, bar. Outdoor pool, children's pool. $

GRANVILLE

Founded in 1805 by settlers who moved here from Granville, Massachusetts and Granville, Connecticut, this city retains a classic small-town American charm.

Information: www.granville.oh.us

RESTAURANTS

★★★Buxton Inn Dining Room
313 E. Broadway, Granville,
740-587-0001;
www.buxtoninn.com
This restaurant serves classic dishes like porterhouse steaks or salmon with lemon caper sauce. The tavern serves a more casual menu of bar favorites like burgers or French onion soup. American, French menu. Lunch, dinner, Sunday brunch. Closed Monday. Bar. **$$**

HAMILTON
Originally Fort Hamilton, an outpost of the Northwest Territory, this city became an industrial center in the 1850s with the completion of the Miami and Erie Canal. Much of Hamilton's 19th-century heritage is preserved in the restored homes in several historic districts.
Information: Greater Hamilton Convention and Visitors Bureau, 201 Dayton St., 513-844-1500, 800-311-5353; www.hamilton-ohio.com

HOTELS

★★ Hamiltonian Hotel
1 Riverfront Plaza, Hamilton,
513-896-6200, 800-522-5570;
www.hamiltonianhotel.com
120 rooms. Pets accepted. Restaurant, bar. Outdoor pool. **$**

KENT
Home to Kent State University, this small town outside Akron is a typical college town with plenty of restaurants and boutiques catering to the many students who attend the school.
Information: Kent Area Chamber of Commerce, 155 E. Main St., 330-673-9855; www.kentbiz.com

HOTEL

★★University Inn
540 S. Water St., Kent,
330-678-0123;
www.kentuniversityinn.com
107 rooms. Restaurant. Outdoor pool. **$**

RESTAURANTS

★★Pufferbelly Ltd.
152 Franklin Ave., Kent,
330-673-1771;
www.pufferbellyltd.com
American menu. Lunch, dinner, Sunday brunch. Bar. Children's menu. Casual attire. Reservations recommended. **$$**

LANCASTER
Centrally located in the middle of the state, this city of 35,000 has a well-preserved historic downtown. General William Tecumsah Sherman, the famed union Civil War leader, was born in Lancaster.
Information: Lancaster Fairfield County Visitors and Convention Bureau, 1 N. Broad. 740-653-8251, 800-626-1296; www.lancoc.org

HOTELS

★AmeriHost Inn
1721 River Valley Circle N., Lancaster,
740-654-5111;
www.amerihostinn.com
60 rooms. Complimentary continental breakfast. Fitness room. Indoor pool, whirlpool. **$**

152

OHIO

★

★

★

★

★

★★★Glenlaurel
14940 Mount Olive Rd., Rockbridge,
740-385-4070, 800-809-7378;
www.glenlaurel.com
This Scottish country inn is located on a 140-acre estate and has a series of waterfalls, a private gorge and 50-foot rock cliffs on its grounds.
16 rooms. Children over 12 years only. Complimentary full breakfast. Restaurant. **$$$**

RESTAURANTS
★★★Shaw's
123 N. Broad St., Lancaster,
740-654-1842, 800-654-2477;
www.shawsinn.com
This charming restaurant is located in historic Lancaster. The menu features regional specials from Southwestern to country French. Fresh fish is flown in from Boston, and tangy ribs and steaks are cooked to perfection.
Continental menu. Lunch, dinner. Bar. Outdoor seating. **$$**

LEBANON
Some of the early settlers around Lebanon were Shakers who contributed much to the town's culture and economy. Though their community, Union Village, was sold more than 50 years ago and is now a retirement home, local interest in the Shakers and their beliefs still thrives.
Information: Chamber of Commerce, 25 W. Mulberry., 513-932-1100

HOTELS
★★★Golden Lamb
27 S. Broadway,
Lebanon,
513-932-5065;
www.goldenlamb.com
This national historic inn, built in 1803, has an outstanding collection of authentic Shaker antiques, many of which are used daily in the dining room.
18 rooms. Complimentary continental breakfast. Restaurant, bar. **$**

RESTAURANTS
★★Golden Lamb Restaurant
27 S. Broadway, Lebanon,
513-932-5065;
www.goldenlamb.com
American menu. Lunch, dinner. Bar. Children's menu. **$$**

★★Houston Inn
4026 Hwy. 42 S., Lebanon,
513-398-7377
American menu. Lunch, dinner. Closed Monday; late December-early January. Bar. Children's menu. Business casual attire. **$$**

LIMA
This small-town northwestern Ohio town is a farming center, most often visited as a stopping point along I-75, which runs through the town.
Information: Lima-Allen County Convention and Visitors Bureau, 147 N. Main St. 419-222-6075, 888-222-6075; www.allencvb.lima.oh.us

HOTELS
★★Holiday Inn
1920 Roschman Ave., Lima,
419-222-0004, 800-465-4329;
www.holiday-inn.com
150 rooms. Pets accepted. Restaurant, bar. Fitness room. Indoor pool, whirlpool. **$**

RESTAURANTS
★★Milano Cafe
2383 Elida Rd., Lima,
419-331-2220
American, Italian menu. Lunch, dinner. Bar. Children's menu. **$$**

MANSFIELD

A pioneer log blockhouse, built as protection against Native Americans during the War of 1812, still stands in South Park in the city's western section. Named for Jared Mansfield, U.S. Surveyor General, this is a diversified industrial center 75 miles southwest of Cleveland. John Chapman, better known as Johnny Appleseed, lived and traveled in Richland County for many years. Pulitzer Prize–winning novelist Louis Bromfield was born here and later returned to conduct agricultural research at his 914-acre Malabar Farm.

Information: Mansfield-Richland County Convention and Visitors Bureau, 124 N. Main St., 419-525-1300, 800-642-8282; www.mansfieldtourism.org

HOTELS

★Comfort Inn

500 N. Trimble Rd., Mansfield, 419-529-1000, 800-424-6423; www.comfortinn.com

114 rooms. Pets accepted; fee. Complimentary continental breakfast. Bar. Indoor pool. $

★★Holiday Inn

116 Park Ave. W., Mansfield, 419-525-6000, 800-465-4329; www.holiday-inn.com

120 rooms. Restaurant, bar. Fitness room. Indoor pool, whirlpool. $

MARIETTA

General Rufus Putnam's New England flotilla, arriving at the junction of the Muskingum and Ohio Rivers for western land-buying purposes, founded Marietta, the oldest settlement in Ohio. Its name is a tribute to Queen Marie Antoinette who offered French assistance to the American Revolution. Most of the landmarks are along the east side of the Muskingum River. Front Street is approximately the eastern boundary of the first stockade, which was called Picketed Point. Later, the fortification called Campus Martius was erected and housed General Putnam, Governor Arthur St. Clair and other public officials.

One of the most important Ohio River ports in steamboat days, Marietta is now a beautiful tree-filled town and the home of Marietta College.

Information: Tourist and Convention Bureau, 316 Third St, 740-373-5176, 800-288-2577; www.marietta-chamber.com

HOTELS

★Comfort Inn

700 Pike St., Marietta, 740-374-8190, 800-424-6423; www.comfortinn.com

120 rooms. Pets accepted; fee. Complimentary continental breakfast. Restaurant, bar. Fitness room. Indoor pool. Airport transportation available. $

★★Holiday Inn

701 Pike St., Marietta, 740-374-9660, 800-465-4329; www.holiday-inn.com

109 rooms. Restaurant, bar. Outdoor pool, children's pool. $

★★Lafayette Hotel

101 Front St., Marietta, 740-373-5522, 800-331-9336; www.lafayettehotel.com

78 rooms. Pets accepted; fee. Restaurant, bar. Airport transportation available. $

RESTAURANTS

★★★The Gun Room

101 Front St., Marietta, 740-373-5522; www.lafayettehotel.com

The traditional American menu at this Lafayette hotel restaurant is as much a draw as the room's ornate, 19th-century riverboat decor and antique gun collection. The adjacent Riverview Lounge offers great Ohio River views.

American, seafood menu. Breakfast, lunch, dinner, Sunday brunch. Bar. Children's menu. $$$

MARION

Both agricultural and industrial, Marion's growth was influenced by the Huber Manufacturing Company, which introduced the steam shovel in 1874. Marion is also the center of a major popcorn-producing area. Its best-known citizen was Warren G. Harding, owner and publisher of the Star. Later, he became a state senator, lieutenant governor and 29th president of the United States.

Information: Marion Area Convention and Visitors Bureau, 1952 Marion-Mount Gilead Rd., 740-389-9770; 800-371-6688. www.marion.net

WHAT TO SEE AND DO
President Warren G. Harding Home and Museum
380 Mt. Vernon Ave., Marion,
740-387-9630, 800-600-6894

Built during Harding's courtship with Florence Mabel Kling, this was the site of their marriage in 1891. Harding administered much of his 1920 "front porch campaign" for presidency from the front of the house. The museum, at the rear of the house, was once used as the campaign's press headquarters. Memorial Day weekend-Labor Day weekend: Wednesday-Sunday; April-May and after Labor Day-October: Saturday-Sunday.

HOTELS
★Comfort Inn
256 Jamesway, Marion,
740-389-5552, 800-424-6423
www.comfortinn.com

56 rooms. Pets accepted; fee. Complimentary continental breakfast. Indoor pool, whirlpool. $

MASON

This Cincinatti suburb is the home of the vast amusement park Kings Island, which is known for its cutting-edge roller coasters.

Information: Mason Area Chamber of Commerce, 316 W. Main St., 513-336-0125; www.masonchamber.org

WHAT TO SEE AND DO
Paramount's Kings Island
6300 Kings Island Dr., Mason,
513-754-5700, 800-288-0808;
www.pki.com

Premier seasonal family theme park. Facility includes 350 acres with more than 100 rides and attractions, such as the Outer Limits thrill ride and Flight of Fear, an indoor roller coaster. Late May-early September: daily; mid-April-late May: weekends; early September-October: selected weekends.

HOTELS
★★★Marriott Cincinnati Northeast
9664 Mason-Montgomery Rd., Mason,
513-459-9800, 800-228-9290;
www.marriott.com

This hotel is ideal for both business travelers and visitors to nearby Kings Island. Other local attractions include the Beach Waterpark and the Golf Center at Kings Island.

302 rooms. Restaurant, bar. Fitness room. Indoor pool, outdoor pool. Business center. $

★★★Kings Island Resort & Conference Center
5691 Kings Island Dr., Mason,
513-398-0115, 800-727-3050;
www.kingsislandresort.com

155

OHIO

★
★
★
★
★

Located across the street from Paramount's Kings Island theme park, this 288-room resort offers 13,000 square feet of meeting space and various recreational facilities.

Visit the Main Street Grill for the weekend prime rib buffet.
288 rooms. Restaurant, bar. Fitness room. Indoor pool, outdoor pool, whirlpool. Tennis. **$**

MENTOR

Site of the first Lake County settlement, Mentor was once an agricultural center. James A. Garfield lived here before his election as U.S. president. The town is now a popular commuter community for those who work in Cleveland.
Information: Mentor Area Chamber of Commerce, 7547 Mentor Ave., 440-946-2625; www.mentorchamber.org

WHAT TO SEE AND DO

Lawnfield James A. Garfield National Historic Site
8095 Mentor Ave., Mentor,
440-255-8722;
www.nps.gov-jaga
This was the 20th president's last house before the White House. The house includes two floors of original furnishings and a memorial library containing Garfield's books and desk. On the grounds are his campaign office, carriage house and picnic area. Daily.

HOTELS

★★Radisson Hotel & Suites Cleveland- Eastlake
35000 Curtis Blvd., Eastlake,
440-953-8000, 800-333-3333;
www.radisson.com
126 rooms. Restaurant, bar. Fitness room. Indoor pool. Business center. **$**

RESTAURANTS

★★Molinari's
8900 Mentor Ave., Mentor,
440-974-2750;
www.molinaris.com
Italian menu. Lunch, dinner. Closed Sunday-Monday. Bar. **$$**

156

MIAMISBURG

Located near Dayton, this city is home to large corporations such as LexisNexis. The Miamisburg Mound, a large conical structure attributed to the Adena culture can be found here.
www.ci.miamisburg.oh.us

HOTELS

★★Courtyard by Marriott
100 Prestige Plaza, Miamisburg,
937-433-3131, 800-321-2211;
www.courtyard.com
146 rooms. Restaurant, bar. Fitness room. Indoor pool, whirlpool. **$**

★★Holiday Inn
31 Prestige Plaza Dr., Miamisburg,
937-434-8030, 800-465-4329;
www.holiday-inn.com

195 rooms. Pets accepted, some restrictions; fee. . Restaurant, bar. Fitness room. Indoor pool, outdoor pool, children's pool. **$**

RESTAURANTS

★Bullwinkle's Top Hat Bistro
19 N. Main St., Miamisburg,
937-859-7677;
www.usbistroco.com
American menu. Lunch, dinner. Bar. Children's menu. **$$**

MILAN

Settlers from Connecticut founded Milan, building houses using the hallmarks of New England architecture. A canal connecting the town with Lake Erie was built in 1839, making Milan one of the largest shipping centers in the Midwest at that time. The town is the birthplace of inventor Thomas Edison.

Information: Chamber of Commerce, 419-499-9929; www.milanohio.com

WHAT TO SEE AND DO
Thomas A. Edison Birthplace Museum
9 Edison Dr., Milan,
419-499-2135;
www.tomedison.org

This is the two-story red brick house where the inventor Thomas Edison spent his first seven years. Contains some original furnishings, inventions and memorabilia. Guided tours. April-October: Tuesday-Sunday; February-March and November-December: Wednesday-Sunday; hours vary by month.

HOTELS
★Comfort Inn
11020 Milan Rd., Milan,
419-499-4681, 800-424-6423;
www.comfortinn.com
102 rooms. Indoor pool, outdoor pool, whirlpool. $

MILLERSBURG

This tiny central Ohio town has a population of less than 4,000. Its historic downtown has been well preserved and features many shops and businesses emblematic of the ideal small American town. The location in Amish country makes Millersburg ideal for exploring the area.

Information: www.millersburgohio.com

SPECIALTY LODGINGS
Bigham House Bed & Breakfast
151 S. Washington St.,
Millersburg,
330-6231-6819, 866-689-6950
Located in the heart of Amish country. Private baths and TVs in every room.
5 rooms. $$

Lamplight Inn Bed & Breakfast
5676 Township Rd. 362, Berlin,
330-893-1122 , 866-500-1122
Located within walking distance of historic downtown Berlin. All rooms have private entrances and baths.
5 rooms. No children allowed. $

The Barn Inn Bed & Breakfast
6838 County Rd. 203, Millersburg,
330-674-7600, 877-674-7600
Located in the picturesque Honey Run Valley, this bed-and-breakfast was once home to a dairy farm. 7 rooms. $$

RESTAURANTS
★★Chalet in the Valley
5060 State Route 557, Millersburg,
330-893-2550;
www.chaletinthevalley.com
Continental menu, Swiss and Amish specialties. Lunch, dinner. Closed Monday; January-mid-March. $

MOUNT VERNON

Descendants of the first settlers from Virginia, Maryland, New Jersey and Pennsylvania still live in this town. The seat of Knox County, Mount Vernon is in the largest sheep-raising county east of the Mississippi.

Johnny Appleseed owned two lots in the original village plot at the south end of Main Street. Daniel Decatur Emmett, author and composer of "Dixie," was born here. Many buildings in town feature Colonial-style architecture.

Information: Knox County Convention and Visitors Bureau, 107 S. Main St., 740-392-6102, 800-837-5282; www.knoxohio.org

HOTELS

★★Historic Curtis Inn on the Square
12 Public Square, Mount Vernon,
740-397-4334
72 rooms. Pets accepted; fee. Restaurant, bar. $

★★★White Oak Inn
29683 Walhonding Rd., Danville,
740-599-6107, 877-908-5923;
www.whiteoakinn.com
Enjoy the peace and quiet at this inn, which is located in a turn-of-the-century farmhouse with original white oak woodwork. Breakfast and dinner are served daily. 10 rooms. Children over 12 years only. Complimentary full breakfast. $$

NEW PHILADELPHIA

New Philadelphia, the seat of Tuscarawas County, and its neighbor, Dover, still reflect the early influences of the German-Swiss who came here from Pennsylvania. Some of the earliest town lots in New Philadelphia were set aside for German schools.

Information: Tuscarawas County Convention and Visitors Bureau, 124 E. HigHAve., 330-602-2420, 800-527-3387; www.neohiotravel.com

HOTELS

★★Holiday Inn
131 Bluebell Dr. S.W., New Philadelphia,
330-339-7731, 800-465-4329;
www.holiday-inn.com
107 rooms. Pets accepted, some restrictions; fee. Restaurant, bar. Fitness room. Indoor pool, outdoor pool, whirlpool. $

★★★Atwood Lake Resort and Conference Center
2650 Lodge Rd., New Philadelphia,
330-735-2211, 800-362-6406;
www.atwoodlakeresort.com
This hilltop resort overlooking a lake provides a unique retreat. Each room has either a view of the lake or countryside. Boat rentals are available through the hotel, and harbor cruises are available through the nearby marina. Private airstrip, heliport. A Muskingum Watershed Conservancy District facility. 104 rooms. Restaurant, bar. Children's activity center. Fitness room. Indoor pool, outdoor pool, whirlpool. Golf, 27 holes. Tennis. Airport transportation available. $

NEWARK

This industrial city on the Licking River attracts many visitors because of its large group of prehistoric mounds. Construction of the Ohio and Erie Canal began here on July 4, 1825, with Governor DeWitt Clinton of New York as the official groundbreaker and speaker. The Ohio Canal was then built north to Lake Erie and south to the Ohio River.

Information: Greater Licking County Convention and Visitors Bureau, 29 S. 2nd St., 740-345-8224; 800-589-8224. www.lccvb.com

WHAT TO SEE AND DO

Newark Earthworks
S. 21st St. and Hwy. 79, Newark,
740-344-1920, 800-600-7174
This group of earthworks was originally one of the most extensive of its kind in the country, covering an area of more than four square miles. The Hopewell society used their geometric enclosures for social, religious and ceremonial purposes. Remaining portions of the Newark group are Octagon Earthworks and Wright Earthworks, with

158

OHIO

many artifacts of pottery, beadwork, copper, bone and shell exhibited at the nearby Moundbuilders Museum.

Moundbuilders State Memorial

65 Messimer Dr., Newark,
740-344-1920, 800-600-7174
The Great Circle has walls from eight to 14 feet high with burial mounds in the center. Museum containing Hopewell artifacts. Memorial Day-Labor Day: Wednesday-Sunday; after Labor Day-October: weekends only. Park April-October.

Octagon Earthworks

N. 30th St., Newark,
740-344-1920, 800-600-7174
The octagon-shaped enclosure encircles 50 acres that include small mounds and is joined by parallel walls to a circular embankment.

Wright Earthworks

James and Waldo Streets, Newark,
740-344-1920, 800-600-7174
One-acre earthworks has a 100-foot wall remnant, an important part of the original Newark group.

HOTELS

★★Cherry Valley Lodge

2299 Cherry Valley Rd., Newark,
740-788-1200, 800-788-8008;
www.cherryvalleylodge.com
120 rooms. Pets accepted. Check-in 4 p.m., check-out noon. Restaurant, bar. Fitness room. Indoor pool, outdoor pool, whirlpool. **$$**

★★Buxton Inn

313 E. Broadway, Granville,
740-587-0001;
www.buxtoninn.com
26 rooms. Complimentary continental breakfast. Restaurant. **$**

RESTAURANTS

★★Cherry Valley Lodge Dining Room

2299 Cherry Valley Rd., Newark,
740-788-1200;
www.cherryvalleylodge.com
American menu. Breakfast, lunch, dinner, brunch. Bar. Children's menu. **$$$**

★Damon's

1486 Granville Rd., Newark,
740-349-7427;
www.damons.com
American menu. Lunch, dinner. Bar. Children's menu. Casual attire. **$$**

★Natoma

10 N. Park, Newark,
740-345-7260
American, steak menu. Lunch, dinner. Closed Sunday. Bar. **$$**

NILES

This southwestern Ohio town, located on the Mahoning River, was named in the 1840s for the editor of a Baltimore newspaper. The town has a stadium that hosts the Mahoning Valley Scrappers, the AA farm team for the Cleveland Indians.
Information: www.thecityofniles.com

RESTAURANTS

★★★Alberini's

1201 Youngstown-Warren Rd., Niles,
330-652-5895;
www.alberinis.com
Husband-wife team Richard and Gilda Alberini preside over this popular Italian restaurant. The restaurant has a cigar room and a pleasant, glass patio.
Italian menu. Lunch, dinner. Closed Sunday. Bar. Business casual attire. Reservations recommended. **$$**

159

OHIO

OBERLIN

Oberlin College and the town were founded together. Oberlin was the first college to offer equal degrees to men and women and the first in the United States to adopt a policy against discrimination because of race. The central portion of the campus forms a six-acre public square, called Tappan Square, in the center of the town.

Charles Martin Hall, a young Oberlin graduate, discovered the electrolytic process of making aluminum in Oberlin. The Federal Aviation Agency maintains an Air Traffic Control Center here.

Information: Lorain County Visitors Bureau, 611 Broadway, Lorain, 440-245-5282, 800-334-1673; www.lcvb.org

HOTELS

★★Oberlin Inn
7 N. Main St., Oberlin,
440-775-1111, 800-376-4173;
www.oberlininn.com
76 rooms. Pets accepted. Restaurant. Airport transportation available. $

OXFORD

This small town exists primarily because of Miami University, which was founded here in 1809. The university was established following a land grant in 1792 from George Washington for a western college, and was named after the Miami Indians who lived in the area. The campus is considered one of the most picturesque in the country, with almost all buildings built in the same brick neo-Georgian style. Miami has been called everything from a "public ivy" for its academic excellence to the "cradle of coaches" for its outstanding football program. Famous alumni include 23rd President Benjamin Harrison and Pittsburgh Steelers quarterback Ben Roethlisberger.

Information: Visitors and Convention Bureau, 30 W. Park., 513-523-8687; www.oxfordchamber.org

HOTELS

★Best Western Sycamore Inn
6 E. Sycamore St., Oxford,
513-523-0000, 800-523-4678;
www.bestwestern.com
61 rooms. Complimentary continental breakfast. Fitness room. Indoor pool, whirlpool. $

★Hampton Inn
5056 College Corner Pike, Oxford,
513-524-0114, 800-426-7866;
www.hamptoninn.com
66 rooms. Complimentary continental breakfast. Fitness room. Indoor pool, whirlpool. $

★★Hueston Woods Resort
5201 Lodge Rd., College Corner,
513-664-3500, 800-282-7275;
www.huestonwoodsresort.com
92 rooms. Restaurant, bar. Children's activity center. Fitness room. Indoor pool, outdoor pool, children's pool. Golf, 18 holes. Tennis. $

PAINESVILLE

This northeastern Ohio town is located close to Cleveland and a short drive from Lake Erie beaches.

Information: Lake County Visitors Bureau, 1610 Mentor Ave.,440-354-2424, 800-368-5253; www.lakevisit.com

HOTELS

★★★Renaissance Quail Hollow Resort

11080 Concord Hambden Rd., Painesville, 440-497-1100, 800-468-3571; www.renaissancehotels.com

Located outside Cleveland, this resort has 36 holes of golf, a spa and many other onsite recreational facilities. The elegant dining room serves classically prepared dishes. 180 rooms. Restaurant, bar. Fitness room. Indoor pool, outdoor pool, whirlpool. Golf, 36 holes. Tennis. Business center. **$**

SPECIALTY LODGINGS

Riders Inn

792 Mentor Ave., Painesville, 440-354-8200; www.ridersinn.com

Original stagecoach stop and historic stop on the Underground Railroad, this inn has some authentic antiques. 10 rooms. Complimentary full breakfast. Restaurant. Airport transportation available. **$**

RESTAURANTS

★★Rider's Inn

792 Mentor Ave., Painesville 440-942-2742; www.ridersinn.com

Lunch, dinner, Sunday brunch. Bar. Children's menu. Features fare from original 19th-century recipes. Outdoor seating. **$$**

PORT CLINTON

This lakeshore town is the departure point for ferries to the Lake Erie islands.
Information: Chamber of Commerce, 110 Madison St., 419-734-5503; www.portclintonchamber.com

HOTELS

★Fairfield Inn

3760 E. State Rd., Port Clinton, 419-732-2434, 800-228-2800; www.fairfieldinn.com

64 rooms. Complimentary continental breakfast. Indoor pool. **$**

RESTAURANTS

★★Garden at the Lighthouse

226 E. Perry St., Port Clinton, 419-732-2151; www.gardenrestaurant.com

American menu. Dinner. Closed Sunday September-May. Bar. Children's menu. Outdoor seating. **$$**

PORTSMOUTH

Portsmouthis the leading firebrick and shoelace center of southern Ohio. At the confluence of the Ohio and Scioto rivers, 100 miles east of Cincinnati, it is connected to South Portsmouth, Kentucky, by bridge. The Boneyfiddle historic District in downtown Portsmouth includes many antique and specialty shops. Portsmouth was the childhood home of cowboy movie star Roy Rogers and baseball's Branch Rickey.
Information: Convention and Visitors Bureau, 341 Front St., 740-353-1116; www.portsmouthcvb.org

HOTELS

★★Days Inn

3762 Hwy. 23, Portsmouth, 740-354-2851, 800-329-7466; www.daysinn.com

100 rooms. Pets accepted; fee. Restaurant, bar. Outdoor pool. **$**

★★Ramada

711 2nd St., Portsmouth, 740-354-7711, 800-272-6232; www.ramada.com

119 rooms. Pets accepted; fee. Complimentary continental breakfast. Restaurant. Fitness room. Indoor pool, children's pool, whirlpool. **$**

161

OHIO

★
★
★
★
★

PUT-IN-BAY

On South Bass Island in Lake Erie, this village is an all-year resort that can be reached by ferry from Port Clinton. The area claims the best smallmouth black bass fishing in America in spring, and walleye and perch fishing at other times of the year. In summer, the area teams with boaters who come here to party at the many bars and restaurants near the town's marina.

Information: Put-in-Bay Chamber of Commerce, 419-285-2832; www.put-in-bay.com

WHAT TO SEE AND DO

Perry's Cave
979 Catawba Ave., Put-in-Bay,
419-285-2405;
www.perryscave.com

Commodore Perry is rumored to have stored supplies here before the Battle of Lake Erie in 1813; later, prisoners were kept here for a short time. The cave is 52 feet below the surface and is 208 feet by 165 feet; the temperature is 50 F. It has an underground stream that rises and falls with the level of Lake Erie. Picnic area available, no water. Twenty-minute guided tour. June-Labor Day: daily; spring and fall: weekends; rest of year: by appointment.

Perry's Victory and International Peace Memorial
2 Bay View Ave., Put-in-Bay,
419-285-2184

This Greek Doric granite column is 352 feet high and commemorates Commodore Oliver Hazard Perry's 1813 victory over the British naval squadron at the Battle of Lake Erie, near Put-in-Bay. The United States gained control of the lake, preventing a British invasion. The 3,986-mile U.S.–Canadian boundary, which passes near here through the lake, is the longest unfortified border in the world. Children under 16 only with adult. May-mid-October: daily.

162

OHIO

SANDUSKY

On a flat slope facing 18-mile-long Sandusky Bay, this town stretches for more than six miles along the waterfront. Originally explored by the French, the town was named by the Wyandot "Sandouske," meaning "at the cold water." When the amusement park Cedar Point opened here in 1870, Sandusky became a center for summertime tourism.

Information: Sandusky-Erie County Visitor and Convention Bureau, 4424 Milan Rd., Suite A., 419-625-2984, 800-255-3743; www.buckeyenorth.com

WHAT TO SEE AND DO

Cedar Point
1 Cedar Point Dr., Sandusky,
419-627-2350;
www.cedarpoint.com

This amusement park consistently wins awards for its roller coasters—the park currently has 17 coasters. Other diversions include a variety of rides, live shows, restaurants, Soak City water park, Challenge Golf miniature golf course and the Cedar Point Grand Prix go-cart race track, (additional fee). Price includes unlimited rides and attractions, except Challenge Park. Early May-Labor Day: daily; after Labor Day-October: weekends only.

HOTELS

★★Best Western Cedar Point Area
1530 Cleveland Rd., Sandusky,
419-625-9234, 800-528-1234;
www.bestwestern.com

106 rooms. Check-in 3 p.m., check-out 11 a.m. Restaurant. Outdoor pool. **$**

★Fairfield Inn
6220 Milan Rd., Sandusky,
419-621-9500, 800-228-2800;
www.fairfieldinn.com

63 rooms. Complimentary continental breakfast. Indoor pool. **$**

★★Holiday Inn
5513 Milan Rd., Sandusky,

419-626-6671
175 rooms. Restaurant, bar. Fitness room.
Indoor pool, outdoor pool. **$**

★★Rivers Edge Inn
132 N. Main St., Huron,
419-433-8000, 800-947-3400
65 rooms. Complimentary continental
breakfast. Restaurant, bar. Fitness room.
Indoor pool, whirlpool. **$**

RESTAURANTS
★★Bay Harbor Inn
1 Cedar Point Dr., Sandusky,
419-625-6373
Seafood menu. Dinner. Closed Sunday
October-April. Bar. Children's menu

SIDNEY
This area was once the forested hunting grounds of the Shawnee and Miami Indians. Later,
it was farmed by American settlers. The historic downtown contains the Louis Sullivan–
designed People's Savings and Loan building.
Information: Sidney-Shelby County Chamber of Commerce, 100 S. Main.,
937-492-9122; www.sidneyoh.com

HOTELS
★★Holiday Inn
400 FolkertHAve., Sidney, 937-492-1131,

800-465-4329; www.holiday-inn.com
134 rooms. Restaurant, bar. Fitness room.
Outdoor pool. **$**

SPRINGFIELD
Indian Scout Simon Kenton,
an early settler, set up a
gristmill and sawmill on the
present site of the Navistar
International plant. his wife
gave the village its name.
When the National Pike came
in 1839, Springfield came to
be known as the "town at the
end of the National Pike."

Agricultural machinery gave
Springfield its next boost. A
farm journal, *Farm and Fire-
side,* published in the 1880s
by P. P. Mast, a cultivator-
manufacturer, was the start of
the Crowell-Collier Publishing
Company. The 4-Hmovement
started here in 1902 by A. B.

163

OHIO

★
★
★
★
★
★

Graham, and hybrid corn grown by George H. Shull had its beginning in Springfield. A
center for some 200 diversified industries, Springfield is in the rich agricultural valley of
west central Ohio.
Information: Convention and Visitors Bureau, 333 N. Limestone St.,
937-325-7621; www.valleyvisitor.com

HOTELS

★★Courtyard Springfield Downtown
100 S. Fountain Ave., Springfield,
937-322-3600, 800-321-2211,
www.courtyard.com
124 rooms. Restaurant, bar. **$**

RESTAURANTS

★★Casey's
2205 Park Rd., Springfield,
937-322-0397.
American menu. Dinner. Closed Sunday.
Bar. **$$**

STEUBENVILLE

In 1786, the fledgling U.S. government established a fort here in 1786 and named it for the Prussian Baron Friedrich von Steuben, who helped the colonies in the Revolutionary War. It later became Steubenville.

Although its early industries were pottery, coal, wool, glass and shipbuilding, the mills of Wheeling-PittsburgHSteel and Weirton Steel started Steubenville's economic growth. The town's most famous resident was Dean Martin, who was born here as Dino Crocetti in 1917.

Information: Jefferson County Chamber of Commerce, 630 Market St., 740-282-6226; www.jeffersoncountychamber.com

HOTELS

★★Holiday Inn
1401 University Blvd., Steubenville,
740-282-0901, 800-465-4329;

www.holiday-inn.com
120 rooms. Restaurant, bar. Outdoor pool.
$

SERPENT MOUND STATE MEMORIAL

3850 State Rte. 73, Peebles, 937-587-2796, 800-752-2757; www.ohiohistory.org-places-serpent.
The largest and most remarkable serpent effigy earthworks in North America. Built between 800 BC–AD 100 by either the Fort Ancient or Adena society, the stone and yellow clay structure curls like an enormous snake for 1,335 feet. An oval earthwall represents the serpent's open mouth, which is aligned with the summer solstice sunset. Observation tower, scenic gorge, museum and picnicking facilities. Park all year, daily 10 a.m.-5 p.m.; museum hours vary.

TOLEDO

The French first explored the Toledo area, at the mouth of the Maumee River on Lake Erie, in 1615. Probably named after Toledo, Spain, the present city began as a group of small villages along the river. During the Toledo War in the 1830s, it was claimed by both Michigan and Ohio, which resulted in Toledo becoming part of Ohio and the Northern Peninsula going to Michigan.

Toledo's large, natural harbor makes it an important port. Railroads move coal and ore to the South, East, and North through the city; grain from the Southwest; steel from Cleveland and Pittsburgh; and automobile parts and accessories to and from Detroit.

Edward Libbey introduced the glass industry to Toledo in 1888, with high-grade crystal and lamp globes. Michael Owens, a glassblower, joined him and invented a machine that turned molten glass into bottles by the thousands. Today, Owens-Illinois, Libbey-Owens-Ford, Owens-Corning Fiberglas and Johns Manville Fiber Glass manufacture a variety of glass products. Metropolitan Toledo has more than 1,000 manufacturing plants producing Jeeps, spark plugs, chemicals and other products. Information: Greater Toledo Convention and Visitors Bureau, 401 Jefferson, 419-321-6404, 800-243-4667; www.toledocvb.com

WHAT TO SEE AND DO

Toledo Botanical Garden
5403 Elmer Dr., Toledo,
419-936-2986;
www.toledogarden.org
This garden has seasonal floral displays; herb, rhododendron and azalea gardens, perennial garden, rose garden, fragrance garden for the visually and physically impaired. Pioneer homestead 1837; art galleries, glassblowing studios. Gift shops. Special musical and crafts programs throughout year. Arts festival fee. Daily.

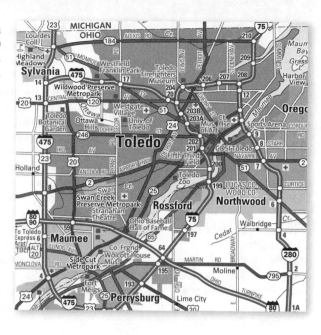

Toledo Museum of Art
2445 Monroe St., Toledo,
419-255-8000;
www.toledomuseum.com
Considered to be one of the finest art museums in the country, this museum has collections from ancient Egypt, Greece and Rome through the Middle Ages and the Renaissance to European and American arts of the present. Included are glass collections, paintings, sculptures, decorative and graphic arts; Egyptian mummy, medieval cloister, French chateau room, African sculpture, Asian art and Southeast Asian and Native American art. Art reference library; cafe; museum store. Tuesday-Sunday.

Toledo Symphony
1838 Parkwood Ave., Toledo,
419-246-8000, 800-348-1253;
www.toledosymphony.com
This symphony presents classical, pop, casual, chamber and all-Mozart concerts.

Performances at different locations. Mid-September-May.

Toledo Zoo
2700 Broadway, Toledo,
419-385-5721;
www.toledozoo.org
On exhibit are nearly 2,000 specimens of 400 species. The zoo has fresh and saltwater aquariums, a large mammal collection, reptiles, birds, a children's zoo, botanical gardens and a greenhouse. Daily.

HOTELS

★★Clarion Hotel Westgate
3536 Secor Rd., Toledo,
419-535-7070, 800-424-6423;
www.clarionhotel.com
305 rooms. Restaurant, bar. Fitness room. Indoor pool, whirlpool. Business center. $

★★Courtyard by Marriott
1435 E. Mall Dr., Holland,
419-866-1001, 800-228-9290;
www.courtyard.com
149 rooms. Restaurant, bar. Fitness room. Indoor pool, whirlpool. Airport transportation available. $

165

OHIO

★
★
★
★
★
★

★★★Hilton Toledo
3100 Glendale Ave., Toledo,
419-381-6800, 800-445-8667;
www.hilton.com
Situated on the campus of the Medical
College of Ohio, this hotel offers easy
access to nearby attractions. A fitness center, tennis courts, pool, and a jogging track
are available.
213 rooms. Restaurant, bar. Fitness room.
Indoor pool, whirlpool. Tennis. Airport
transportation available. **$**

RESTAURANTS
★★★Fifi's
1423 Bernath Pkwy., Toledo,
419-866-6777;
www.fifisrestaurant.com
Fifi's offers a wide array of regional and
traditional dishes prepared with a creative
flair. house specialties are soups, such as
traditional vichyssoise or gourmet fruit
soups served as dessert.
French menu. Dinner. Closed Sunday; holi-
days. Bar. **$$$**

★★Mancy's
953 Phillips Ave., Toledo,
419-476-4154;
www.mancys.com
Seafood, steak. Lunch, dinner. Closed
Sunday. Bar. Children's menu. **$$**

★Tony Packo's Cafe
1902 Front St., Toledo,
419-691-6054;
www.tonypackos.com
Hungarian menu. Lunch, dinner. Bar. Chil-
dren's menu. **$$**

VERMILION
Perched on the shore of Lake Erie between Cleveland and Toledo, this small town is popu-
lar with summer boaters and vacationers alike.

Information: Chamber of Commerce, 5495 Liberty Ave. 440-967-4477;
www.vermilionohio.com

RESTAURANTS
★★★Chez François
555 Main St., Vermilion,
440-967-0630;
www.chezfrancois.com
Located in a small, Lake Erie harbor town,
this French restaurant has a formal dining
room and a more casual, outdoor dining
area with a view of the Vermilion River.
French menu. Dinner. Closed Monday; also
January-mid-March. Jacket required. Out-
door seating. **$$$**

WAPAKONETA
This small northwest Ohio town is the birthplace of astronaut Neil Armstrong, the first man
to set foot on the moon. A museum dedicated to space exploration and named in his honor
is located here.
Information: Wapakoneta Chamber of Commerce, 16 E. Auglaize St.,
419-738-2911; www.wapakoneta.com

WHAT TO SEE AND DO
Neil Armstrong Air and Space Museum
500 S. Apollo Dr., Wapakoneta,
419-738-8811;
www.ohiohistory.org-places-armstrong
This museum displays everything from
early planes to spacecraft, showing aero-
space accomplishments; audiovisual presentation; other exhibits. Tuesday-Sunday.

HOTELS
★★Best Western Wapakoneta
1510 Saturn Dr., Wapakoneta,
419-738-8181, 800-528-1234;

94 rooms. Pets accepted; fee. Complimentary continental breakfast. Restaurant, bar. Fitness room. Outdoor pool. **$**

WARREN

In 1800, Warren became the seat of the Western Reserve and then the seat of newly formed Trumbull County. At one of its stagecoach inns, the Austin house, Stephen Collins Foster is said to have begun writing "Jeannie with the Light Brown hair." According to local lore, while walking along the Mahoning River, Foster found the inspiration for "My Old Kentucky home."

Information: Youngstown-Warren Regional Chamber of Commerce, 160 E. Market, 330-393-2565; www.regionalchamber.com

HOTELS

★Comfort Inn
136 N. Park Ave., Warren,
330-393-1200, 800-424-6423;
www.comfortinn.com
54 rooms. Pets accepted, some restrictions; fee. Complimentary continental breakfast. Fitness room. **$**

★★★Avalon Inn Resort and Conference Center
9519 E. Market St., Warren,
330-856-1900; 800-828-2566;
www.avaloninn.com
Rooms at this inn are decorated in a colonial style. The resort offers 36 holes of golf, an Olympic-sized pool, and tennis, raquetball and volleyball courts.
140 rooms. Pets accepted; fee. Complimentary full breakfast. Two restaurants, two bars. Fitness room. Indoor pool, whirlpool. Golf, 36 holes. Tennis. Airport transportation available. **$**

167

OHIO

WOOSTER

Wooster claims to have had one of the first Christmas trees in America, introduced in 1847 by August Imgard, a young German immigrant. Disappointed with American Christmas, he cut down and decorated a spruce tree, which so pleased his neighbors that the custom spread throughout Ohio and the nation.

The town is located in farm country and near AmisHcommunities. The College of Wooster, a small liberal arts school, is located here.

Information: Wayne County Convention and Visitor Bureau, 428 W. Liberty St., 330-264-1800, 800-362-6474; www.wooster-wayne.com-wccvb

HOTELS

★★★Wooster Inn
801 E. Wayne Ave., Wooster,
330-263-2660;
woosterinn.wooster.edu
It seems impossible, but it's true: a college-owned hotel that offers more than dorm-style service. The Wooster Inn is a quaint country inn offering comfortable rooms and Colonial decor.
15 rooms. Closed early January. Pets accepted; fee. Restaurant. Golf, 9 holes. **$$**

SPECIALTY LODGINGS

Inn at Honey Run
6920 County Rd. 203,
Millersburg,
330-674-0011, 800-708-9394;
www.innathoneyrun.com
This is an arts-centered inn located in the heart of Amish Country.

39 rooms. Complimentary continental break fast. $$

RESTAURANTS
★★TJ's
359 W. Liberty St., Wooster,
330-264-6263
American menu. Lunch, dinner. Closed Sunday. Children's menu. $$

★★★Wooster Inn
801 E. Wayne Ave., Wooster,
330-263-2660;
woosterinn.wooster.edu
Dinner at this inn is served in the main dining room, which overlooks a nine-hole golf course and driving range. In the fall, there is a guest chef series. American menu. Lunch, dinner, Sunday brunch. Closed Monday; also early January. $$

YOUNGSTOWN

Youngstown, located five miles from the Pennsylvania line, is the largest city in Ohio's southwestern coal mining and steel manufacturing region. This is not an area known for its tourism, but rather is prominent for its role in the production of goods from clothing to lightbulbs.

Youngstown's steel history started in 1803, with a crude-iron smelter. The first coal mine began operating in the valley in 1826; in 1892, the first valley steel plant, Union Iron and Steel Company, opened.

Information: Youngstown-Mahoning County Convention and Visitors Bureau, 100 Federal Plaza E., 330-747-8200, 800-447-8201; www.youngstowncvb.com

WHAT TO SEE AND DO
Mill Creek Park
7574 Columbiana-Canfield Rd., Canfield,
330-702-3000;
www.millcreekmetroparks.com
This park has more than 3,200 acres of gorges, ravines and rolling hills from the Mahoning River to south of highway 224. A Western Reserve pioneer woolen mill (1821) is now the Pioneer Pavilion used for picnics and dancing. May-October: Tuesday-Sunday; April and November: weekends

HOTELS
★★Best Western Meander Inn
870 N. Canfield Niles Rd., Youngstown,
330-544-2378, 800-937-8376;
www.bestwestern.com
57 rooms. Pets accepted; fee. Complimentary continental breakfast. Restaurant, bar. Outdoor pool. $

★Quality Inn
4055 Belmont Ave., Youngstown,
330-759-3180, 800-221-2222;
www.qualityinn.com
144 rooms. Complimentary continental breakfast. Restaurant, bar. Indoor pool. Airport transportation available. $

168

OHIO

ZANESVILLE

Ebenezer Zane, surveyor of Zane's Trace through the dense Ohio forests and great-great-grandfather of Zane Grey, writer of Western novels, selected Zanesville's site at the junction of the Muskingum and Licking Rivers. First called Westbourne, it was the state capital from 1810 to 1812.

Today, beautiful pottery is made here, as well as transformers and automobile components. The "Y" Bridge, which a person can cross and still remain on the same side of the river from which he started, divides the city into three parts.

Information: Visitors and Convention Bureau, 205 N. 5th St.,740-455-8282, 800-743-2303; www.zanesville-ohio.com

HOTELS

★Comfort Inn
500 Monroe St., Zanesville,
740-454-4144, 800-424-6423;
www.comfortinn.com
81 rooms. Pets accepted, some restrictions; fee. Complimentary continental breakfast. Fitness room. Indoor pool, whirlpool. $

★★Holiday Inn
4645 E. Pike, Zanesville,
740-453-0771, 800-465-4329;
www.holiday-inn.com
130 rooms. Pets accepted; fee. Restaurant, bar. Fitness room. Indoor pool, whirlpool. $

★

★

★

★

★

INDEX

170

INDEX

171

INDEX

★
★
★
★
★

172

INDEX

173

INDEX

★

★

★

★

174

INDEX

★
★
★
★
★

175

INDEX

★ ★ ★ ★ ★

177

INDEX

★

★

★

☆

☆

179

INDEX

★
★
★
★
★

180

INDEX

181

INDEX

NOTES

182

★
★ ★
★ ★
★ ★
★

NOTES

183

INDEX

★
★
★
★
★

NOTES

★
★
★
★
★